YANKEE SAINTS
and
SOUTHERN SINNERS

YANKEE SAINTS
and
SOUTHERN SINNERS

BERTRAM WYATT-BROWN

LOUISIANA STATE UNIVERSITY PRESS

Baton Rouge and London

Library of Congress Cataloging in Publication Data

Wyatt-Brown, Bertram, 1932–
   Yankee saints and Southern sinners.

   Includes index.
   1. Slavery—United States—Anti-slavery movements—
Addresses, essays, lectures. 2. United States—Social
conditions—To 1865—Addresses, essays, lectures.
3. Southern States—Civilization—1775–1865—Addresses,
essays, lectures. 4. United States—History—Civil War,
1861–1865—Causes—Addresses, essays, lectures.
I. Title.
E449.W97   1985   973.7   85-8112
ISBN 0-8071-1244-5

For My Friends
Lawrence J. Friedman
Stanley L. Engerman
David Hackett Fischer
William L. Marbury
Kay Williams

CONTENTS

PREFACE AND
ACKNOWLEDGMENTS

THE BOOK is divided into two parts, approximately equal in length though not in number of chapters. All but the last chapter have been published before, but each of them has been substantially revised and updated to take account of the latest scholarly developments. In Part One, "Yankee Saints," I first explore the interpretation that Stanley Elkins offered in *Slavery* regarding the nature of the abolitionist movement and the character of Yankee society. It is followed by an attempt to place the abolitionist leaders' identity in the context of a larger, religious movement in the North. I examine the way the reformers and a parallel group, the foreign missionaries, were raised and found their calling. To show the evolutionary character of child-rearing in a reform family, I have devoted some pages to the Tappans. The history of that reform clan contrasts in some respects with the much more psychologically curious upbringing of John Brown. His antinomian politics and religion are the subject of the last portion of Part One. Brown's death more than life roused a nation to the "sin" of slaveholding in ways that neither the Tappans nor other abolitionists could ever have accomplished. All of Part One is devoted to the common theme of antislavery as a Christian—and destabilizing— enterprise, one which aimed at the creation of a new Republic based on universal rather than local and variant principles.

Parallel with the analysis of Elkins' contribution, the opening chapter of Part Two, "Southern Sinners," is historiographical. It appraises W. J. Cash's *The Mind of the South* and argues that despite its lingering Menckenian tone, the work should still command respect forty years after its original publication. Cash called the southern mode of domination the "Savage Ideal," but it could be recast, as it is here, under the rule of honor. In its various forms, that elusive concept helped to provide the South with an easy conscience about slavery. But honor expressed itself best in actions—in florid oratory or bursts of violence—rather than in cool terms of rational discourse. To meet the intellectual deficiency during the thirty years before war, a proslavery argument developed—romantic, even fantastic in its assertions. The penultimate essay deals with this vain effort to carry the southern cause into enemy territory, win conservative friends, and make southern ideology explicit, sophisticated, and harmonious with contemporary Anglo-American thought. The last and longest chapter offers a fresh interpretation of why the South seceded. It employs a cultural definition of honor that helps to clarify the nature of southern political language as well as the process of departure from the Union itself. A brief epilogue sums up the ethical thrusts of the two antebellum sections and suggests the continuities in this realm that persist, to inspire and afflict us still, at home and also abroad.

Over the years, so many individuals—librarians, archivists, and fellow historians—have given their time, expertise, or critical skills to help in the preparation of these essays that their names must be omitted. I am particularly grateful, though, to those to whom the book is dedicated, most especially Stanley L. Engerman, who read more versions of my work than he probably wishes to recall. Kay Williams is mentioned here as a most warmhearted friend during and after our departure from Cleveland; her contributions to the intellectual and aesthetic life of her city deserve much more recognition than this modest acknowledgment can convey. William L. Marbury, Dave Fischer, and Larry Friedman have provided high standards of intellectual achievement, an inspiration and a challenge. In addition, I thank Ronald G. Walters, Drew Gilpin Faust, David Van Tassel, James M. McPherson, Eugene D. Genovese, Dickson Bruce, and James Brewer Stewart, readers of particular sections of the book.

Raimund Goerler, George Crawford, John Cimprich, Daniel J. Singal, Philip S. Paludan, Dickson D. Bruce, Jr., and Kenneth S. Greenberg made contributions to this volume either by providing specific sources of information or by sharing their thoughts on particular topics. My wife Anne's contribution lies in whatever felicity of language and thought the collection has. Also, I gratefully acknowledge the advice and friendship of C. Vann Woodward.

A number of foundations have also been instrumental over the period when these writings were compiled and revised: the American Philosophical Society, the National Endowment for the Humanities, the John Simon Guggenheim Foundation, the Woodrow Wilson Center for International Scholars, the Shelby Cullom Davis Foundation of Princeton, and the Charles Rieley Armington Program of Case Western Reserve University. I also praise the typing skills of Cheryl Combs and the help of the staff at the Department of History, the University of Florida.

YANKEE SAINTS
and
SOUTHERN SINNERS

INTRODUCTION

THE THEME of this collection of essays is easily stated. A great moral chasm separated the antebellum North and South on the eve of the Civil War. So evident a proposition might seem hardly worth stating. Nowadays, we *assume* that freedom and slavery were incompatible and that they always were or at least should have been. Quite naturally such a view of the past would also require us to place Yankees on the side of the angels and southerners at the nether reaches. Yet historians are rightly skeptical of such easy divisions between Good and Evil and other poles of sanctity and vice. What, then, is the correct way to approach the moral dilemmas that our ancestors faced? Should we use their standards or ours or none at all?

For years the debate over the morality of war and the methods of Reconstruction was an academically popular enterprise. Then, there descended a historiographical silence so profound that Eric Foner, one of the most thoughtful and consistent explorers of this unhappy terrain, felt constrained to protest. In his introduction to *Politics and Ideology in the Age of the Civil War*, Foner complained that the mid-century calamity "had been relegated to the wings." He attributed the disappearance of Civil War political themes to a preoccupation with the rise of social history. Under the inspiration of new methods of quantification and theories imported from the French Academy, social historians of the 1970s pushed aside political questions, Foner reasoned. Concentrating on local situations in which ethnic and cultural factors loomed larger in the 1840s and the 1850s than did national issues of slavery and sectionalism, political historians practically forgot that secession and war were about to engulf the nation. As a result, a coherent interpretation of Civil War causation was no longer sought, needed though it was.[1]

Scholarly rejection of topics in Civil War political ideology had another cause. The moral uncertainties of the 1970s that Americans faced as a people made it hard to deal with so great a tragedy as the Civil War. It was a time of Watergate politics, military interventions in Asia and the Middle East, and a general sense of masterlessness over domestic economic and social crises. We had lost self-confidence. Retreat into less public spheres of interest was a natural reaction to the shouts and raised fists of the turbulent 1960s. Disillusionment with the possibilities of reform affected American historians, whether they realized it or not. Like the Supreme Court, scholars tend to follow the headlines.

Yet, Foner's lament turned out to be premature. Since 1980, when his essays on the Civil War appeared, there has been a remarkable resurgence in the field. James M. McPherson's *Ordeal by Fire* is by far the most comprehensive and trenchant single-volume narrative to be produced in a quarter century. To match Eric Foner's own *Free Soil, Free Labor, Free Men* (1970), we now have Jean H. Baker's masterly study, *Affairs of Party*. William J. Cooper, Jr., has retraced the southern political path to disunion in his provocative *Liberty and Slavery*. These authors do not hide from the tough questions. They aim at the big target: how the nation came to blows in 1861.[2]

Gratifying though the revival of Civil War studies has been, a mood of intellectual uncertainty still lingers—not so much in the books mentioned above but in the work of others. Their tentativeness contrasts with the truculence of the liberal and radical stance of scholars in the black rights and anti-Vietnam decade. At that time, Howard Zinn, Staughton Lynd, and others asserted that all white

1. Eric Foner, *Politics and Ideology in the Age of the Civil War* (New York, 1980), 4.
2. James M. McPherson, *Ordeal by Fire: The Civil War and Reconstruction* (New York, 1982); Eric Foner, *Free Soil, Free Labor, Free Men: The Ideology of the Republican Party Before the Civil War* (New York, 1970); Jean H. Baker, *Affairs of Party: The Political Culture of Northern Democrats in the Mid-Nineteenth Century* (Ithaca, 1983); William J. Cooper, Jr., *Liberty and Slavery: Southern Politics to 1860* (New York, 1983).

Americans were equally blameworthy for the racism manifest in the Civil War era. By that formula, Abraham Lincoln emerged as cold-hearted a nationalist as Count Cavour or Otto von Bismarck, willing to sacrifice the black people's freedom or expatriate them one and all, for the sake of creating a capitalistic and lily-white Union; the anti-slavery elements in and out of the Republican party sought chiefly to keep blacks from migrating north or west; white Reconstructionists were charged with too little meddling in southern affairs rather than too much. So thick were the accusations that degrees of wrongdoing were not at all clear. Many were sinners, and saints were hard to find.

That state of affairs has now been modified. For a number of scholars, there has been a strange blending of conservative and radical views that has muddied, more than clarified, the moral dynamics of Civil War causation. By and large the scholars involved are those who once might have been more radically inclined but now find themselves in a conservative national milieu. Two approaches are particularly evident. The first is a questioning of sectional distinctiveness in all spheres of human endeavor, and of nearly all aspects of the economy except free and slave labor. Rather than condemn the North for being too "southern" in the cataloging of regional characteristics, historians have reversed the pattern. We find southerners portrayed as Yankees in disguise. In terms of economic, social, and institutional structures, according to Edward Pessen, among others, there was no difference between the sections.[3] As a result, we learn to admire the planter's regularity and bourgeois values which were at least no worse than those of an early Yankee industrialist. The southerner, rich or poor, slaveholder or slaveless, seems less alien, morally and culturally, than he did a decade or two ago. But he was not exactly just like us. The writers make it clear that they are not apologizing for slavery but are placing it in the context of a capitalism which was itself a dismally exploitative regime. The point has validity. Yet the retreat from the moral indignation of the 1950s and 1960s should be clear. Something is lost in the withdrawal from abolitionist premises even if slavery has been situated in a larger historical and more objective framework.

3. Edward Pessen, "How Different from Each Other Were the Antebellum North and South?" *American Historical Review*, LXXXV (1980), 1119–49.

The second approach in this amalgamation of conservative and liberal interpretation is to stress the theme of crisis in institutional politics. Partisan structure collapsed, especially in the 1850s, because of both sectional divisions and internal strains. The investigators of party politics have illuminated how political ties became unraveled, but sometimes such concentration upon particular situations and upon struggles among rival factions, ethnic as well as ideological, has obscured the great moral dichotomies that led to secession and war. A resurgent southern Jacksonianism appearing in the 1850s, for instance, has served for some as explanation for the strident anticentralism, the defense of slavery, and the drive toward secession. But Jacksonian tenets were securely based upon old cultural and moral foundations. The principles that the Tennessee hero's admirers revered had been evolving from rather aristocratic (or, at least, plutocratic) roots toward a new synthesis of democracy, liberty, and honor—for white men only. Without full recognition that politics was a means to an end, a way to hold fast to heartfelt principles of collective southern life, one tends to make rational and therefore less visceral the antagonisms separating northerner from southerner.

The fact is that the rival sections had grown more, not less, distinctive in ethical and certainly political perspectives as the storm clouds of armed conflict approached. Based on the concept of modernization, a catchword for rate of growth toward economic and cultural complexity, McPherson's factual sketch in the opening chapters of *Ordeal by Fire* puts sectional differentiations as clearly as any historian ever has. In regard to transportation, educational commitments, urban development, economic diversification, numbers of immigrants and ability to accommodate them, and a host of other criteria, the sections were becoming more institutionally complex at different rates of change. In a microcosmic and equally impressive way, William H. Pease and Jane H. Pease have pointed out similar discrepancies in the textures of life in Boston and Charleston over the course of the antebellum era.[4] Additional comparative work in the years ahead will no doubt result in further evidence of North-South distinctions. By no means does this imply that the South failed to move forward

4. William H. Pease and Jane H. Pease, *The Web of Progress: Private Values and Public Styles in Boston and Charleston, 1828–1843* (New York, 1985).

4

toward a more complex society, only that the process was hobbled by a greater concern for the exigencies of slavery, race control, and tradition.

Given the present state of historical thinking about the Civil War, the purpose of this work is to explore not the material differences but the moral understandings of the two sections. There is no claim for covering the entire subject. Instead an effort has been made to restore the ethical dimension by means of selective examples as diverse as child-rearing and political rhetoric. Some chapters focus on the way certain writers have approached sectional ethics, and others deal with the way contemporaries reacted.

On the face of it, the title of this work might seem to be a simple-hearted reversion to the old abolitionist dichotomy by which Hermann von Holst and Henry Wilson, writing for the first post–Civil War generation a hundred years ago, celebrated the Union triumph over the Great Slave Power.[5] My intention, however, is to compare the social values of a segment of Yankee society with the slaveholding element of the South. Of course the term *saints* refers to the northern abolitionists. To be sure, some southerners, even today, would prefer to label them devilish fanatics rather than saints. They were by no means free of imperfection.

Like the British emancipationists of the same period, the American reform leaders were generally bourgeois in their social attitudes—concerned less with exploitations of the poor at home than with the fate of blacks far away. Some years ago the economic historian Eric Williams provocatively argued that the British abolitionists were guilty of grievous hypocrisies. They condoned "wage slavery" but lamented bondage, he surmised, while investing profits from West Indian sugar in British industrialization. David B. Davis and others have been attracted to the theory. As Seymour Drescher has noted, "If the abolitionists were distilled and marketed as a band of 'saints,' by their own epic tradition it is but a small dialectic step to emphasize antislavery as the preserve of capitalistic evangelicals, not as part of a broader and democratic heritage." Nonetheless, skep-

5. Hermann Eduard von Holst, *The Constitutional and Political History of the United States, 1750–1861* (6 vols.; Chicago, 1877–92); Henry Wilson, *History of the Rise and Fall of the Slave Power in America* (3 vols.; Boston, 1872–77).

ticism about humanitarian impulses can be pushed too far. There can be no denying that the abolition causes in both Great Britain and America acquired what Drescher calls "*sacralizing* power," especially in the United States after the war was won and slavery abolished.[6]

For the antislavery reformers on both sides of the Atlantic, the endeavor was a holy enterprise. Even today one would hesitate to challenge that opinion. By the usual standards of Christian life over the ages, the American abolitionists fit the criteria of a sacred band rather well. As always in such cases, the number of truly dedicated "saints" was small. Yet without their polemics, thought, and activity, there would have been no Civil War, a much longer life for the brutalizing institution of slavery, and a substantial slackening of the drive toward a freer society for all Americans. Even if abolitionists were selective in their philanthropies and even if free-labor distress received too little attention, the very concept of reform—as opposed to both inaction and revolution—was enhanced by the abolition movements in England and America. It is a circumstance that entitles the reformers to equal place with those whom they called sinners (in the organization of this volume), though one represented only an "elect" and the other a chief force in southern life. The proportion of saints to sinners has never been much greater than that anyhow, particularly if the old Calvinists were accurate about the rarity of divine attributes in mankind.

Since radical idealisms are almost by nature beyond the comprehension and workaday interests of Everyman, antislavery had to be an unpopular cause not only in the South but in the North, too. Perhaps Horace Greeley, editor of the New York *Tribune*, had his own reasons for saying so, but he was probably correct when he told a fellow Republican in 1858, "I do not believe that the People of the Free States are heartily Anti-Slavery. Ashamed of their subserviency

6. Eric E. Williams, *Capitalism and Slavery* (Chapel Hill, 1944); Seymour Drescher, "Cartwhip and Billy Roller: Antislavery and Reform Symbolism in Industrializing Britain," *Journal of Social History*, XV (1981), 18, 24n73; David Brion Davis, *The Problem of Slavery in Western Culture* (Ithaca, 1966), and *The Problem of Slavery in the Age of Revolution* (Ithaca, 1974), 346–68. Davis seems to have modified his position in his *Slavery and Human Progress* (New York, 1984), 162–91, 335n121, and stresses religious over economic motives in the emancipation cause.

to the Slave Power they may well be; convinced that Slavery is an incubus and a weakness, they are quite likely to be; but hostile to Slavery as wrong and crime, they are not, nor (I fear) likely soon to be."[7] If the standard for beatification was abolitionism, then few candidates, even in the Republican party, could have stepped forward for canonization.

To nominate the slaveholder as a sinner may seem a violation of historical judgment, too. But in some respects, the term does apply, although here it is meant only in a general sense. All men fall short of divine command, and it would be the height of historical hubris to lambaste southern whites because they refused to match the abolitionists' search for truth and God. In a collective way, however, they were burdened in a fashion other Americans were not, even if they did not feel much guilt for wielding the racial power they did. In any case, southerners themselves took pride in a virility and martial spirit that they believed was rooted in Christianity itself. Yet, from any other perspective, southern attitudes of this kind seemed at war with the social implications of the gospel. They worshipped the same Protestant God that Yankees did, but they claimed a regional freedom from the cant of Yankee Pecksniffs and from the heretical and perfectionist *isms* that romantic clergymen and sentimental schoolmarms espoused. If antislavery convictions increased one's chances of heaven, then a good many slaveholders would have resigned themselves to an eternity in hell, rather than admit to wrongdoing.

The choice of title, though, matters much less than a somewhat more concrete and serious moral distinction: sectional attitudes toward freedom and equality, the twin precepts of American political culture. As will be seen, these basic concepts had both similar and different meanings in the sectional conflict. For nearly all antebellum Americans, there was an abiding mistrust of outside authority: freedom from government or from self-serving interests beyond local community surveillance was thought to be the foundation of human equality. Slaveholders and yeomen, Yankee reformers and

7. Horace Greeley to Salmon P. Chase, September 18, 1858, quoted in Richard H. Sewell, *Ballots for Freedom: Antislavery Politics in the United States, 1837–1860* (New York, 1976), 350.

7

conservatives—ordinary folk from all walks of life—shared this faith. But in the South, equality was associated with sectional parity in the management of the federal apparatus. Liberty meant freedom from the potential coercions of the state, especially on matters of race and slavery.

In explaining why liberty, equality, and slaveholding were interdependent, some southerners, at least, recognized that they presented an unformed, hastily constructed case. In fact, one writer in 1857 candidly pointed out that along with other, more material signs of southern inferiority in demographic and economic terms, they suffered from intellectual weaknesses as well. "Our place in the Union is provincial, and as such our peculiarities will have to be defended, excused, ridiculed, pardoned. We can take no pride in our national character, because we must feel that from our peculiar position we do not contribute to its formation." Deprived of an authentic native philosophy and unable to utilize imported ones, "we can not live honestly in the Union because we are perpetually aiming to square the maxims of an impracticable philosophy with the practice which nature and circumstances force upon us." Likewise George Randolph, at the Virginia secession convention in 1861, observed how the abolitionist argument was by then hoary with age, whereas the proslavery philosophy "is recent—it is comparatively a thing of yesterday— it has not been inculcated in early life—it is not backed by sympathy abroad—it has hardly had time to be understood and appreciated by our own people."[8] Randolph meant not that the South's moral posture was defective, merely that methods for asserting it effectively were deficient. Mutuality of sectional respect, such southerners believed, had to be based on a willingness to preserve the appearance of moral and political equality, despite the clear imbalances. For them it was a matter not of expediency but of honor.

In addition to a different understanding of sectional equity, southerners were slower than antebellum northerners to relinquish the eighteenth-century—and earlier—tradition of status as a major

8. *Russell's Magazine*, May, 1857, quoted in Ulrich B. Phillips, *The Course of the South to Secession* (New York, 1939), 142; Randolph quoted in William W. Freehling, "The Editorial Revolution, Virginia, and the Coming of the Civil War: A Review Essay," *Civil War History*, XVI (1970), 70.

function of personal identity. In his Commonwealth Fund lectures of 1963, David M. Potter, the great Civil War historian, put the matter in general terms: "Alone, [man] cannot orient himself in a universe of overwhelming immensity, but in his relations with others, a realization of their awareness of him helps to steady and focus his awareness of himself. Indeed, it might be said that every person's sense of his own identity is derived from this awareness of other people's perceptions of his identity." Although that was applicable throughout the antebellum nation, in the South the individual was intensely alive to his place in what Potter calls the "social web of his community."[9]

The preoccupation with social relationships (somewhat at the expense of solitary, private experience) was partly a matter of environment. The southerner lived in rural circumstances—sometimes barely cleared wilderness—where institutions were few and reliance on family and neighborhood great. Such conditions existed in the North as well (though urbanization and heterogeneous mixings of peoples from abroad weakened the force of small-scale community culture). But unlike life in the free states, community involvement in determining an individual's status was so great because of slavery and the presence of blacks. The latter possessed no status, a circumstance that in negative ways helped to define and place those who did.

I have called this set of personal and group codes of behavior the ethic of honor. The term implies hierarchy, subordination, and other Old World prescriptions. Although hostile to hereditary titles and monarchy, southerners managed to reconcile honor as status with egalitarianism and liberty. They did so by insisting that honors or entitlements be fairly won in competition for public favor, from a governorship to a militia captain's rank. Even ordinary men had their portion of respect as well, if only because of their white skin. This concept which linked honor to equality and freedom is summed up in the famous Huey Long slogan Every Man a King. The phrase means that no man—that is, no white man—should have his selfhood insulted or his right to improve his position denied. As I argue in the last chapter, at the core of the secession movement and Yankee reactions to it lay antagonistic notions of honor.

9. David M. Potter, *Freedom and Its Limitations in American Life*, ed. Don E. Fehrenbacher (Stanford, 1976), 22, 24.

For the abolitionists, on the other hand, liberty and equality had more deeply Christian and abstract meanings, ones that can be distinguished from the rather eighteenth-century concepts prevailing in the South. The crusaders' aim was to establish moral uniformity throughout the land, especially with regard to these twin precepts. Personal liberty for all became, in the abolitionist mind, inseparable from equal protection under the law. As legal historian William Nelson argues, the concept involved an expanded role for the central government, much more so than the early abolitionists foresaw. But their insistence upon moral uniformities pointed toward the kind of activism that was, for instance, later manifested in the Progressive movement. The possible uses of government, however, counted much less in their critique of slavery than the immediate "sinfulness" of slaveholding. That system, the reformers declared, provided all power, honor, and glory to one race and not a fragment for the underclass. The followers of William Lloyd Garrison and Theodore Dwight Weld perceived arbitrary power less as a problem of governmental despotism in America than as a personal one. The slave master's unchecked coerciveness was a violation not just of natural law, according to the Declaration of Independence, but also of God's. The Deity was affronted by the arrogations of unlimited rule that masters, in fact all white Americans, possessed over blacks. Finding a sense of community in their own radical groups of associates, the abolitionists discovered honor not in status but in defiance of racist conventions. "Deliver us from a boastful, vain-glorious, self-confident spirit," intoned William Lloyd Garrison, "but, oh! what dignity there is in christian independence! . . . Let us use, then, the dialect of christian conquerors."[10] Garrison was accustomed to employ the imagery of honor and chivalry in its most Christian context, but that kind of crusade was poles away from the southern perception of political and racial morality. Liberty, equality, and honor all had different connotations in the North and the South. For that reason, the nation went to war.

10. William E. Nelson, *The Roots of American Bureaucracy, 1830–1900* (Cambridge, Mass., 1982), 41–61, esp. 51; William Lloyd Garrison to Samuel J. May, January 17, 1836, in Louis Ruchames (ed.), *The Letters of William Lloyd Garrison: A House Dividing Against Itself, 1836–1840* (6 vols.; Cambridge, Mass., 1971), II, 14.

10

PART ONE

YANKEE SAINTS

I

STANLEY ELKINS AND NORTHERN REFORM CULTURE

IN NO AREA of study has historical understanding been so volatile as in nineteenth-century American racial and sectional history. In a parallel chapter in the second part of this study, the work of W. J. Cash provides an introduction to the way southerners differed from their northern compatriots. In this chapter, the focus is on the once highly influential typology that Stanley Elkins offered for understanding abolitionist behavior and the society which helped to shape it. For over two decades, a veritable eternity by professional standards, his monograph, *Slavery*, enlivened undergraduate class lectures and graduate seminars, usually in outraged dissent. Owing to the racial tensions of the day and to Elkins' own imaginative analysis of how servitude and servility were intimately connected, critics focused almost exclusively upon the first three-quarters of the book.[1] Elkins' last chapter, which concerned the character of the pre–Civil War North, drew little fire, although it provided a novel interpretation of the origins of the sectional conflict. Now that suburban liberalism and black insurgency have shriveled away, his views may be

Previously published, in slightly different form, as "Stanley Elkins' Antislavery Interpretation: A Re-examination," in *American Quarterly*, XXV (1973), 154–76. Copyright 1973, Trustees of the University of Pennsylvania.

1. Stanley M. Elkins, *Slavery: A Problem in American Institutional and Intellectual Life* (Chicago, 1959); Aileen S. Kraditor, "A Note on Elkins and the Abolitionists," in Ann J. Lane (ed.), *The Debate over "Slavery": Stanley Elkins and His Critics* (Urbana, 1971), 87–101.

entertained with some detachment so that we comprehend the role of "sainthood" or moral commitment in the nineteenth-century North.

Like his interpretation of the highly individualistic American form of slaveholding, his criticism of the abolitionist cause is based on a particular predisposition for reason over moral passion and for faith in the ordinary institutions of society over grand moral absolutes. After all the difficulties of the recent past and the current antinomian terrors—Iran, Northern Ireland, Lebanon, assassinations, and bombings everywhere—his predilection seems more congenial now than it did in the early 1960s. One either appreciates the romantic temperament that antislavery exemplified or, with Elkins, turns from it in dismay. Northrop Frye once declared that "to say with T. E. Hulme: 'I object to even the best of the Romantics' is much like saying 'I object to even the best battles of the Napoleonic War.'"[2] Consciously or not, we cannot escape a similarly visceral reaction either to Elkins or to the men and women of whom he disapproved. But to avoid the dangers of partisanship as much as possible, I will first present the basic argument of Chapter 4; second, examine the strengths and then the weaknesses of Elkins' strategy; and third, ascertain the purpose of the work as whole.

Despite a familiar stress upon American "frontier" individualism, Elkins presented the case in a highly original way.[3] As he explained it, individual Americans, struggling against each other but sometimes joining in casual unities, swept aside long-standing institutional checks which might otherwise have afforded a structured approach to the "peculiar institution." By 1830, he claimed, whatever stability the country enjoyed was confined to the centrifugal momentum of atoms more or less moving in the same direction.

Elkins drew from these premises the conclusion that Americans were unprepared for dealing with slavery. They not only lacked the institutional means, they also lacked the proper intellectual frame

2. Northrop Frye, "The Drunken Boat: The Revolutionary Element in Romanticism," in Frye (ed.), *Romanticism Reconsidered: Selected Papers from the English Institute* (New York, 1963), 2–3.
3. Stanley Elkins and Eric McKitrick, "A Meaning for Turner's Frontier: Democracy in the Old Northwest," in Richard Hofstadter and Seymour M. Lipset (eds.), *Turner and the Sociology of the Frontier* (New York, 1968), 120–51.

of mind for reasonable action on any pressing social question. "For Americans of this [1830s] generation," he declared, "the very concept of power—its meaning, its responsibilities, its uses—was something quite outside their experience."[4] Frustrated by the absence of proper channels to effect change, a band of philosophers and abolitionists forced the nation off course. The fragile institutions, which they so ruthlessly denounced, flew apart. Motion became commotion. The nation went to war, a bloody, needless tragedy.

There was a striking parallel between Stanley Elkins' approach to social issues and that of the Founding Fathers, which a rough characterization of the eighteenth-century view may help to demonstrate. In intellectual terms, the period was typified by a sense of orderliness in human and divine affairs. Men of the Enlightenment thought that selfish instincts could be controlled through ecclesiastical and civil institutions, age-old habits, and a general sense of rightness about one's status and allegiances. Under stable conditions, moral progress, humanitarian advance, and other noble aspirations were possible, but only so long as the proponents of change deferred to the limitations of power, wisely distributed among neatly adjusted "orders" and institutions. Order, balance, and progress were the trinity of Enlightenment hopes. The crumbling of any of these would bring down the others, even to the point of anarchy or tyranny.

Of course, Elkins found this institutional approach congenial not because of an affectation but because of a correspondence with attitudes current in the academic milieu in which *Slavery* was composed, as the following passage illustrates: "Institutions with power produce the 'things' not only upon which one leans but also against which one pushes; they provide the standards whereby, for men of sensibility, one part of society may be judged and tested against another. The lack of them, moreover, removes the thinker not only from the places where power resides but also from the very *idea* of power and how it is used."[5]

Elkins tied the concept of power directly to those institutions which he and other scholars of the 1950s considered the most acces-

4. Elkins, *Slavery*, 34.
5. *Ibid.*, 143.

sible—the national government, the university centers, and the interlocking network of urban social elites. Twenty-five years of growing governmental interest in various scholastic enterprises had encouraged the notion that the most practicable solutions for social ills came through ventures uniting government and intellectual leaders. It was both natural and logical for Elkins to transfer the idea of scholar-as-bureaucrat into eighteenth-century parlance. In a manner of speaking, *brain truster*, a crude term, became gently translated into the archaic but appropriate designation "men of sensibility" in the passage above.

Elkins' strategy was well designed for a profound criticism of the romantic temperament in American political reform. He began with these assumptions: that order is preferable to violence; that small gains peaceably won are better than high ambitions leading to shattering disillusionment; that men in their imperfectibility can only delude themselves in zealotry. Given this framework, abolitionism, the most thoroughly romantic of the host of antebellum causes, appeared as the offspring of Byronic impulse and evangelical soulfulness.

Indeed, abolitionists were, as Elkins claimed, inspired with an antinomian vision. In accordance with that theological concept, they stressed the primacy of intuition over intellect, the imperative of immediacy, the commitment to self-discovery through anti-orthodox engagement, and finally the justification of deed by direct reference to an absolute ideal, privately ascertained. Although indebted to some of the expansive themes of the Enlightenment, they replaced a faith in traditional mechanisms with a zeal that others either rejected or misunderstood. Like Edmund Burke in his attacks on French Revolutionary enthusiasms, Elkins offered the reasons for the inevitable self-defeat that romantics prepared for themselves. Ironically, his perspective may yet prove more resistant to criticism than did his approach to slave psychology, which met a different fate.[6]

6. David B. Davis, "The Emergence of Immediatism in British and American Antislavery Thought," *Mississippi Valley Historical Review*, XLIX (1962), 209–230; see Stanley Elkins, "Slavery and Ideology," in Lane (ed.), *The Debate over "Slavery,"* 361–78; George M. Fredrickson, *The Inner Civil War* (New York, 1965); R. Jackson Wilson, *In Quest of Community: Social Philosophy in the United States* (New York, 1968). Fredrickson and Wilson utilize the same definition of *institution* that Elkins employs.

Three major portions of his argument have borne the test of further research in the social sciences and history especially well: first, that American society entered the nineteenth century in an iconoclastic, ego-centered, and anxious mood; second, that abolitionists and Transcendentalists shared similar moral and intellectual views, including a suspicion of conventional attitudes and institutions; third, that Transcendentalists and abolitionists alike were opposed to the racial sins of their fathers and their own generation because of a deep-seated sense of personal guilt.

In regard to American self-serving dynamism, few historians would dispute that the manifold changes in the ways men made their living helped to transform basic ideological patterns during the antebellum period. Most important was the commercializing of agriculture. Subsistence farming and its customs were restricted to backwaters; cash-crop settlers of the North and the South developed the vast hinterlands. This transformation made possible the rise of cities, industry, and improved means of distribution, travel, education, and communication.

Under these circumstances, Americans—always restless—became more mobile, so much so that values could no longer be entrusted to the broken integrity of family and kin, community tradition, and outworn elites of tenured clergy and squires. Robert H. Wiebe in *The Search for Order* observed, "Already by the 1870s the autonomy of the community was badly eroded." The process had begun with American independence and accelerated in the 1830s. The task of cementing society to common aims fell largely to such mass devices as political parties, common schools, benevolent agencies, and quickly gathered assemblies for specific objects. Fraternal associations, social clubs, and religious activities provided a measure of security. Yet, as Elkins rightly stressed, there was a paradoxical urge for individuality. With some flamboyance but essential truth, Max Lerner in 1957 argued that the archetypal American was the supreme modern man: "Hungering for a sense of personal worth, he is torn between the materialisms he can achieve and the feeling of wholeness which eludes him. . . . He is the double figure in Marlowe, of Tamerlane and Dr. Faustus, the one sweeping like a footloose barbarian across the plains to overleap the barriers of earlier civili-

17

zations, the other breaking the taboos against knowledge and experience, even at the cost of his soul." In attempting to master his environment and himself, the antebellum American played so many roles at once and in such rapid sequence (witness Melville's *The Confidence-Man*) that loyalties lost former relevance. New and rather unstable ones appeared, sometimes, as David B. Davis explained, in formulations of a negative character. Occasionally mob action and the rooting out of supposed conspiracies of "aliens" testified to the anxieties that shifts in commitment helped to generate.[7]

Turning to anthropology, we find further support for Elkins' interpretation. Mary Douglas, a leading anthropologist, has worked out a typology rather helpful in understanding the Jacksonian era as Elkins perceived it: when allegiances to a homogenous "group" (a New England village, for instance) decline, a "grid" or a set of adaptive rules governing the relations between ego-centered individuals offers more meaning than community, family custom, and routine. As a result of this imbalance between "grid" and "group," she observed, men look upon institutions as merely temporary agencies to further ambitions and aspirations. Institutions or, more precisely, regulative conventions no longer afford psychic comforts, nor do they help the individual to know precisely his relationship to the world around him. Under these circumstances, Douglas continued, men find anchors of faith in their own bodies and inner feelings while alienating themselves from traditions rapidly losing former sacredness. The immortal self seems to provide surer hooks into "reality" than do commitments to family, business partnerships, charities, or time-honored religious customs. As Douglas explained, preoccupations with personal hygiene, dietary regulations, moral dogmas, and introspective yearnings—all newly adopted realms of spirit and body—frequently become replacements for a flagging respectfulness for long-standing authorities in times of social transition. Applying this view to Jacksonian America, one is reminded of the temperance

7. Robert H. Wiebe, *The Search for Order, 1877–1920* (New York, 1967), viii; Max Lerner, *America as a Civilization: Life and Thought in the United States Today* (New York, 1957), 63; David B. Davis (ed.), *The Fear of Conspiracy: Images of Un-American Subversion from the Revolution to the Present* (Ithaca, 1970), 9–22.

cause, the Grahamite regimen, the sexual asceticism and experimentation of utopians, and the quest for new identities in communitarian fellowship. Lawrence Friedman, in his study *Gregarious Saints*, amplified this aspect of the movement—the bonding that occurred. In forming their "clusters" of activists, leaders like Garrison, Tappan, and Gerrit Smith, for example, failed to overcome their essential powerlessness, a point on which Elkins and Friedman are agreed. Nonetheless, the abolitionists' sense of political weakness itself was an ingredient in the forming of their distinct but interrelated circles. The opposition and indifference of the masses helped in the uniting of the self and the small, manageable groups of antislavery radicals.[8]

Given this context, Elkins was wise to uphold his original observations, though granted an opportunity to retract in Ann Lane's anthology a decade later. "In America," Elkins reaffirmed, "a major cultural fact was the general inability to see any clear relationship, except perhaps a negative one, between institutions and individual character." Institutions (by which Elkins also meant customary usages and conventional ways of thinking as well as formal civil structures) were conceived to be "at best a convenience," and even the family was "not really a given, something that one inherited and in which one assumed a place; it was rather something one created anew . . . and subsequently maintained, as it were, through force of individual will." His commentary has support not only from other historians but from social psychologists as well.[9]

The second contribution that Elkins offered was a persuasive argument for abolitionist and Transcendental affinities, one that grew out of the cultural setting itself. Antislavery crusaders and the Concord school were part of the same philosophical revolt against Enlightenment rationalism and religious orthodoxy, both of which accepted human weakness as an eternal part of the universal order.

8. Mary Douglas, *Natural Symbols: Explorations in Cosmology* (New York, 1970), vii, 19–23, 70–71, 82–83, 149–55; Ronald G. Walters, "The Erotic South: Civilization and Sexuality in American Abolitionism," *American Quarterly*, XXV (1973), 177–201; Lawrence J. Friedman, *Gregarious Saints: Self and Community in American Abolitionism, 1830–1870* (New York, 1982).

9. Elkins, "Slavery and Ideology," 374; Douglas, *Natural Symbols*, 33–36, 38; David C. McClelland, *The Achieving Society* (Glencoe, Ill., 1961), 13, 48–49.

Elkins underlined this point in the Lane anthology when he quoted with approval R. Jackson Wilson: "The perfectionism of Garrison and other reformers was, like Transcendentalism, insistently antinomian; both implied a thorough, even ruthless criticism and repudiation of existing institutions." [10] The Boston heresy represented a disillusionment with the prevailing "common sense" theology and seeming hypocrisy, evasions, and ordinary muddle of the American churches.

The radical reformer invariably believes that institutions should enfold the ideal, when by their consensual nature, they can only reach for it. In any case, the best minds in the antislavery venture left the denominations and the faiths of their fathers for a more liberating gospel of "free religion," a secular trend in keeping with their stress upon the divinity of the self. No scholar has yet explored this abolitionist trend, one that began in the late 1830s; the phenomenon, however, substantiates Elkins' views. To be sure, Gerrit Smith, La Roy Sunderland, Elizur Wright, and the Weld-Grimké family failed to join Garrison's anti-evangelical circle in the 1840s. Yet they and many others repudiated the theology as well as the formal ecclesiastical structure of contemporary religious life. Instead, they prophesied the need for "a higher, purer theology," as Joshua Giddings exclaimed, to "cast aside" institutions which were "inert, inefficient and worn out." Someone like Giddings, a congressman from the Western Reserve of Ohio, could hardly have matched the Transcendentalists in learning and sophistication. But the kind of abolitionist he represented shared Emerson's and Thoreau's contempt for church conventionalities in the common pursuit of means for glimpsing the future and condemning the present.[11]

Thousands of evangelical Christians and their leaders remained true to the circumspect abolitionism of 1833, but a trend was under way. Even within the evangelical movement in the 1840s, Charles G. Finney's revival doctrine of sanctification of men in present life transcendentalized, so to speak, Methodist Arminianism. Abolitionists, like the Tappan brothers, adopted Finney's theology. These and other

10. Elkins, "Slavery and Ideology," 364.
11. James B. Stewart, *Joshua R. Giddings and the Tactics of Radical Politics* (Cleveland, 1970), 253; Ralph Waldo Emerson, "New England Reformers," in Edwin C. Rozwenc (ed.), *Ideology and Power in the Age of Jackson* (New York, 1964), 171.

indications of romantic desires to impute a measure of divinity to mankind showed that transcendentalism and abolitionism were emphatically moving in the same direction. Elkins, limited by inadequate secondary resources, did not explore the religious tendencies of the age very knowledgeably, but his sketch was consistent with more recent scholarship on the subject.[12]

Likewise, Elkins correctly observed the abolitionists' responsibility for weakening public regard for *some* institutions. Some years ago, historian Aileen Kraditor disputed this argument, complaining that most crusaders "did not repudiate institutions or institutional means to effect desired change"; they merely sought to replace corrupted ones. Yet, who could argue that these reformers did not seek a radical change in existing relationships between whites and blacks, Yankees and southerners? This undertaking inevitably clashed with current notions of American nationality, based as they were upon racial hierarchy and sectional parity. In fact, abolitionists were like Reformation Lutherans who rejected the magical assumptions of Catholic ritual, an exercise that inescapably challenged church structure as well. Similarly, Garrison's public burning of the Constitution, for instance, profaned the central icon of romantic patriotism. In that act he consummated what a Reformation sectarian did by proving saint's blood to be nothing more than a vial of colored water. Garrison's contemporaries were horrified or jubilant because they rightly understood its shattering symbolism. Whether reformers remained within a given body to amend it to well-doing or "came out" from corrupt institutions, they were engaged in a form of subversion. One may feel compelled to approve or repudiate the policy, but the reformers' disruption of accepted norms is a matter of record. Although historians now tend to see abolitionists as rather typical or "bourgeois" on social questions apart from race, the very *intensity* of their conventionalities—notions of work, temperance, duty, conscience, and purity of

12. Ronald G. Walters, *The Antislavery Appeal: American Abolitionism After 1830* (Baltimore, 1976), 40–51; Bertram Wyatt-Brown, *Lewis Tappan and the Evangelical War Against Slavery* (Cleveland, 1969), 310–12; J. R. Jacob, "La Roy Sunderland: The Alienation of an Abolitionist," *Journal of American Studies*, VI (1972), 1–17; Ernest R. Sandeen, *The Roots of Fundamentalism: British and American Millenarianism, 1830–1930* (Chicago, 1970); Lewis Perry, *Childhood, Marriage, and Reform: Henry Clarke Wright, 1797–1870* (Chicago, 1980).

thought, for instance—were carried to the point of disruptiveness, a position that certainly influenced reactions to them, even in other conventional and Victorian circles.[13]

In addition, Elkins saw clearly the tragic costs that were exacted in the practice of romantic antinomianism. Moralists of this kind are often burdened with simple Manichean extravagances and suspicions, intolerance, and an abstract way of thinking. They are animated by an individualistic sense of responsibility for historical conditions and contemporary policies. This moral acuity precludes an orderly approach to power. The stress upon immediacy and national depravity limited the responses of slaveholders and conservatives, no matter how benevolent or open-minded they might have been. A planter could have chosen to join abolitionist forces, as James G. Birney did, or, as Elkins said, "he might simply discharge his sense of guilt by turning on his tormentors." In any event, whether motivated by guilt or, more likely, by shame and anger, southerners predictably closed ranks and turned inward. This form of "consensus" in the South, Elkins observed, withdrew "one kind of liberty [but] conferred in its place another kind which had not previously been there. The mind could now conceive the enemy in any size or shape it chose; specters were utterly free to range, thrive and proliferate."[14]

Meanwhile, abolitionists reworked the definition of a Christian. Slaveholding became the cardinal sin in the antinomian theology, for men were judged solely according to their relationship to slavery, a radical departure in scriptural interpretation. Thereafter it was easy—all too easy—to distinguish the saints from the fallen. Non-slaveholding churchgoers could take refuge from their own spiritual vacuity by condemning others for what environment, circumstances, and inclination shielded them from ever doing. Moreover, there were some impoverished efforts to supply new symbols of beatitude and damnation to replace conventional sermon imagery, preoccupied as most clergymen were with submission to divine will and with neigh-

13. Kraditor, "A Note on Elkins and the Abolitionists," 92; Douglas, *Natural Symbols*, 48–49; Walters, "The Erotic South," 177–201; W. J. Rorabaugh, *The Alcoholic Republic: An American Tradition* (New York, 1979), 214–16; James B. Stewart, *Holy Warriors: The Abolitionists and American Slavery* (New York, 1978), 43–49.
14. Elkins, *Slavery*, 212, 217.

borly, familial virtues. In contrast, abolitionists stressed distant empathies. Primitive woodcuts of lustful masters and abject slaves became the gargoyles and relics of a gothic revival. And there was even a kind of Protestant rite of indulgence performed in the purchase of a suitably decorated lamp-mat or a pamphlet from Knapp & Garrison. They were false representations, crude compositions for a complex and highly personal set of relationships in the South. Doubtful churchmen were not simply justifying their own timidity when they reproached abolitionists' portrayals of a southern purgatory and the blessedness of the antislavery child prattling pieties on her deathbed. In the eyes of some churchmen it seemed that God himself was soon to be worshipped as a dispenser of tracts. Something of the dignity and awesomeness of divinity, as it had been perceived for centuries, was displaced by an identification of sin with certain cultural arrangements and virtue with others.[15]

Proslavery ministers, however, were likewise disposed in behalf of pious slaveholding patriarchalism. Yet pietists could well argue that in the long span of human travail, God had not seen fit to excite men about slavery. Why should he have chosen 1831 for the year of new revelations and the pages of the *Liberator* for a revised Mosaic law? Like Elkins, conservatives were discomfited by the abolitionists' arrogation of divine authority. Wisely they feared that religion—or religious fanaticism, as they saw it—would lead to a bloodbath. It had happened before, and Americans, these critics knew, had not left human passion on the other side of the Atlantic.

Yet there are two major problems with Elkins' notion of antislavery reform: first, his identification of transcendentalism with antislavery radical activity; and second, his misinterpretation of abolitionist psychology. The first criticism has been presented effectively by Anne C. Rose in a reappraisal of the New England circle of intel-

15. James H. Moorhead, *American Apocalypse: Yankee Protestants and the Civil War, 1860–1869* (New Haven and London, 1978), 88–96, a good summary of prewar ambivalence about slavery and abolitionism; Thornton Stringfellow, "A Brief Examination of Scripture Testimony on the Institution of Slavery," in Drew Gilpin Faust (ed.), *The Ideology of Slavery: Proslavery Thought in the Antebellum South, 1830–1860* (Baton Rouge, 1981), 136–67; William S. Jenkins, *Pro-Slavery Thought in the Old South* (Chapel Hill, 1935).

lectuals. She argues that the relationship between the Transcendentalists and the reformers was at best ambivalent when not desultory. At times there was genuine hostility. For instance, Henry Thoreau withdrew in disgust from the all-too-familiar and gratuitous manner of Henry C. Wright, a veteran Garrisonian, whom Peter Walker has called "more royal than the king." Thoreau recorded in his diary that Wright was the kind of individual who seeks to "cuddle up and lie spoonfashion with you" and even to "wrap you about with their bowels. . . . Men's bowels are far more slimy than their brains." Such personal antipathies aside, neither Thoreau nor Emerson took an active part with the radicals in the great cause of the day and seldom did they or others in the loosely banded literary movement have much influence upon the immediatists they knew. Rose illustrates the point well, but on the questionable grounds that Theodore Parker was not a Transcendentalist, she leaves out the great thinker and orator whom Elkins better appreciated.[16] Abolition and transcendentalism were similar but not interchangeable, as Elkins implied.

In regard to his misreading of reform psychology, Elkins overlooked the generational factor in assessing the nature of abolitionist polemics. Correctly he observed that "a gnawing sense of responsibility for the ills of society appears to be experienced most readily in this country by groups relatively sheltered" from the sources of power.[17] No one who witnessed the anti–Vietnam War protest a decade ago would doubt his contention. But, like those engaged in denouncing the American effort in Southeast Asia, abolitionists, some Transcendentalists included, were chiefly young men and women at the time of their recruitment or conversion. The young seldom have access to the levers of power, nor do they fully grasp the mechanisms of governance. Limited in experience and often uncertain of their own untested gifts, they sometimes compensate for such deficiencies with a volatile and abstract idealism. As the abolitionists matured they generally became more moderate, less given to shouting into

16. Anne C. Rose, *Transcendentalism as a Social Movement, 1830–1850* (New Haven and London, 1981), 217n46, 219–20; Thoreau and the appraisal of Wright are both quoted from Peter Walker, *Moral Choices: Memory, Desire, and Imagination in Nineteenth-Century American Abolition* (Baton Rouge, 1978), 278, 279.
17. Elkins, *Slavery*, 161.

the wind, and much more political than religious in the sources of their inspiration.

These remarks fail, however, to invalidate Elkins' point. Naïve modes of thought may linger in the American psyche beyond the days of romantic youthfulness chiefly because of the long tradition of religious and moral expectancy in our society. For instance, Frederic C. Howe, a Progressive reformer, recognized that "it was with difficulty that realism got lodgment in my mind; early assumptions as to virtue and vice, goodness and evil remained in my mind long after I had tried to discard them." As a result, he said, he, like other reformers, had placed faith "in men rather than institutions," spread a gospel of coercive evangelism, and sought "a moralistic explanation of social problems and a religious solution for most of them."[18]

Steeped in the Protestant impulse to mount a pulpit, abolitionists found in reform not only an occasion for pious work but also a means for channeling inner doubts toward morally satisfying ends. These existential fears and hopes were peculiarly associated with the youthful crises of faith and identity about which William James wrote so sensitively in *The Varieties of Religious Experience*. By applying James's insights, Elkins could have added another dimension to his analysis of reform. Instead, his comments about such Transcendentalists as William Henry Channing, Margaret Fuller, and George Ripley recorded their accustomed gloom without speculation on its causes. Having already used psychological theory to explain master-slave relations, Elkins missed an opportunity to do likewise with reform and institutional connections. Nevertheless, he was clearly accurate in perceiving a commonality of spirit in Transcendental reform thought—"its overtone of guilt," abstraction, and introspectiveness.[19]

A favorable verdict on many aspects of Elkins' *Slavery* cannot, however, hide a disappointment. His distaste for the antinomian personality was not only historically unfair but also distracting and un-

18. Warren I. Susman, "The Persistence of American Reform," *Journal of Human Relations*, XV (1967), 97–98.
19. William James, *The Varieties of Religious Experience: A Study in Human Nature* (New York, 1902); Elkins, *Slavery*, 156.

essential to his argument. He failed to balance his preference for institutional checks with a discriminating sympathy, one that would have led to greater precision and persuasiveness. After all, these sensitive men and women were caught up in the traumas of the birth of the modern world; they were surrounded by the shifting and perplexing social forces that Elkins himself had so well described. Given these circumstances, it was hardly a wonder that abolitionists were romantics, racked with feelings they did not fully understand. Even so, the inner compulsions of guilt, ambition, and personal despair can hardly explain the entire antislavery movement. A tension between inner doubts and aspirations may have deepened abolitionist convictions, but Elkins did not show how emotional factors were the ultimate determinants of an allegedly irresponsible reform. The causal relationship was implied in a rather mechanistic way. The links between cause and result are ever complex, sometimes unfathomable. Of course, mental anguish played a role, but the examiner of the evidence must resist the temptation of reductionism, a proposition that invariably cheapens the fullness of human experience. Elkins' problem in the final chapter was not an overapplication of psychology but a lack of historical charity. The reformers appeared chiefly as victims of their own psychic misfortunes, the reasons for which Elkins morally did not condone. But after all, these earnest thinkers were also fashioners of a destiny for themselves and their world, and they moved toward that goal on the basis of a hope *born* of their inward doubt.

In any event, abolitionists were better able to cope with conditions around them than Elkins acknowledged. For the most part, the crusaders did not comprehend the exigencies of practical politics, but they did see the potentiality of new means of communication as a weapon of wide influence. As Aileen Kraditor has so ably shown, they built their reform upon the mechanisms that the sudden rise of mass democracy made available: the national press, mass rallies and mass campaigns, including the postal and petitions effort in the early years and, later, the widespread dissemination of polemics about the Great Slave Power and its designs against liberty. Antislavery programs of all sorts—even the Garrisonian—were suited to purposes of public instruction. Sensationalism was a major way to overcome popular indifference, though hardly one to appeal to those at the center of traditional power. As David C. McClelland observed, "The value of using the mass media for educational purposes lies precisely in the fact that they come to represent a new 'voice of authority' replacing the authority of tradition."[20] Elkins understood the agitational process, but rather than merely describing how abolitionists educated the masses about slavery, he deplored the effort as a creation of pure fantasy from first to last.

In this connection, compare Donald G. Mathews' explanation of antislavery growth in the Methodist church with Elkins' view of the general procedure. Mathews illuminated the way that Methodist reformers led their northern brethren to consider themselves "'responsibly' opposed to slavery," an arduous and lengthy task. "The vagueness and generality of the position," Mathews said, "had the virtue of uniting a maximum number of people under an antislavery banner." Abolitionists were unsatisfied with the meager result, but they had helped to provide Methodists "with a battle hymn in their greatest moment of national crisis."[21] Thus, the radical dogma of abolitionism eventually came to serve as a source of comfort and communal security as well as an inspiration for conducting war, even as the reformers personally remained outside the realms of power.

With much less detachment, Elkins described the advance of antislavery ideas as the gradual universalizing of a "fellow-traveler" sympathy. The reference meant an accumulation of corollary issues—the debate over free speech and gag rules, for example—matters around which moderates rallied as they drew closer to the abolitionist position. The point was valid, but the "fellow-traveler" label demeaned it. Mathews cited the sociological work of Lewis Coser; Elkins borrowed from the rhetoric of anticommunism. Actually, Elkins and Mathews were essentially agreed, for both historians

20. McClelland, *The Achieving Society*, 193; Aileen S. Kraditor, *Means and Ends in American Abolitionism: Garrison and His Critics on Strategy and Tactics, 1834–1850* (New York, 1969); Eric Foner, *Politics and Ideology in the Age of the Civil War* (New York, 1980), 42–43.

21. Donald G. Mathews, "The Methodist Schism of 1844 and the Popularization of Antislavery Sentiment," *Mid-America*, LI (1969), 21–22.

stressed the rise of a new ideology hastened by the expansion of mass communications, the fragmentation of national bodies, and the reduction of the antislavery gospel to its lowest common denominator, a murky but visceral dislike of things southern—and "sinful." [22]

Elkins also failed to concede that much of what abolitionists had to say about the psychic horrors of slavery were points which he himself had so graphically portrayed in other portions of *Slavery*. Nurtured in Calvinism and fed by their own romantic meditations, abolitionists guessed with some precision the effects of total masterhood and bondage. Slavery, they claimed, *could* make children out of men, broodmares out of women, and disposable chattel out of infants. Consistently they attacked the slaves' lack of accessibility to normal aspirations. All those institutional restraints and opportunities that Elkins rightly described as necessary for healthy psychic development could be found in the reformers' catalog of what was wrong with slavery. Of course, their vision included a gothic terror that granted masters and slaves less than their due as human beings. An antislavery tract was like a Brontë novel: a mixture of revealing insights into evil and thrusts into popular bathos.

Moreover, Elkins deplored what many others would consider praiseworthy in abolitionist political theory. Exuberant breast-beating and lusty indignation did not exhaust the antislavery reformers' repertoire. They realized that ancient racial folkways were being rapidly incorporated into all those agencies transforming America into a modern state. Abolitionists made war upon both church and party at a time when these institutions were just developing. Hoping to make changes before the hour passed, abolitionists urged church bodies and political parties to be morally consistent, in conformity with their claims of national representativeness. [23]

In sum, antebellum reformers were determined to make the coun-

22. Elkins, *Slavery*, 175–93; see John B. Lentz, "The Antislavery Constituency in Jacksonian New York City," *Civil War History*, XXVII (1981), 101–122, on the workers as "fellow-travelers."

23. John Higham, *From Boundlessness to Consolidation: The Transformation of American Culture, 1848–1860* (Ann Arbor, 1960); Arthur K. Bestor, "Patent-Office Models of the Good Society: Some Relationships Between Social Reform and Westward Expansion," *American Historical Review*, LVIII (1953), 505–526.

try as homogeneous and puritanical as possible, to eliminate the evil of folk racism but to strengthen the heritage of Christian idealism. In Talcott Parsons' terms, they were the most comprehensive advocates of a "universalistic-achievement" society in American history. They opposed all compromises with "particularistic-ascriptive" folkways to which southern culture tenaciously clung. The doctrines were flavored with the stingy paternalism, sectional chauvinism, suspicion of godless party spirit or "faction," and mustiness of Connecticut Sundays—all aspects of ancient New England custom. Yet abolitionism was eventually, though imperfectly, incorporated into the northern or at least the Republican system of values. Conservatives questioned the fantasies of a "higher law," but the ideals reflected were much more appropriate to the secular aspirations of the free-labor North than were the pieties of a bygone day. Given the transfer of power from local squires to national constituencies, it made supreme sense that Americans submit to a single cultural pattern. With communications growing more interstitial, it mattered very much that moral uniformities keep pace with nationwide transformations, especially in regard to the universal spread of law and the protections of a common, civil religion.[24] Elkins' bias induced him to prefer a declaration of ideological change, even though society was moving rapidly forward.

Intent upon polarizing rational behavior and antinomian vagary, Elkins also took little notice of the conventionalities of nineteenth-century reform. Even antinomians must breathe the common air and accept many of the normal conditions of earthly existence. In the first place, men like Garrison and Henry C. Wright—complex figures— were not American Jacobins. Antislavery methods were often quite mundane and peaceful. Lewis Tappan's notion of radical behavior was to seize a summer hotel lobby as a forum for antislavery discussion, no matter what fellow vacationers thought.[25] Elkins made aboli-

24. Talcott Parsons, *Social Structure and Personality* (London, 1970), and *The Social System* (Glencoe, Ill., 1951), 196–200; Eric Foner, *Free Soil, Free Labor, Free Men: The Ideology of the Republican Party Before the Civil War* (New York, 1970), 302–304; Stewart, *Holy Warriors*, 182–94.
25. Bertram Wyatt-Brown, "William Lloyd Garrison and Antislavery Unity: A Reappraisal," *Civil War History*, XIII (1967), 5–24; James B. Stewart, "Garrison Again,

tionists' actions seem much more quixotic and flamboyant than could actually have been sustained for the thirty years of the prewar aspects of the crusade.

In like manner, Transcendentalists were less consistently opposed to conventional arrangements and values than Elkins suggested. Both groups of reformers seldom quarreled with traditional ideals—family integrity, temperate habits, respect for others—reasoning that American society was moving away from such ageless goals. They chiefly quarreled with what they discerned as the diminishing quality of American experience. Despite Anne Rose's questioning of Elkins' characterization of transcendentalism, he rightly pointed to an anti-institutional tendency in their criticisms. Yet qualifications were not supplied in his account. Emerson's anti-institutionalism, for instance, bordered on cryptic piety. In his personal life he was jealous of simple comforts of a traditional kind. Sensitive to public opinion, Emerson never spoke against slavery when he was on tour. Unlike the gregarious Lewis Tappan, he submitted only reluctantly to the lucrative lyceum circuit out of a sense of democratic obligation, a duty "to roll with the river of travellers, & live in hotels." [26]

One reason for Elkins' displeasure with the Jacksonian radical reformers was his own almost romantic faith in the capabilities of modern-day established or academic intellectuals. He alleged that "when a society is confronted by a problem [such as slavery] one supposes that all the wisdom available . . . should strain toward its solution," a duty that antebellum thinkers irresponsibly shunned. How much wisdom a "solution" may require is always a highly subjective matter. Presumably John Adams and the intellectual patriots of 1776 fell short of Elkins' standards, since neither they nor the institutionally minded British leaders were able to settle matters, short of

---

and Again, and Again . . . ," *Reviews in American History*, IV (1976), 539–45; Susan A. Tappan to Julia Tappan, June 5, 1848 [copy], in Lewis Tappan Papers, Library of Congress.

26. Rose, *Transcendentalism as a Social Movement*, 219–20; compare Michael Fellman, "Worldly Transcendentalists," *Reviews in American History*, XI (1983), 68; Ralph Waldo Emerson to Thomas Carlyle, April 29, 1843, in Joseph Slater (ed.), *The Correspondence of Emerson and Carlyle* (New York, 1964), 341–42; Elkins, *Slavery*, esp. 147, 148, 151, 156.

war. But the question remains, were the Concord thinkers peculiarly deficient in statecraft? Borrowing Elkins' reliance on analogy for the moment, one might pose them against their English counterparts, the authors of the *Lyrical Ballads*. After a brief, youthful flirtation with French Revolutionary thought in 1790, William Wordsworth and Samuel Taylor Coleridge subsided into poetic repose without much interest in antislavery or any other philanthropy of the day. Shelley and Byron were more active in politics and radical thought. Yet one would hardly have expected to find them devising committee-room plans for social uplift. Alienation, the Romantic thinker believed, was a function of the poetic temperament. The notion was hardly peculiar to the Concord elite. Like their transatlantic counterparts, the Transcendentalists were concerned with matters of principle, not power.[27]

Elkins' bias, as the comparison helps to show, led him into errors regarding the chronological setting. One must agree with him that the members of the Concord circle rejected the normal channels of power, but their position was related to the temper of the times, not solely to a unique and tragic American flaw as Elkins suggested. Confusion was also evident in Elkins' comparison of the British and American emancipation movements. Other critics have noted the inappropriateness of his contrast between the freeing of West Indian slaves by distant Parliamentarians and the American struggle over slavery on native soil. But Elkins also overlooked the parallel chronologies of transatlantic reform. Like the American movement to free northern slaves, the English endeavor against the slave trade began in the late eighteenth century along traditional, moderate lines. After 1815, both movements became increasingly romantic, mass-oriented, and anti-institutional. Nonconformists in England replaced the Clapham group in the leadership of the antislavery movement, particularly after the restructuring of Parliament of 1832. These Dissenters were by no means congenial allies of the Anglican and Tory establishment, as Elkins asserted, nor did they believe that "the ruling class [was] fluid enough in its recruitment" to satisfy

27. Elkins, *Slavery*, 140; M. H. Abrams, "English Romanticism: The Spirit of the Age," in Frye (ed.), *Romanticism Reconsidered*, 52–72.

their self-conscious aspirations. In fact, as the English historians Roger Anstey and Howard Temperley and other antislavery experts note, British abolitionism was based on a growing sense of imperialistic destiny and industrial progress benefiting all classes, but especially the Nonconformist middle and lower classes. Abolition sentiment, scarcely confined to the rich and wealthy elite, appealed most broadly to those long restrained by aristocratic hegemony.[28]

The Emancipation Act of 1833 was intimately connected with various reform causes that challenged landed-gentry rule. Quakers and Methodists saw a direct analogy between their civil distresses and restrictions at home and the more tragic plight of West Indian slaves. Their rhetoric and styles of agitation resembled those of the contemporaneous American cause. The contexts, though, obviously diverged sharply. Elkins stressed the earlier stage of the English campaigns under the Evangelical members of the Church of England, efforts comparable to the work of Federalist manumissionists in the eighteenth century and of Whiggish colonizationists in the early nineteenth century. A more valid analogy for the post-1830 period of reform would have linked Joseph Sturge, the Quaker philanthropist of Birmingham, with the American evangelicals—John Greenleaf Whittier and Orange Scott, for example—and George Thompson, the British leader, with Garrison and Wendell Phillips. Moreover, we are now aware that the working classes in both countries were involved in antislavery work, although leadership was largely in the hands of the middle classes in the two nations. Yet, one is forced to agree with Elkins that English reformers were more respectful of tradition and privilege than American activists usually were. The very fact that English antislavery became a respectable

28. Elkins, *Slavery*, 202; Roger Anstey, "The Patterns of British Abolitionism in the Eighteenth and Nineteenth Centuries," in Christine Bolt and Seymour Drescher (eds.), *Anti-Slavery, Religion and Reform: Essays in Memory of Roger Anstey* (Folkstone, Eng., and Hamden, Conn., 1980), 19–42, and the essays therein by James Walvin, C. Duncan Rice, and Howard Temperley; Seymour Drescher, "Cartwhip and Billy Roller: Antislavery and Reform Symbolism in Industrializing Britain," *Journal of Social History*, XV (1981), 3–24; Edith Hurwitz, *Politics and Public Conscience: Emancipation and the Abolitionist Movement in Great Britain* (London, 1973), 42–43.

form of vicarious social protest suggested a caution and obliqueness in the United Kingdom not to be found in Garrison's America.[29]

Nevertheless, Elkins had misread the British reform situation. As a result, he treated the American abolitionists more harshly than they deserved. The most telling example was his contrast between the gentle octogenarian William Wilberforce, patriarch of British emancipationism, and William Lloyd Garrison. Evangelicalism of eighteenth-century England belonged to the world of Whig estates and drawing-room prayers. Garrison was a child of romantic zeal and provincial puritanism. Elkins asked, "In contrast to these planners, these intellectuals, these men of affairs [of Clapham Commons], what plans had he? What were *his* resources—other than the impotent fury of his own poisoned pen?" Garrison was, as Elkins added, very "poor," but he was also very young. (Wilberforce was fifty years his senior when their reform efforts crossed.) Yet Elkins meant pathetic, not penurious. Adjectives bore the weight of argument.[30]

A truly just evaluation of American immediate emancipationism would have placed it squarely in the context of a romantic spirit abroad in the early-nineteenth-century Western world. No country, particularly on the Continent, escaped the impact of antinomian, even revolutionary, thought. The bastions of feudal institutionalism and particularistic loyalties were inexorably crumbling in France, Germany, Austria, and Italy. As in America, economic change, nationalism, and mass culture were modernizing the old nations. Tocqueville, to whom Elkins referred for supporting a case for American peculiarities, actually saw America as an example of the European future, one in which traditional ties, intimacies, and arrangements surrendered to mass uniformities, restless dynamism, and ideo-

29. Lentz, "The Antislavery Constituency," 101–122; Eric Foner, "Abolitionism and the Working Class," in Bolt and Drescher (eds.), *Anti-Slavery, Religion and Reform*, 254–71; C. Duncan Rice, *The Scots Abolitionists, 1833–1861* (Baton Rouge, 1981), 197–98; Betty Fladeland, *Men and Brothers: Anglo-American Antislavery Cooperation* (Urbana, 1972), 400–409; Davis, "The Emergence of Immediatism," 209–230; G. R. S. Kitson Clark, "The Romantic Element, 1830–1850," in John H. Plumb (ed.), *Studies in Social History: A Tribute to G. M. Trevelyan* (London, 1955), 209–239; Elkins, *Slavery*, 202–204.

30. Elkins, *Slavery*, 202–205 (quotation, 204–205).

logical mobilization. America, the French observer believed, was a promise and a warning to the Old World.[31] Elkins, however, reduced Tocqueville's observations to a simple contrast between European stability and American anarchy. By failing to embrace a large vision of romantic intellectualism, Elkins narrowed his theme unduly and provoked his critics to question most of his profound analysis. But the reason why he failed to sustain a strategy of impartiality was perhaps as interesting as anything he said about slaves, comparative institutions, and Yankee life.

To understand *Slavery* we must place this brilliant achievement in the context of the period of its composition. Elkins was inevitably influenced by the hopes and disappointments of the Eisenhower era. Historians of that generation have been called "consensus" scholars; the term was vague and somewhat misleading. Yet there was a common mood reflected in their writings, a general mistrust of ideology— and for good reason. The rise of Stalinist Russia, Nazi Germany, militarist Japan, and finally Communist China was a wrenching experience. Given the political extremism of mindless McCarthyism at home and cold-war rhetoric in all parts of the world, it seemed to this generation of intellectuals to matter little if men willed their own slavery to dictatorships of Right or Left. Both forms of rule achieved the same stultification and horror. As Daniel Bell observed, the academicians of the 1950s had once been "intense, horatory [*sic*], naive, simplistic, and passionate, but, after the Moscow trials and the Soviet-Nazi pact, disenchanted and reflective; and from them and their experiences we have inherited the key terms which dominate discourse today: irony, paradox, ambiguity, and complexity." Taking chill comfort from the new skepticism, a few rejoiced in an "end of ideology," but most longed "for 'a cause to believe in,'" although they were self-consciously aware that "the desire for 'a cause' itself is self-defeating." Attention was therefore given to American diversity, pluralism, pragmatic politics, and, to a degree, anti-intellectuality—

31. *Ibid.*, 160*n*49; J. P. Mayer, *Alexis de Tocqueville: A Biographical Study in Political Science* (New York, 1960), 29–38; R. Jackson Wilson, "Gentlemen Democrats at Home and Abroad," in Howard Quint and Milton Cantor (eds.), *Men, Women, and Issues* (2 vols.; Homewood, Ill., 1980), I, 150–69.

sources of strength for some and of weakness as perceived by others. To a greater or lesser extent, however, these intellectuals were suspicious of the romantic mode. Thus Elkins' distaste for anti-nomianism and his almost pessimistic view of man resulted partly from his training at Columbia under those of the "twice-born" generation, as Bell labeled them, and partly from his own reactions to the climate of the times.[32]

Elkins' *Slavery* reflected these sentiments in some measure. Man's best chance for progress, the work implied, lay in pragmatic, non-ideological, and structured benevolence. Chiliasm offered nothing but violence and disillusionment. Blind, unrestrained reaction was self-defeating. Remaining hope focused upon rational social science skillfully coordinated with institutions of power. The promise of that kind of public activity proved illusory a few years after Elkins' work appeared. The mistakes of scholar-bureaucrats and the misfortunes of their foreign and domestic programs may even have hastened the appearance of the antinomian radicalism that followed. Yet a faith in the concreteness, the seeming substantiality of the social sciences offered Elkins and his contemporaries a reason for creativity and a way for the intellectual to help order and guide the future. A degree of arrogance was involved, but the intentions were inspired and worth being tested.

Elkins, however, was not merely an echo of "consensus" scholars like Richard Hofstadter or Daniel Boorstin. Most particularly, Boorstin failed to delve very far into issues regarding the twin American tragedies of the Civil War and slavery. Rather, Elkins was much more sensitive to the moral and sectional dilemmas that the nation faced in the nineteenth century than were his somewhat older colleagues, then stressing the optimism and consensual nature of the American experiment. Whereas Boorstin, for instance, saw European obsession with abstraction and ideology in contrast to a stable and hopeful America, Elkins reversed the mirror. Moreover, he was not satisfied with the usual narrative form of historical writing. More than most

32. Daniel Bell, *The End of Ideology: On the Exhaustion of Political Ideas in the Fifties* (New York, 1965), 300.

of his contemporaries, he dealt with *mentalité* and social structure, both seen in a behavioral science fashion. Given later historiographical developments, Elkins' *Slavery* was a pioneer study foreshadowing the rise of anthropological approaches to social history in America.[33]

An advantage of his social-science style was that it permitted a much less morally charged examination of slavery than that by such scholars as Kenneth Stampp, author of *The Peculiar Institution*, in the mid-1950s. In addition, the behavioral approach offered Elkins a useful vocabulary and set of concepts, including such terms as institution, open systems, social control, power, responsible action, sensibility. These constructions had their opposites in anti-institutionalism, closed systems, insensibility. These rather benign words for what some might call fanaticism, bloodthirstiness, and the like were applicable to masters or to their Yankee critics, according to one's moral perspective.

Another break with traditional history-writing was the employment of analogy, an elaborate and extended metaphor. Elkins' use of the Nazi attempt at Faustian supremacy illustrated the point. The tone of the hardheaded statement of fact disarmed the reader while it highlighted the torment and inner corruption of ideology run amok. A characterization of southern means of race control was likewise placed next to the appealing portrait of a benevolent, restrained Hispanic culture. In the last chapter, however, Elkins revealed more clearly what his moral purpose was. Therein, the intellectual distance sometimes broke down, partly because the analogies were less gripping in themselves and partly because emotive words appeared more frequently, as evinced in the Garrison-Wilberforce comparison. Thus Elkins banked the fires of conviction, but his moral commitment shone through, especially in Chapter 4.

If hyperbole is permitted, one could say that *Slavery* was a four-

33. Louis Hartz, *The Liberal Tradition in America* (New York, 1955); Daniel J. Boorstin, *The Americans: The National Experience* (New York, 1965); Jack P. Diggins, "The Perils of Naturalism: Some Reflections on Daniel J. Boorstin's Approach to American History," *American Quarterly*, XXIII (1971), 153–80, and "Consciousness and Ideology in American History: The Burden of Daniel J. Boorstin," *American Historical Review*, LXXVI (1971), 110–11.

chapter sermon. Among other things, *Slavery* was a rational, carefully constructed exposition of the evils of selfish individualism, dogmatism, antinomian self-possession, ideological waywardness, and thirst for total power. Elkins' looseness of organization, of which critics have complained, was the result of his decision not to draw these judgments together.[34] To do so would have reversed his nonideological strategy. Nevertheless, he assumed throughout the book that civilization died the moment full authority was vested in the individual actor. He might be an SS guard at Dachau, a plantation overlord on the Mississippi River, or a dreamer on the outskirts of Boston. What all three shared was rejection of institutional restraints. The absence of ideological boundaries was the collective failure of their respective societies. Yet it was no less tragic for being so widespread. Elkins implied that each of these antinomian types, so to speak, guard, slaveholder, and reformer, represented man out of control, pursuing his uninhibited and devilish ends.

According to this rendering of the historical verdict, men have an inordinate drive for power and a capacity for self-delusion. They will resort to psychological devices of terror to master their fellows and their own destiny. Such mechanisms are possible because men participate in their own humiliation and even learn to enjoy it. Accordingly, Sambo was a metaphor in *Slavery*, one representing this trait as well as the consequences of tyranny unchecked by traditions, history, and institutions. As symbols, the docile slave and the concentration-camp inmate were luminous images, like figures in stained glass—frozen, one-dimensional, but evocative. Elkins himself seemed a little uncertain about whether he intended a literal characterization or a literary archetype. But metaphors cannot serve a scientifically verifiable function. They are iconographic, not factual. Yet as a means of casting moral light on man's condition, metaphors, whether couched in poetic or scholarly language, can burn the inner consciousness. For that reason alone, *Slavery* must be consid-

34. David Donald, Review of Elkins' *Slavery*, in *American Historical Review*, LXV (1960), 921–22; Robert Durden, Review of Elkins' *Slavery*, in *South Atlantic Quarterly*, LX (1961), 94–95.

ered a major achievement. The use of metaphor as a strategy in American historiography has not often been attempted. Elkins' pioneering in the field must be appreciated.

Indeed, historians are still living under the shadow of interpretations and styles offered by social scientists of the 1950s. Their distrust of easy solutions to problems present and past, their sense of irony, and their creative yearning for truly workable answers to ancient woes set them apart from their Progressive forebears and from the less reflective breed of the 1960s.[35] With rare subtlety and innovation, historians such as Elkins explored areas of American experience.

The one failing that Elkins did not fully overcome was parochialism, which his borrowings from other Western cultures did not assuage. Philosophically, he differed from the Progressive scholar Frederick Jackson Turner, but like him he overstressed American uniqueness. As a result, he was too concerned with the American tragedy of civil war to observe that other nineteenth-century nations also bore the weight of moral weakness, arrogance, and culpability. For instance, Elkins could be granted that Latin white colonials faced some modest checks upon masterhood that Americans lacked. Perhaps Brazilian slaveholding was more "open," a pleasant word, and society less racist, as he claimed. Yet even in imagination, one cannot import the best a society has to offer, without accepting the less attractive corollaries as well. From Elkins' critics we learned that Latin America had its special contributions to make to human travail. Racism, it seems, was overwhelmed in squalor and the utter misery of practically everybody. Whatever problems Americans have experienced with slavery and prejudice, they have escaped evils present elsewhere. Whatever comforts may be elicited from that state of grace must be balanced against the brutal costs of racial violence and sorrow.

Despite his willingness to compare our institutional breakdowns with equally tragic ones in other places, Elkins' moral position is unassailable. If government, laws, history, and genial habits were respected because they deserved to be, and if intelligence and responsi-

35. See Aileen S. Kraditor, "American Radical Historians on Their Heritage," *Past & Present*, No. 56 (1972), 136–52.

bility held passion in rein, wars and oppression would cease or at least be subject to less tragic consequences. Elkins sought to demonstrate that the United States had failed to match its potentiality in the antebellum years, and his argument was more than a simple moral lesson from the past. His was a study of American character and its romantic tendencies.

Elkins was not so much wrong about a fractured and atomistic society, however, as his depiction was incomplete. Indeed, American institutions were undergoing fierce strains, in company with those of Western civilization itself. But the old order, based upon folkways, localistic virtues, and simple ties of community and family, had to make way for a new and universalistic system of stateways. The modern industrial nation, as historians have long understood, was formed in the crucible that Theodore Parker and his indignant colleagues helped to fashion. In his final chapter, Elkins pointed mostly to the losses, but surely there were great gains as well. Still more important, those gains and defeats were each shaped and distorted, restrained and released in such a way that anomaly or contradiction formed the texture of the experience. Like the slaveholder who saw only the Sambo in the slave, like the abolitionist who saw only southern sin and un-Yankee particularism in slavery and not human beings in their infinite varieties, Elkins perceived an experiential aspect of national life, griefs and unrealized possibilities, and assumed it was the whole.

We must acknowledge Elkins' bold uses of behavioral techniques. But men, in isolation and collectivity, seldom fit comfortably into the formulas and abstractions provided for comprehending them. A society capable of raising up such complex, admirable men as Emerson, Wendell Phillips, and John C. Calhoun might well have done worse. In the long run, Elkins would be happy to agree. After all, his purpose was not to advocate blind conformity. He did not use Great Britain's institutionalism to propose a similar social structure for America. Moreover, he did not in any way approve of the baser impulses he so tellingly described. To the contrary, he offered his analogies and his strategy of detachment and pragmatic expectancy in the interests of graciousness, equity, and racial harmony.

His message resembled that of Hannah Arendt: modern man recognizes no limits to conquest of self, others, and environment. Convinced of their own pure motives, abolitionists and masters alike demanded unrestrained access to power. There was little humility or reflection on either side of the Potomac. With the bankruptcy of Enlightenment sensibilities, the sacredness of simple obligations, consensual prejudices, and social deference did collapse. A new militance arose with freedom and democracy. The march of northern armies crushed one form of arrogance. Yet it is hard to say that the Union victory transformed the American conscience and unfolded a new era of utopian promise, even though it resolved the anomaly of slavery in a free society.

Elkins' *Slavery* reminds us of some ancient truths of human nature by means of a strategic appeal of reason. Occasionally his bias became too overt. Yet as long as men perceive either war or enslavement as cause for moral outrage, the historian is obliged to judge if freedom is worth the price paid in blood and treasure. Most scholars are not afraid to offer their moral views which coincide with their political convictions. But the passage of time and changes in world opinion seem to mock the historians' certainties of what was right and wrong. Few in the profession have dared to leave problems and events of the past unresolved, in a state of tension without message or purpose. As David B. Davis observes, "For those of us who still think of history as a kind of moral philosophy teaching by examples, it is precisely the multiple character of truth—the varied angles of vision that are also the subject of imaginative literature—that one must seek to capture."[36] Explanations must be offered for the sound in the Marabar Caves, to borrow E. M. Forster's image. Otherwise, historians would imply a future as well as a past without meaning. Few if any have yet striven for the kind of experiential truthfulness of a novelist or a poet, though Elkins seemed to be working toward this aim. Instead, the historian, like his readers, chooses sides or else serves as referee. The means for making contradictions, wayward irresolutions the essence of the historical process have so far escaped

36. David B. Davis, *Slavery and Human Progress* (New York, 1984), 154.

us. Glibly expository, our best works are written in the manner of Trollope, not Faulkner. We remain prisoners of moral certitudes and conventions; the humanness of the past fades into grand abstraction. In some measure Elkins is such a prisoner too, but the situation is common. In any case, the quality of his moral conviction, not his technique alone, has rendered his study the battleground for rewarding contention. A sense of engaged morality made *Slavery* one of the most vigorous, perceptive, haunting volumes in recent American history.

II

CONSCIENCE AND CAREER:
Young Abolitionists and Missionaries Compared

FOR ALL the innovations of *Slavery*, Stanley Elkins' portrayal of abolitionism conformed with long-standing popular and academic opinion about the fanatical and destructive nature of the cause. Shortly after the book's appearance, though, a much more favorable perception emerged. In the era of civil rights crusades, the reformers seemed noble prophets of modern racial justice. The revision was long overdue, but it was distorting. The new approach rather neglected the religious foundations of antislavery and instead stressed its secular and political side. Historians could thus praise the abolitionist host as "freedom-fighters" and still criticize leaders of other reforms as ideologues for capitalism and middle-class morality that used religion to impose social controls upon an unruly lower class. That tradition has continued. David Rothman's *The Discovery of the Asylum*, Paul Johnson's *A Shopkeeper's Millennium*, and Paul Boyer's *Urban Masses and Moral Order in America* exemplify the persistent skepticism of professional historians throughout the 1970s.[1]

Previously published, in slightly different form, as "Conscience and Career: Missionaries and Abolitionists Compared," in Christine Bolt and Seymour Drescher (eds.), *Anti-Slavery, Religion and Reform: Essays in Memory of Roger Anstey* (Folkstone, Eng., and Hamden, Conn., 1980). Used with permission.
    1. David J. Rothman, *The Discovery of the Asylum: Social Order and Disorder in Jacksonian America* (Boston, 1971); Joseph Gusfield, *Symbolic Crusade: Status Politics and the American Temperance Movement* (Urbana, 1972); Michael Katz, *The Irony of*

How easy it is to find fault, for instance, with the foreign mission movement. It was an evangelical enterprise as romantic and adventuresome as abolitionism, with which it had closer ties than we have ordinarily thought. Like the teetotalers, prison and asylum advocates, tractarians, and other apostles of repression, the missionaries can be called narrow busybodies who imposed a shabby culture on helpless aborigines and opened the doors for imperialism. Thus, the antislavery humanitarians were allegedly breaking chains while others in far-off places were forging them. Nonetheless, both groups stood for the same things—especially the end of bondage, whether it was suttee or the southern auction block. Because of their doctrinal and social similarities, the missionaries for emancipation and for pagan conversion are worth comparing.

First, neither group was very subtle or circumspect about what it wanted: universal moral discipline and restraint on the one hand and personal autonomy and freedom from ancient sins and passion on the other. Foreign missionaries sought to elevate "heathen" women and other dependents so appallingly maltreated. The abolitionists wished to uplift the "bleeding" slave. Foreign missionaries were probably more condescending toward the native peoples than abolitionists were in regard to American slaves, but both groups had their egalitarian saints and their racially haughty sinners. Second, the foreign missionaries and emancipationists agreed that literacy should not be used as a means for rulers, priests, and their allies to hold others in the bondage of ignorance. Education, these Christian Yankees insisted, should be available to all, the ordinary people of other continents as well as the blacks at home. Both kinds of reformers hoped to create new Yankeedoms in places of darkness, firmly convinced that their common culture could be exported. Third, from a theological point of view, foreign missionaries and antislavery advocates championed the Second Coming and were naïve enough to think the goals achievable in a matter of years. Despite these similarities, political

---

Early School Reform: Educational Innovation in Mid-Nineteenth Century Massachusetts (Cambridge, Mass., 1968); Paul E. Johnson, A Shopkeeper's Millennium: Society and Revivals in Rochester, New York, 1815–1837 (New York, 1978); Paul S. Boyer, Urban Masses and Moral Order in America, 1820–1920 (Cambridge, Mass., 1978).

perspectives of the causes and their leaders have muddled our understanding of who the abolitionists and the foreign missionaries were.

The most important single factor uniting missionary with abolitionist was that most unwelcome New England export: the evangelical conscience. To that purpose, we should start as life does itself—at the beginning. Three crucial areas of moral development were significant: the instilling and growth of conscience in the child; the adolescent problems of religious belief and intellectual ambition; and the stresses of choosing the career in benevolence, when political differentiation seemed to emerge.

The evangelical style of child-raising was an alternative to an older means that relied on shame, open humiliation, and physical pain to curb presumed depravity. The latter doctrine has been associated with Calvinism, but actually the idea that children were all but incorrigible and required stern handling should not be identified too narrowly with any sectarian or theological position. In any case, an enlightened approach to child-rearing had developed by 1800, and those practicing it chiefly belonged to evangelical faiths. The new religious sensibility reflected a concern with the atonement of Christ more than the illimitable sovereignty of God, affection as well as obedience in human relations, the inner life more than the outward appearance, and personal integrity over demands for conformity. Of course, in the treatment of children, families adopted all sorts of patterns and methods, whether they were Quakers, Methodists, predestinarian Congregationalists or belonged to some other denomination. On the whole, the children of evangelical parents were subjected to a scheme that for all its faults, had a specific rationale, a clear expectation of what the results should be, and an attentiveness to the child that contrasted with the preemptiveness that so often had marked the parental ways of the past. This interpretation denies Philip Greven's identification of authoritarian patriarchy with the evangelical faith. Of course, the parents, especially the father, still controlled the household, but the emphasis was upon rational persuasion informed by love, the notion that parents know best, not upon simple obedience for its own sake.

Shame was a device that employed overt exposure to ridicule. In contrast, conscience internalized moral precepts. It also repressed unacceptable impulses and channeled aggressions toward objectives thought socially and personally useful.[2] To accomplish these ends, parents, under religious guidance, learned that explaining the purposes of their decisions and pointing out the consequences for wrongdoing impressed the child. Stirring feelings of anxiety was a part of the disciplinary process, but it contrasted with the uncalculating, inconsistent, reactive style of the past: abrupt demands for total obedience, a heavy beating or ear-boxing, or an unwarranted indulgence to soothe or compensate the child. Joseph Waite, Samuel Shaw, and Richard Baxter, English Evangelical divines of the seventeenth century, groped toward these ideas. Especially popular was Baxter's series of works offering practical Christian advice. John Locke had made the new child-rearing prescriptions still more explicit. By the beginning of the nineteenth century, many evangelical families were convinced that children were quite malleable. If parents would begin with their children when they are young, suggested a minister's wife in 1813, they might "mould" them into any frame they choose. Laymen cared very little about such abstruse arguments as that regarding infant damnation, a topic that clergymen debated. What mattered was the child's earthly sojourn as a creature of God.[3]

The parents of little John Mooney Mead exemplified the new approach: they sought to build character in the boy by denial and distraction. Such means, they asserted, taught the child to postpone gratifications, to control physical and emotional impulses, and to think of others' needs, not just his own. The regimen included "withholding from him whatever he cried for, and when he was fretful,

2. Philip Greven, *The Protestant Temperament: Patterns of Child-Rearing, Religious Experience, and the Self in Early America* (New York, 1977), 21–150; Jay Fliegelman, *Prodigals and Pilgrims: The American Revolution Against Patriarchal Authority* (Cambridge, Eng., 1982), 159–60, 269n2; Gerhart Piers and Milton B. Singer, *Shame and Guilt: A Psychoanalytic and Cultural Study* (New York, 1953); Helen M. Lynd, *On Shame and the Search for Identity* (New York, 1958), 13–71.
3. Lydia Maria Child, *The Mother's Book* (Boston, 1832), 7, 10, 16–17; Richard Baxter, *The Christian Directory*, vols. II–VI of *The Practical Works of Richard Baxter*, ed. William Orme (23 vols.; London, 1830), IV, 175–90; C. John Sommerville, "English Puritans and Children: A Socio-Cultural Explanation," *Journal of Psychohistory*, VI (1978), 113–37; Nancy F. Cott, *The Bonds of Womanhood: "Woman's Sphere" in New England, 1780–1835* (New Haven, 1977), 47.

they did not pacify him by caresses, or by bestowing what he desired, but by directing his attention to something else." John Mead's father, a Congregational minister, and mother used physical punishment but once in his short life of four years, when he was fourteen months old. Parental violence, they urged, merely promoted similarly harsh responses in the child. He would learn not to turn the other cheek or control anger but simply take out his feelings by inflicting on someone else such pain as he had received. Therefore, the couple suggested that "obedience was generally readiest and most cheerful, when the commands were given in the most affectionate manner, seeming rather to ask, than to demand compliance." As occasions presented themselves, they encouraged John Mead to share toys and treats with playmates. The habit of giving could not be learned too soon, they felt.[4]

Prescriptive literature, such as this memorial volume, as well as daily practice ascertained from letters and diaries, indicated a growing conviction that calculated, rational, and predictable behavior toward the child shaped good character and willing obedience. The contradiction was an inherent aspect of the evangelical spirit. The system did not encourage overt shows of affection—for fear of spoiling the child. But in most cases, there was love, and from it a sense of self-confidence developed in the child. Rigorous, a little cheerless, and overly regimented, evangelical child-rearing tried to link godliness with consistency, love with conscience, individuality with order, and benevolence toward others with sacred duty.[5]

Abolitionists, along with other evangelical inheritors, were raised within this framework. To be sure, there were variations, exceptions, and degrees of laxity, strictness, and success. But a similarity of aims, a roughly common understanding of moral boundaries, and a willingness to give attention to the child had evolved. Freedom and

4. *Memoir of John Mooney Mead, Who Died in East Hartford, April 7, 1831, Aged Four Years, 11 Months, and 4 Days* (Boston, 1832), 7, 9, 10–11; Greven, *The Protestant Temperament*, 32–55.
5. Anne L. Kuhn, *The Mother's Role in Childhood Education* (New Haven, 1947), 27; Nancy F. Cott, "Notes Toward an Explanation of Antebellum Childrearing," *Psychohistory Review*, VI (1978), 4–20; Mary P. Ryan, *Cradle of the Middle Class: The Family in Oneida County, New York, 1790–1865* (Cambridge, Eng., and New York, 1981), 157–62.

discipline, parents and advisors agreed, had to be held in equilibrium. To evangelicals' distress, old ethical standards that revered male honor and glorified male self-indulgences prevailed and even found wide dissemination. Quite correctly, they saw the dangers of temptation that a fast-changing democracy offered their young. Establishing good habits had to begin early. Therefore they sought to protect the children, especially the boys, from male pressures to conform as a way of demonstrating manhood: wenching, gambling, drinking, and fighting. As slums and the vices associated with them multiplied, the evangelicals grew increasingly troubled, and by the 1820s they sought with almost desperate seriousness ways to prepare youngsters to resist temptations. The uncontrollable character of democracy was worrisome, but rather than expect a return to some puritan order, evangelicals determined to counteract the trends by posing a Christian ethic against the traditional male ethic of tavern, penny sheet, and public meeting-place.

Reflecting this determination, Lydia Maria Child, moral preceptor as well as abolitionist, put the matter of conscience and character versus male honor and prerogative in this way: "Everything in school books, social remarks, domestic conversation, literature, public festivals, legislative proceedings, and popular honors, all teach the young soul that it is noble to retaliate, mean to forgive an insult, and unmanly not to resent a wrong. Animal instincts, instead of being brought into subjection to the higher power of the soul, are thus cherished into more than natural actions."[6]

At the heart of evangelical child-rearing was the role of the mother. The authority for disciplining and making decisions about the children had formerly been in the father's hands. By the end of the American Revolutionary era, the mother had gained the means and the ideology for devoting full attention to child-rearing. Previously she had been preoccupied with such soul-wearying, endless drudgeries as weaving cloth and making soap. But the developing economy provided her not only such comforts as factory textiles but also the time for making plans about child-rearing. Instead of just hastily re-

6. Child quoted in *American Whig Review*, I (1845), 67.

acting to the crises of the moment, mothers could concentrate upon becoming professional child-raisers. It was a calling that every evangelical writer in the new Republic assured them was both divinely ordained and patriotic. Through pious clubs called "maternal associations," Sunday school and church sewing societies, and other newly developed organizations, northern mothers, whatever their station, could leave the house to enjoy the exchange of child-rearing ideas and gossip. They could also display an active piety which would instruct their own children. Benevolence, all agreed, should be taught by example as well as by precept.[7]

The mother's preeminence over the father was not, of course, peculiar to households from which abolitionists would later emerge. Yet it appeared in most such homes. Abolitionist Thomas Wentworth Higginson, for instance, remembered that he owed his mother his most cherished principles: a "love of personal liberty, or religious freedom, and of the equality of the sexes." John Greenleaf Whittier, antislavery poet, also declared, "I felt secure of my mother's love, and dreamed of losing nothing and gaining much," but his father was to him an elderly, austere presence. In similar fashion Higginson had little positive to say of his father, who had died when Higginson was eleven. "I was unfortunately too young at that time to feel my loss much."[8]

One could dismiss these examples as mere recollections of childhood summoned up for adult reasons—to fit the emphasis upon motherhood and domesticity that accompanied the growth of Victorian sentiment and sensibility. But social attitude and actual experience seemed to coincide. As jobs became more specialized and carried the father to employments outside home and field, women had to take charge of all aspects of child-rearing including discipline, both physical and hortatory. The shift worried some observers. The Reverend Erastus Hopkins of Troy, New York, for instance, warned evangelical fathers not to lose their claims upon "filial affection" through neglect. In the evangelical ministers' view, however, power in the

7. Ryan, *Cradle of the Middle Class*, 89–91.
8. Mary T. Higginson, *Thomas Wentworth Higginson: The Story of His Life* (Port Washington, N.Y., 1971), 7; Samuel T. Pickard, *Life and Letters of John Greenleaf Whittier* (2 vols.; Boston and New York, 1894), I, 26.

nursery and on the playground belonged to women. They were supposed to be best equipped both emotionally and spiritually for the
difficult and vital business. In a sense, the delegation of authority to
the mother was itself a kind of career specialization and expansion of
opportunity rather than simply a means of yoking women to insignificant burdens.[9]

This self-conscious, inventive role for mothers encouraged the selection of one child or perhaps two for extraordinary attention. Quite
early on, the youngsters learned that they must begin plans for the
future, even though their careers were years away. Kenneth Keniston, the Yale psychologist, has called this emphasis upon the child's
moral and career success the creation of "a sense of specialness." In
traditional fashion, boys heard about pious and benevolent work for
men. The future missionary Adoniram Judson, for instance, was frequently encouraged to play at gospel preaching when only four. Likewise, the future abolitionist orator Wendell Phillips—to parental
delight—enjoyed haranguing playmates seated beneath his "pulpit"-
chair. More unexpectedly, evangelical mothers sometimes urged
daughters to think of serving Jesus as missionary wives. That career
combined domesticity with romantic adventure and service to others.
Children's literature included anecdotes from the lives of such missionary heroines as Harriet Newell and Harriet Wadsworth Winslow.
The Reverend Gardiner Spring, biographer of the missionary Samuel
J. Mills, put the matter this way: "Many a godly mother can say, —'I
have had peculiar solicitudes respecting *this* child. Even before its
birth, I dedicated it to the Lord.'" Whatever the choice would later be,
the child discovered that benevolence and career, when practiced in
play, elicited parental blessing. In addition, the youngster became
aware that he or she had been selected for a special destiny.[10]

The subtleties involved can scarcely be recaptured from reminiscences, but occasionally one glimpses the sense of specialness aris-

9. Hopkins quoted in Daniel Calhoun, *The Intelligence of a People* (Princeton,
1973), 165; *Mother's Magazine* (Utica, N.Y.), II (1834), 143; compare Jay Mechling, "Advice to Historians on Advice to Mothers," *Journal of Social History*, IX (1975), 44–63.
10. Kenneth Keniston, *Young Radicals: Notes on Committed Youth* (New York,
1968), 44–51, 55–60; David Elkind, "The Origins of Religion in the Child," *Archives de
Psychologie*, XL (1969), 15–24; Gardiner Spring, *Memoirs of the Rev. Samuel J. Mills,
Late Missionary to the South Western Section of the United States* (New York, 1820),
10–11; Carlos Martyn, *Wendell Phillips: The Agitator* (New York, 1890), 30.

ing, particularly among the acutely sensitive and especially when the child had committed some wrong. Isaac Hecker's Methodist mother, for instance, had only to express some mild displeasure to plunge her boy into spasms of abject submission. Everton Judson, missionary to northern Italy, recalled his mother telling him at age six or seven, "My son, I wish I could see you as much engaged in serving Jesus Christ as you are at your play." He put down his toy and burst into sobs.[11]

These illustrations were indicative of a pattern. By no means were they significant in themselves. Yet, they point toward a sense of special grace and of special failure and anxiety. There was a tension between pleasing mother and God and dreading the disappointment of those formidable figures. That early feeling of despair, and then recovery, was to have many parallels in the child's later development. Moreover, it presaged the dynamic mixture of hope and fear for creating a better world that adult missionaries and abolitionists shared.

In shaping the child's conscience toward benevolence and piety, the evangelical mother well knew the importance of stirring up anxiety. From fear of disapproval and from desire for praise and love, sometimes withheld as penalty, the child learned to listen to his or her inner voice. Fear of death, a greater reality for children then than now, was occasionally enlisted to serve the purpose. David Marks, an evangelist to the West, recalled that his Calvinistic Baptist mother nightly tucked him into bed with the words, "Soon my son you will exchange the bed for the grave, and your clothes for a winding sheet." As adults, many evangelicals expressed resentment against such morbid laments. Yet the remarks met the purpose intended. Anxiety, fear of meaninglessness and abandonment by God and loved ones, became a spur to life. Strangely, this kind of anxiety seemed to encourage self-confidence and grittiness, not despair or lassitude. The price, however, was the painful goad to do good, as child and adult. The effort was often taxing, and the individual felt driven.[12]

11. Vincent F. Holden, *The Early Years of Isaac Hecker (1818–1844)* (Washington, D.C., 1939), 9; E. P. Barrow, Jr., *Memoir of Everton Judson* (Boston, 1852), 21–22.
12. Mrs. Marilla Marks, *Memoirs of the Life of David Marks, Minister of the Gospel* (Dover, N.H., 1846), 14; Henry C. Wright Journal, May 22, 1835 (MS in Henry C. Wright Papers, Houghton Library, Harvard).

Nonreformers and nonabolitionists—ordinary churchgoers—were raised in the same fashion. The difference was that some children took the lessons of conscience and the burden of inner doubt with unusual seriousness. They were not necessarily prissy or submissive. As a rule, however, the future well-doer was more aware of moral strictures than were other youngsters. Theodore Parker, later a leading Garrisonian, offered an insight into his own upbringing. Once, at age five, he nearly killed a turtle. Racing home, he breathlessly asked his mother Hannah why he had not struck it. She exclaimed, "'Some men call it conscience, but I prefer to call it the voice of God in the soul of man. If you listen and obey it, then it will speak clearer and clearer . . . but if you turn a deaf ear or disobey, then it will fade out . . . and leave you all in the dark and without a guide.'" Parker concluded the recollection, "No event in my life has made so deep an impression upon me."[13]

The tale was not so important as the tendency it represented. Likewise in abolitionist biographies and other sources, there were frequent references to parental kindnesses and sympathies toward a local black, a fugitive slave, or some other victim of prejudice and ridicule. The most impressive example was the early history of Samuel Joseph May, a leading Garrisonian abolitionist and Unitarian clergyman in later years. When he was four, May saw his brother Edward fall from a chair during their barnyard play. A splintered post fatally punctured the six-year-old under the arm. Too young to understand the reality of death, Samuel refused to leave Edward. Stern Calvinists though his Boston parents were, they did not interfere when, as May recalled, "I kissed his cold cheeks and lips, pulled open his eyelids, begged him to speak to me, and cried myself to sleep because he would not." He remained in the room with the body that night until he fell asleep and his parents could at last take him away. After the burial, an uncle took him to the family vault and opened a coffin in which lay another dead sibling. He wanted to show Samuel the corruption of the flesh while assuring the boy that Edward and all the others there entombed enjoyed in heaven an immortality of

13. John Weiss, *The Life and Correspondence of Theodore Parker* (2 vols.; New York, 1864), I, 25.

spirit. For several nights thereafter, Samuel dreamed that Edward came to lie with him as he had in life, declaring that he was happy in his new celestial home. Samuel's fears and grief at last subsided. Two years later, May himself had a severe accident. He fell in the road and struck his head on a rock. When he awoke, he found himself in his house with "a large black woman" looking down at him. She had picked him up and brought him to the house. Agonized with worry and busy washing away the blood, his mother did not even thank the black Samaritan, as it were. The stranger had disappeared, and despite many searches the family never saw her again. No doubt May's later interest in emancipation had much to do with the two incidents of death, guilt, shock, and rescue. But more remarkable was the sensitivity of May's family. Had they not complied with the child's importunings to sleep with his brother, May could well have carried a grim burden of unconscious guilt for his own survival. Instead, their approach to his pain, as much as the black's good deed, prepared him for his eventual antislavery commitment. That reform was dedicated to the memories of his own good fortune and his brother's fate, but it transcended them both.[14]

Few other abolitionists had experiences as dramatic as May's to bring them to the cause, though many could recall some act of kindness by a black, some incident of racial prejudice that stirred their early indignation. But there can be no question about the depth of piety, concern for justice in the abstract, and sensitivity to the needs of others that these incidents came to symbolize. By such pleasing recollections, one often links the past with present interest. For antislavery reformers, the memories were especially consoling.[15]

Intelligent, strong-willed, and benevolent though many of these evangelical mothers were, they exhibited a certain ambivalence about their children, too. The Calvinist heritage in New England was powerful. Intellectually gentler theologies—Arminianism or

14. *Memoir of Samuel Joseph May* (Boston, 1874), 5–12.
15. See Anna D. Hallowell, *James and Lucretia Mott: Life and Letters* (Boston, 1896), 4–5, 14; Pickard, *Life and Letters of Whittier*, I, 39; John Brown to Henry L. Stearns, July 15, 1857, in Oswald Garrison Villard, *John Brown, 1800–1859: A Biography Fifty Years After* (Boston, 1910), 4; William B. Gravely, *Gilbert Haven, Methodist Abolitionist* (New York, 1973), 15.

Unitarianism, for example—could be adopted as the family religion, but emotionally religious and concerned parents alternated between hope and doubt that human beings could overcome evil. Mothers knew that pampering the young was no way to prepare them for a world of sin and sorrow. Love was offered provisionally, with little spontaneity. Theodore Parker's mother, for instance, had given the boy warmth and warning in equal measure.

Even when a mother was affectionate, her nurturing could be off-set by the severity of the father. William McLoughlin, the historian of American religion, argues that evangelical parents produced "immense amounts of anxiety, self-doubt, and dependence," so that there was a constant and unhealthy desire to please the father, an unrequited effort lasting a lifetime. In some instances, that was the result. John Greenleaf Whittier vividly recalled seventy years afterward how he had quailed before a weekly trip with his taciturn, unloving father. The Quaker farmer of Massachusetts and his five-year-old son had to climb a steep hill at the top of which a screeching gander always waited. As they approached, the boy grew terrified that the goose would peck at him with a fury to match the squawk. The resentments Whittier felt toward his domineering father prevented him from expressing his fear. He never asked his father for help or sympathy on this or any other occasion. Encouragement would not have been forthcoming. The fretful patriarch, then fifty-three, had already been complaining of his son's unmanly sensitivities and later ridiculed his writing poetry. In Whittier's case, the burden of special holiness and the equally intense agony of introspection, reticence, and suppressed rages, as Perry Miller has noted, lasted nearly a lifetime. Henry C. Wright, the reformer and abolitionist whom Thoreau had found so oppressively intimate, had a similarly taciturn, aloof father, who was a carpenter in western New York. Having lost his mother, whose memory the son romanticized, Henry Wright felt, his perceptive biographer says, as if his throat, in the hands of Seth, his father, "was endlessly vulnerable to Abraham's knife." It would be wrong to assume that the experiences of Whittier and Wright were representative of what happened to others in the abolition cause. Conscience-stricken, even intensely anxious, such figures as these were anything but narcissists, nor were they timid conformists. Their concern for others, not their disappointments with themselves, was to give meaning to their lives.[16]

However much paternal repressiveness affected Whittier, one must be careful to judge each reformer's background separately rather than assume Oedipal longings and resentments as the impetus toward reform. Certainly such tortured struggles were evident in the relationship of Theodore Dwight Weld, a leading abolitionist, and the Reverend Ludovicus Weld, his formidable and unpleasable father. According to Robert Abzug, Weld was torn between a love of order and godly restraint and a sometimes uncontrollable impulse toward freedom and romantic self-fulfillment. Nevertheless, early experiences and their lingering effects varied too much for Freudian generalizations. Childhood hardships and fears came often in many shapes. For instance, William Lloyd Garrison's father, Abijah, a lowly sailor, deserted Fanny Lloyd Garrison, a woman of enormous piety— and girth—leaving her in dire straits. Certainly Abijah bore no resemblance at all to Weld's father. Instead, it was Garrison's mother who dominated her son and warned him constantly of the sins of drink and irresponsibility, a lesson the boy learned well and applied in his later career.[17]

Other kinds of childhood difficulties appeared in reform backgrounds. Abolitionist Sydney Howard Gay came from people as substantial as Garrison's were obscure. His father Ebenezer was a banker in Hingham, Massachusetts, and his mother was an Otis of the famous Revolutionary clan. Locally prominent though they were, the Gays persistently rued lost opportunities in the grander sphere of Boston. "We are indeed, what is a little mortifying to our pride to ac-

16. William G. McLoughlin, "Evangelical Childrearing in the Age of Jackson: Francis Wayland's View on When and How to Subdue the Willfulness of Children," *Journal of Social History*, IX (1975), 21; Pickard, *Life and Letters of Whittier*, I, 26; Charles A. Jarvis, "Admission to Abolition: The Case of John Greenleaf Whittier," *Journal of the Early Republic*, IV (1984), 161–76; Perry Miller, "John Greenleaf Whittier: The Conscience in Poetry," *Harvard Review*, II (1964), 8–24; Lewis Perry, *Childhood, Marriage, and Reform: Henry Clarke Wright, 1797–1870* (Chicago, 1980), 75.

17. Walter M. Merrill, *Against Wind and Tide: A Biography of Wm. Lloyd Garrison* (Cambridge, Mass., 1963), 2–3, 5–12; Robert Abzug, *Passionate Liberator: Theodore Dwight Weld and the Dilemma of Reform* (New York, 1980), 3–20.

knowledge, a decayed family," wheedled Mrs. Gay in 1841, hoping for some patronage from John Quincy Adams. "The generation that knew us are passing away. New families have come to power." Sydney Gay's entry into abolitionism was as tortured as anybody else's. His mother's social worries, which may have affected his mordant character, did not guide him to a specific choice of what to do with himself.[18]

Elijah P. Lovejoy, also an abolitionist editor, grew up in a glum household. His father, a failed minister, was barely able to cleave to sanity. His "unnatural elevation and depression of spirits," his funeral orator bluntly exclaimed, was bound to "occasion an inequality in the character" of his ministry. Lovejoy's mother made it abundantly clear to all that she bore her griefs in a silence louder than words.[19]

All these examples of familial distress early in childhood could be replicated a thousand times in the lives of people quite outside the antislavery orbit. The illustrations are intriguing, for they are most suggestive about the effects of family troubles upon the way individuals developed. In no sense were they predictive of future careers. They were perhaps a factor in predisposing the child toward some kind of dream of self-sacrifice. Certainly, intense anxieties helped to shape personalities. It should be remembered, however, that Wendell Phillips, the Grimké sisters, the Tappans, William Jay, Elizur Wright, and many others had fathers both loving and successful, supportive and yet strict. Elizur Wright, Jr., one of the early immediatists from the Western Reserve in Ohio, was not unusual in recalling the affectionate nature of his father. After his father, a pious churchman, had died in 1845, his son wrote that Elizur Wright, Sr., "bade me climb the height whereon he stood, and eased its steepness with the kindest smile."[20] Like so many others in that generation of mission-minded New Englanders, the son felt the pressures to conform, to listen to conscience, *and* to find his own way to achievement.

18. Mary Otis Gay to John Quincy Adams, January 1, 1841, in Gay-Otis Papers, Loeb Library, Columbia University, New York.
19. Joseph C. Lovejoy and Owen Lovejoy, *Memoir of the Rev. Elijah P. Lovejoy . . .* (New York, 1838), 15.
20. Lawrence B. Goodheart, "Child-Rearing, Conscience, and Conversion to Abolitionism: The Example of Elizur Wright, Jr.," *Psychohistory Review*, XII (1984), 25.

No single family problem or childhood distress, no extraordinarily intense antagonism between father and son or between mother and daughter, distinguished all abolitionists from others of similar upbringing and environment.

Men and women who did not join the holy war against slavery registered similar kinds of childhood strain. "Properly speaking I had no childhood," lamented Orestes Brownson, the Transcendentalist and Catholic convert. The father of Isaac Hecker, also a Catholic leader, was an alcoholic and the object of perpetual family worry. "I knew nothing but fear," stated Clara Barton, founder of the American Red Cross. Each of these individuals had peculiarities of character related to their early experiences. There was no common factor, however, to predict their later lives. In Barton's case, her father was a genial, strong-minded figure, but her mother was excessively temperamental. A maiden aunt, even more dangerously violent, was confined in an upstairs room. Forced to sit for hours in an unheated church as a little girl, Barton recalled "being taken home one bitter Sunday with frozen feet. I had not dared complain and fell in the pew when they set me down." Like Whittier, she had remained silent for reasons of pride, unexpressed fury, and fear of capricious reprimand. Yet these and other signs of family troubles and childhood reaction influenced only personality. They burdened the developing child, but they did not determine future occupation.[21]

Anxiety, so consciously aroused, was a major component of that culture, but it affected no group, abolitionist or otherwise, more than another. Worry about personal righteousness, parental intrusiveness, even severely unhappy childhoods beckoned some to benevolence, others to pious ways within business careers, some to indifference, called "nothingarianism," and a few to outright anti-evangelical "unrighteousness." Yet, those who *did* enter reform came with an instructed conscience, implanted as early as five years of age. The English divine Richard Baxter had told parents, "It is conscience that must watch them in private, when you see them not; and conscience

21. Henry F. Brownson, *Orestes A. Brownson's Early Life* (Detroit, 1895), 4; Percy H. Epler, *The Life of Clara Barton* (New York, 1919), 6 (quotation), 12, 14; Ishbel Ross, *Angel of the Battlefield: The Life of Clara Barton* (New York, 1956), 9.

of God's officer and not yours; and will say nothing to them, till it speak in the name of God." Over a century later, Elizur Wright made the same point, though in somewhat more secular and child-centered terms: "Conscience whispers no in the ear of the child when he is first tempted to tell a lie, or take even a pin that is not his, and then it chokes his utterance and agitates his nerves as he commits the deed." Almost by definition, missionaries and reformers were untranquil souls. They had learned dissatisfaction with themselves and the world. Yet few ever dared curse the parents who had bound them over to "God's officer," a drillmaster as tough and unyielding as any birch stick.[22]

As one could anticipate, these children, singled out for specifically moral purposes, were often intellectually gifted. Parents encouraged study and reading, for two reasons aside from concern for knowledge. First, reading banked the fires of youthful exuberance and passions; second, being a solitary activity, reading was one way to shield the child from bad influences. In those days churchgoing children could scarcely avoid the usual hazings, but an avid thirst to learn became a form of segregation. Antislavery leaders Theodore Parker, Theodore Weld, and Elijah Lovejoy were all remarkable for their early signs of intellectuality. The mother of the great East Asian missionary Adoniram Judson began her boy's literary training at age three. Elizur Wright, Theodore Weld, and David T. Stoddard, a missionary to the Nestorians, stood at the head of their classes. Not only did these and many other reformers and evangelists show intellectual promise, but that promise sped them along the moral, even solitary paths laid out for them by their parents.[23]

Likewise, women in both causes showed uncommon abilities. To be sure, they were not supposed to compete with boys for academic honors or to prepare themselves for independent careers. Nonethe-

22. Baxter, *The Christian Directory*, IV, 178; Goodheart, "Child-Rearing, Conscience, and Conversion to Abolitionism," 25.
23. Joseph P. Thompson, *Memoir of the Rev. David Tappan Stoddard, Missionary to the Nestorians* (New York, 1859), 61; David C. French, "The Conversion of an American Radical: Elizur Wright, Jr., and the Abolitionist Commitment" (Ph.D. dissertation, Case Western Reserve University, 1970), 25–30; Wright Journal, March 12, 1835 (MS in Wright Papers, Houghton Library); Benjamin P. Thomas, *Theodore Weld, Crusader for Freedom* (New Brunswick, 1950), 8–9.

less, many female reform leaders and foreign missionaries showed strong intellects in their formative years. The first women into the foreign mission field, usually as wives of leaders, were also gifted, sometimes even in such unfeminine subjects as mathematics and science. Yet, the road for women was difficult. Even in evangelical households, scholarly competition was meant for boys only. When Elizabeth Cady Stanton, for instance, won academic honors, her father Daniel Cady, grieving for lost sons, exclaimed, "'Ah, you should have been a boy.'" Although he did not wish her to deviate from the submissive role assigned women, he was much less severe with her than was her mother, who deplored Elizabeth's natural intellectual and athletic aggressiveness.[24]

Even for the boys, academic competition was supposedly worldly; they struggled for prizes anyhow. After all, the parable of the talents pointed the way. The result was a tension between demands for godly humility of mind and hope of glory in His name. Though not debilitating in most cases, the dilemma of intellectual hubris and piety proved troublesome for a few adolescents. Charles Torrey's biographer reported that his "two years [at Exeter Academy] not only fitted him for college but well nigh unfitted him for this world and the next." Theodore Weld struggled constantly against pride with intemperate zeal.[25]

During the higher grades of school, the most significant event in the future abolitionist's or missionary's life was the conversion experience. It was an occasion to be cherished for a lifetime. It marked the beginning not just of manhood but of Christian commitment and a godly career (of some as yet unspecified kind). Some went through

24. Theodore Stanton and Harriot S. Blatch (eds.), *Elizabeth Cady Stanton: As Revealed in Her Letters* . . . (2 vols.; New York and London, 1922), I, 3, 22–23, 24–25; Lois W. Banner, *Elizabeth Cady Stanton: A Radical for Women's Rights* (Boston, 1980), 1–14; *The Missionary's Daughter: A Memoir of Lucy Goodale Thurston of the Sandwich Islands* (New York, 1842), 13, 14; Gerda Lerner, *The Grimké Sisters from South Carolina: Rebels Against Slavery* (Boston, 1967), 16.

25. Joseph C. Lovejoy, *Memoir of the Rev. Charles Turner Torrey* . . . (Boston, 1847), 3–5; Thomas, *Theodore Weld*, 159–60; Abzug, *Passionate Liberator*, 3–20; [Miss Lyman], *The Martyr of Sumatra: A Memoir of Henry Lyman* (New York, 1857), 14; Harold Schwartz, *Samuel Gridley Howe: Social Reformer, 1801–1876* (Cambridge, Mass., 1956), 4–5, 9; Ralph R. Gurley, *Life of Jehudi Ashmun, Late Colonial Agent in Liberia* (Washington, D.C., 1854), 18n; Francis Wayland, *A Memoir of the Life and Labors of the Rev. Adoniram Judson, D.D.* (2 vols.; Boston, 1854), I, 13.

the ordeal in conventional fashion, especially when a revival was under way. Then everybody joined in the excitement. Those with special feelings of fervor or declension did not cross the spiritual divide so smoothly. Sensitive souls by inclination, they suffered acutely. At thirteen, for instance, Henry Lyman, "the Martyr of Sumatra," happened to swear aloud in front of friends. They teased him with such remarks as "'Oh! Henry Lyman, what will your father say if he heard that.' . . . My moral nature [quivered and trembled] under the shock like an aspen leaf," he said. "I hear even now that oath ringing in my ears . . . that *horrible heavy* mountain that rolled back upon my soul—that withdrawal of the restraints of divine grace." It was the beginning of Lyman's youthful conversion.[26]

The contrast between the conventional, relatively easy conversion and the missionaries' acute difficulties was most striking in the case of Samuel J. Mills. In 1798, Litchfield, Connecticut, was undergoing a Congregationalist revival. All of Samuel's brothers and sisters gained assurance, as the phrase went, but the introspective fifteen-year-old could not. "With nothing was his dissatisfaction more painful, than the discriminations of the divine favour in showing mercy to those who were around him, while he himself was apparently left to obduracy and ruin," intoned the biographer. For two years more, Mills remained in "a dismal frame of mind," finally confessing his torment to his mother. She angrily replied that he was still unconvinced of his sinfulness. About six months later, while teaching school in another village, he at last surrendered to the "glorious sovereignty." Mills, unlike his kinsmen, had doubted that a conversion under the pressure of a convenient revival was honest and soul-felt. But the intensity of his experience points not only to this sense of specialness but also to his future career. He was the only child in that family to enter the missionary field or, indeed, any similarly sacred calling.[27]

26. Gurley, *Life of Jehudi Ashmun,* 19–20; Wayland, *A Memoir of Adoniram Judson,* I, 25; Ryan, *Cradle of the Middle Class,* 69–72, 98–104; Hillel Schwartz, "Adolescence and Revivals in Ante-Bellum Boston," *Journal of Religious History,* VIII (1974), 144–58; [Lyman], *The Martyr of Sumatra,* 15–16.

27. Spring, *Memoirs of Samuel J. Mills,* 14–16; William James, *The Varieties of Religious Experience: A Study in Human Nature* (New York, 1902), 190; F. E. H. Haines, *Jonas King: Missionary to Syria and Greece* (New York, 1879), 18.

This experience was not idiosyncratic. No doubt, some physicians, businessmen, and politicians also remembered dramatic revival conversions. What matters, however, is that the totality of factors pressed the missionaries and abolitionists toward their destiny. *Few men and women of the mission and antislavery causes failed to experience the conversion rite, or came from religiously indifferent households, or grew up with habits quite out of keeping with the evangelical conscience.* Thus, abolitionist Elijah Lovejoy's wanderings were not peculiar to him. Both inside and outside the antislavery circle, others acted similarly, but seldom with such excessive zeal. He walked all the way from Waterville, Maine, to New York City, eating almost nothing. He suffered from headaches, a result of the strains of his soul as much as the rigorous inadequacy of his diet. His pilgrimage was a penance for not professing faith. The transgressions worried his parents and pious brothers for many years. Selfhood, he appeared to say, could not be forced upon him. Eventually, though, he found relief and regeneration. The delay, if not the depth of agony, was one with which any evangelical could sympathize.[28]

Women abolitionists and reformers also had to suffer at this critical juncture. Raised in an unusually high-minded and pious household in South Carolina, Sarah Grimké at thirteen offered herself as godmother for her baby sister Angelina, though she did not feel wholly adequate to the responsibility. As historian Gerda Lerner says, "She was deeply in earnest in her pledge and, years later, remembered the profound emotions which caused her to shut herself in her room after the [baptismal] ceremony and pray to God to make her worthy of the task she had assumed." Susan B. Anthony, another who fought for slaves' and women's rights, mourned over her "hardened heart" and yearned that she might grow "more and more refined until nothing shall remain but perfect purity."[29]

28. See Raimund E. Goerler, "Family, Psychology and History," *Group Use of Psychology in History Newsletter* [later, *Psychohistory Review*], IV (1975), 31–38, based on his "Family, Self, and Anti-Slavery: Sydney Howard Gay and the Abolitionist Commitment" (Ph.D. dissertation, Case Western Reserve University, 1975); David C. French, "Puritan Conservatism and the Frontier: The Elizur Wright Family on the Connecticut Western Reserve," *Old Northwest*, I (1975), 85–95; Merton L. Dillon, *Elijah P. Lovejoy, Abolitionist Editor* (Urbana, 1971), 9–10.

29. Mildred Danforth, *A Quaker Pioneer: Laura Haviland, Superintendent of the*

Communal pressure to conform affected young girls no less than teenage boys. Both male and female evangelicals had to learn the lesson of self-reliance, of standing apart from the crowd. It was not enough for the ones endowed with specialness to follow the herd. In the process, as William James describes it, the individual often had to overcome despair either by an immediate and overpowering sense of hope, the opposite emotion, or by "getting so exhausted with the struggle that we have to stop,—so we drop down, give up, and *don't care* any longer." Temporary apathy provided the means, he thought, to break down "egoistic worry" and allow "the expansive confidence of the soul of faith" to assume control. Thus one learned to make hard decisions, James suggests. So it was in the case of Harriet Wadsworth Winslow, a missionary to Ceylon. These steps of alienation and restoration gave her a way to cut her dependence upon friends who blamed her for delaying her revival commitment. She took her time, meditating for hours in a garret. Finally, drained by her struggle, she surrendered in a confession to her minister. It was a classic case of achieving evangelical wholeness.[30]

The movement out of declension could take a number of forms, the most untypical being that of Henry C. Wright. His conversion seemed to be associated with early childhood experiences in a very direct way—the yearning for an affectionate mother: "When a boy in my teens, at a Sunday meeting in a country church far in the interior of N.Y. state, a Babe was put into my arms during sermon time, to rest the mother. . . . I sat looking into its face—so fair, so beautiful." The preacher expounded on Original Sin and predestination, but it "*flashed*" upon Wright that God was not in the preacher's voice. Instead, the true divinity was in the sleeping child. The baby, declared Wright in recollection, was "the image of God. . . . It was an era—a marked *Event* of my life." Lewis Perry, however, warns us that Wright's memories of his early years when his mother had died

Underground Railroad (New York, 1961), 19; Lerner, *The Grimké Sisters*, 25; Ida H. Harper, *The Life and Work of Susan B. Anthony* (2 vols.; Indianapolis, 1889), I, 29.

30. Alfred Lee, *A Life Hid with Christ in God: Being a Memoir of Susan Allibone* (Philadelphia, 1856), 22–27; James, *The Varieties of Religious Experience*, 212; Miron Winslow, *A Memoir of Mrs. Harriet Wadsworth Winslow, Combining a Sketch of the Ceylon Mission* (New York, 1835), 11–15.

served special adult purposes; they were part of his public and his private life. More conventional, in any event, was the experience of Jonas King, missionary to Greece. Unimaginatively he claimed to have felt a sudden and permanent state of religious commitment after praying in the woods.[31]

The first crisis of spiritual identity, usually begun and resolved in the teens, did not generally lead to a career decision. One reason was that by the 1820s, New England's sons (and daughters, to some extent) had a variety of options, some requiring additional education. To await further maturing, to provide an emotional resting spot, some of those with a sense of special mission became, for instance, temporary teachers or served as colporteurs for a mission enterprise. Abolitionist Charles Torrey, among others, tried schoolkeeping, but the indifference of his performance led him to mourn: "What shall I do, God knoweth, I do not. . . . Is it my fault that I am not as old as Methuselah? How can I help my youth?" Others delivered inspirational tracts, clerked at national benevolent agency headquarters, edited small reform sheets, joined summer crusades to free the slave, such as Weld's band of Oberlinites. These offered the satisfactions of idealism and commitment, but they were not necessarily permanent.[32]

Ordinarily there was a second crisis of the spirit in the twenties. Though similar to the first in its gyrations of feeling, the second episode concerned career much more than personal identity. The form was the familiar conviction of sin, emptiness, alienation from God, but the question uppermost was, what am I to do in life? Peers, admired elders, perhaps a college professor or more mature student exercised considerable influence in the working out of the problem. Usually the subject put down on paper his innermost feelings, just as he had in the first crisis. The journal made a handy reference for substantiating the unfolding spiritual events, perhaps to please a seminary official. Certainly, memorialists of the missionaries and

31. Henry C. Wright Journal, October 21, 1869 (MS in Henry C. Wright Papers, Boston Public Library); Perry, *Childhood, Marriage, and Reform*, 65–79, 256–57; Haines, *Jonas King*, 18–20; "Memoir of Nathaniel Ripley Cobb," *American Baptist Magazine*, XIV (1834), 316–26.

32. Lovejoy, *Memoir of Charles Torrey*, 29; see also Samuel Gridley Howe Journal, April 21, 1829 (MS in Samuel Gridley Howe Papers, Houghton Library, Harvard).

crusaders found such papers useful in writing up the accounts for public edification. In any case, the young collegian or seminarian felt obliged to undergo the second test of faith, another rebirth, particularly if he was weighing the dangers of foreign work against the conveniences of home.

Just as parents had inculcated conscience, so ministers, church elders, and college faculties guided the young person toward a benevolent career during the period between parental authority and adult autonomy. Religious societies and presses churned out hundreds of sermons, old works and new, all of which not only demanded belief in a saving Lord but also the witness and sacrifice of spreading the gospel.[33]

Being incorporated into a rather sophisticated religious apparatus, the second crisis was both self-conscious and stylized in a way that the more immature first conversion was not. At Amherst College, for instance, Henry Lyman made a show of spurning a religious revival among classmates. On a spring day in 1827, however, a friend saw him meditating and invited him "to a grove of pine, beneath whose shade was a sanctuary." The site was a conscious imitation of a famous haystack near Andover Seminary where Adoniram Judson had led a group of earnest seminarians in 1809 to pledge their lives to the mission cause abroad. Jauntily, Lyman refused, though he admitted to serious religious doubts, especially about the doctrine of election. A few days passed, during which Lyman consulted with President Heman Humphrey, professors, and pious as well as "gay associates." Finally, however, he and his solicitous friend repaired to the appropriate site. Lyman's eyes filled with tears as he confessed, *"I am all in the wrong."* It was the beginning of his second change of heart and purpose: he would become a missionary abroad. The whole

33. The changing nature of ministerial professionalism is explored in Daniel Calhoun, *Professional Lives in America: Structure and Aspiration, 1750–1850* (Cambridge, Mass., 1965), 88–177; Donald M. Scott, *From Office to Profession: The New England Ministry, 1750–1850* (Philadelphia, 1978), esp. 52–75; on collegiate and seminary training, see David F. Allmendinger, *Paupers and Scholars: The Transformation of Student Life in Nineteenth-Century New England* (New York, 1975), esp. 9–12, 45–62. On pressure toward missionary labors, see Hall Harrison, *Life of the Right Reverend John Burrett Kerfoot, LL.D., First Bishop of Pittsburgh* (2 vols.; New York, 1886), I, 26; John S. Stone, *A Memoir of the Life of James Milnor, D.D. . . . .* (New York, 1848), 89–91.

incident—the inquiries of the friend, the sacred location, the consultations with believers and (respectable) unbelievers, the meditations, and finally the intimate and emotional admission of sin to the fellow student—seemed novel and exciting to the participants, but considerable tradition and conscious planning lay behind this second ritual of conversion.[34]

The result of the lengthy, hard-won conversion was that young men and women took enormous pride in the grand work of well-doing that opened before them. Sometimes well before, sometimes long after the second episode of dedication to God, moments of doubt and declension assailed them. Byronic *angst*, particularly about sexual interests, gave rise to thoughts of death. John Humphrey Noyes at Dartmouth College, for instance, noted that "two patients sorely afflicted with the hypo [that is, hypochondria or depression] have applied to me today for consolation. I advised them never to read Byron, never to think of suicide, and above all repeat every five minutes: 'Faint heart never won fair lady.'" Henry C. Wright filled his diary with allusions to the "mansion" of death that lovingly beckoned: "Ye ghastly spectors; I hear a voice, declaring, that I shall *soon be with you* . . . I close my eyes and fold my *arms* in *death*." Sarah Grimké remembered a time when "I craved a hiding-place in the grave. . . . I was tempted to commit some great crime, thinking I could repent and then restore my lost sensibility." Elijah Lovejoy set his miseries in verse.[35]

These self-indulgent, youthful depressions were a passing phase in the process of working out the role of life. They scarcely should be considered a peculiarity of future abolitionists and idealists. Yet they did have a bearing upon later career developments, particularly for those in the foreign mission field and the abolition cause. Both causes

34. [Lyman], *The Martyr of Sumatra*, 38, 33–45; Lois W. Banner, "Religion and Reform in the Early Republic: The Role of Youth," *American Quarterly*, XXIII (1971), 680–82.

35. John Humphrey Noyes Journal, February 18, 1830, in George W. Noyes (ed.), *Religious Experiences of John Humphrey Noyes, Founder of the Oneida Community* (New York, 1923), 22; see also Jonas Evans, *Memoir of Elder George Evans* (Woburn, Mass., 1857), 7, 10–15; Lerner, *The Grimké Sisters*, 53; Wright Journal, 1821 (MS in Wright Papers, Boston Public Library), 10; see "The Wanderer," a poem in Lovejoy and Lovejoy, *Memoir of Elijah P. Lovejoy*, 29–31.

were physically dangerous and emotionally taxing. From Andover Seminary, Henry Lyman, for instance, wrote his sister, "When these four years have rolled around, I shall probably be in my grave, on a sick bed, or on mission ground. Yes, the pleasures of home, and country, and kindred shall be sacrificed. But what do I say? Rather, the pleasure of leading the benighted heathen to Jesus shall not be sacrificed for home, country, or friends. Would that tomorrow's rising sun might witness my final departure from New England."[36]

The consummation of romantic feelings that Lyman typified was the contemplation of a glorious martyrdom. In a sense, men like Lyman were engaged in a spiritual wager: if God granted life, the missionary would perform miracles in his service. If God willed death, He was obliged to recognize the sacrifice by conferring salvation. Their pact was not with Mephistopheles but with the Holy Spirit, and often in the hope of earthly fame as well. The nature of their parent-guided conscience forced them constantly to see this unflattering possibility—the temptation into self-glorification. "The leading influence of my life," recalled Samuel A. Dorrance, one of Theodore Weld's disciples, in 1850, "was the love of admiration. . . . Coarse food, hard bed, labor, long walks, fatigues of any kind [were the means to] get admired." Steeped as they were in theology, such men well knew how close they flirted with the blasphemy of challenging God to deny them his gratitude. As Pliny Fisk, missionary to Palestine, declared before his final career decision, "Many unholy motives may induce a man to desire this work. I wish, therefore, to re-examine all my past resolutions and plans, and inquire anew what I ought to do."[37]

Always self-conscious, but forever restless, the products of the evangelical mode of development were well equipped to meet the clearly marked-out goals of New England piety, love, self-reliance, and hatred of sin. They sought the uplift of communities allegedly

36. Lyman to his sister, November 2, 1828, in [Lyman], *The Martyr of Sumatra*, 69. A small tribe in the Batta country, already weakened by wars with powerful neighbors, killed all of Lyman's party upon their first appearance. Neighboring tribes, with British help, shortly exterminated the offending tribe in revenge.

37. Samuel A. Dorrance to Theodore D. Weld, October 15, 1850, in Theodore Dwight Weld Papers, William L. Clements Library, Ann Arbor; Alvan Bond, *Memoir of the Rev. Pliny Fisk, A.M., Late Missionary to Palestine* (Boston, 1828), 71.

lacking in those virtues. Certainly there was an almost self-absorbed preoccupation involved, but it was in keeping with the early channelings of conscience and aggression imparted during childhood. "By my influence, with God to direct and bless, Africa may be made to arise from her degradation and shake herself from her chains," mused a seminarian and future abolitionist, Amos A. Phelps. This was American "individualism" at a zenith: the single-handed conversion of a continent. Whatever the cause was to be—missions, antislavery, or some other—the evangelical brought to bear a storehouse of energy. Its source lay in his or her dynamic tensions between love and deprivation, humility and pride, joy and depression, hope and despair. Only in this way can one explain the confidence and determination behind the nineteenth-century reformer and missionary. As Julia Ward Howe later satirized in doggerel about her irrepressible, reform-minded husband Samuel:

> Rero rero riddlety rad
> This morning my baby caught sight of her Dad
> Quoth she, "Oh Daddy, where have you been?"
> "With Mann and Sumner a-putting down sin!"

At the same time, there were inherent dangers of overtaxing the body and sometimes even the mind. Theodore Weld, for instance, lost the use of his vocal powers for a number of years, owing to the strains of constant public speaking in behalf of the slave and to psychosomatic causes that only a gifted biographer like Robert Abzug can help us to understand. Remarkably enough, however, one is struck not by the instances of mental breakdown or physical collapse but by the very opposite.[38]

Joseph Kett recently called the evangelical scheme of childraising "a kind of moral and religious pressure cooker," an opinion

38. Amos A. Phelps Journal, January 19, 1828 (MS in Amos A. Phelps Papers, Boston Public Library); see also Bela B. Edwards, *Memoir of Elias Cornelius* (Boston, 1834), 29; Laura E. Richards (ed.), *Letters and Journals of Samuel Gridley Howe* (2 vols.; Boston, 1906–1909), I, 25; Schwartz, *Samuel Gridley Howe*, 328; Abzug, *Passionate Liberator*, 152–54; see also "Life and Works of Stephen Olin, D.D., LL.D.," *New Englander*, XIV (1854), 125–28, 130–37; "Autobiography of the Rev. Amasa Converse," *Journal of Presbyterian History*, XLII (1965), 202–203; Lovejoy, *Memoir of Charles Torrey*, 31–32.

shared by Philip Greven, another historian of child-rearing. If so, it seldom exploded. Although such deviations as sexual misdeeds did arise unexpectedly in evangelical ranks every so often, the number was small. The only notable case among abolitionists was Ray Potter, leader of the Rhode Island chapter of the American Anti-Slavery Society. Potter, a ministerial heretic from the Sixth Principle Baptist sect in Pawtucket, slept with an unmarried member of his church for a number of months before his wife and the neighbors discovered the deception. His disgrace, community ostracism, and jail sentence for adultery led him to publish a lengthy justification. He claimed the superiority of his conscience against the worldly cynicism and unchristian meanness of his former parishioners and friends.[39]

On the other hand, the Reverend Daniel Buttrick, youthful missionary to the Cherokees, displayed uncommon self-control when, after some weeks in the wilderness, he came upon Indian girls bathing nude in a forest stream. He mastered his feelings and committed no sin. Later, word came to him that a retarded girl had wandered from her pioneer family heading west, and these Indian girls had found her body on Raccoon Mountain, near the Indian village of Turkey Town in southeast Tennessee. Buttrick had to go to the site to conduct the burial service. He worried all the way there that he might find her naked and be subjected to renewed sinful thoughts. Much to his relief, the girl had covered herself completely. Yet Buttrick's eventual solution to his sexual discomfort was a somewhat less remarkable exercise of evangelical conscience. In 1827, Buttrick, after a week of courting, decided to marry "dear sister Elizabeth Proctor," a new arrival at the Brainerd station, who had begun schoolkeeping. He prayed, "O dear Jesus wilt thou leave me to sink in sensual indulgence—to be ensnared and taken in the chains of carnal pleasures?" That petition was offered just before Elizabeth accepted.[40]

39. Joseph Kett, *Rites of Passage: Adolescence in America, 1790 to the Present* (New York, 1977), 68; Ray Potter, *Memoirs of the Life and Religious Experiences of Ray Potter* (Providence, 1829), and *Admonitions from "The Depths of the Earth," or the Fall of Ray Potter, Twenty-four Letters* . . . (Pawtucket, 1838).
40. Daniel S. Buttrick Journal, 1819–45, esp. May 31, 1821, and entries for April, 1827 (MS in American Board of Commissioners for Foreign Missions Papers, Houghton Library, Harvard).

Given the strains that evangelicalism imposed upon men and women of this generation, that is, those born between 1780 and 1810 or so, it is remarkable how much they accomplished, how few were broken by the system. The children of these hardy souls, however, were to fare somewhat less well, as the next chapter will suggest. But the difference lay in the fact that these early evangelicals were quite conscious of the alternative style—the hyper-masculine and pa-triarchal order against which they could pose themselves as a means of self-identification. They had had to deal with fistfights, barroom temptation, and peer-group pressures as youngsters in the New En-gland villages. The social order had been crude, the standards rustic. Evangelical upbringing had given them the means to rise to what seemed new heights of refinement and purposefulness. For their sons and daughters born in the 1820s and 1830s, there was already a seg-regation of the classes, with special schools for the religiously minded and certain parts of town where the middle-class child could be shel-tered from evil influences. As a result, the children of the latter gen-eration were separated from the rough-and-tumble. Even missionary children in foreign lands often lived in compounds behind high fences. These were walls, however, that caged as well as protected. The high Victorians were to have emotional difficulties, for these and other reasons, that their energetic and pious parents did not. The evangelical system was too intense for easy transmission through generations.

Finally, there was the matter of a significant difference between the abolitionist and the foreign missionary: the attitude toward poli-tics and the moral state of America. For reasons that had little to do with upbringing but much to do with peers and personal experience, future abolitionists had a predilection for changing the minds of those they knew best, on religious as well as secular topics. Moreover, in contrast to the often squabbling foreign missionaries, they seemed a more gregarious lot, happier in association with each other, a con-cern that Lawrence Friedman cogently argues was paramount for the reformers. One cannot be definitive about the matter, though, for ab-olitionists were well known for their fractiousness even within their "clusters." Yet, it seems that only future abolitionists vexed them-selves over politics. They were provoked by such political issues as Anti-Masonry, nullification, Sunday mail laws, and the like, in con-trast to the apolitical future missionaries. This orientation was, of course, logical and self-selective. They put themselves beyond gov-ernments, some beyond life itself. Jehudi Ashmun and Samuel Bacon, early missionaries to Liberia, carried matters to extremes hard to match in the abolitionist movement. "'I came to these shores to *die*: and any thing better than death is better than I expect,'" de-clared Bacon. Ill from consumption and, as always, severely de-pressed, Ashmun returned to his Liberian post, determined to spend what little remained of life "dwelling among distant savages." They both won quickly the reward they seemed to court so eagerly.[41]

Obviously, someone stimulated by events in Washington and the state capitals was not so likely to go, as Ashmun and Bacon did, off to a fever-ridden country. So, too, a pietistic turn of mind would scarcely be compatible with a cause such as slavery, which was so clearly a matter of law, politics, and social control. For instance, Amos A. Phelps thought of becoming a missionary to Liberia. He shortly changed his mind, having already shown considerable fascination with politics—as well as a repulsion against its alleged corruption. By 1830, his worry over Jacksonian "tyranny," Fanny Wrightism, Cherokee Indian removal, and other issues especially worrisome to evangelicals led him to break with an old schoolmate and friend, William Weeks. In almost a microcosm of Yankee divisiveness over antislavery politics later, Weeks denounced Phelps roundly as a "*Politician Minister*." Once a Congregational ministerial candidate himself, Weeks, a young lawyer, had become a blindly loyal Jackso-nian partisan, receiving a postmastership in Canaan, New Hamp-shire, as reward—and Phelps professed disgust at the news. To com-plete his new self-image, he renounced Congregationalism and joined the Baptists. The set of decisions had its logic, no less than did Phelps's

41. Lawrence J. Friedman, *Gregarious Saints: Self and Community in American Abolitionism, 1830–1870* (New York, 1982); Gurley, *Life of Jehudi Ashmun*, 1–92 (quotations, pp. 27, 88).

combination of Congregational ministry, Anti-Masonry, Sabbatarianism, and eventual antislavery commitment.[42]

Quite different was the evangelical who decided to become a foreign missionary. Like most ministers, even in New England, he had little interest in American political institutions and little knowledge of secular problems that required legislative attention. Although the evidence is strictly impressionistic, one finds few diary references to elections or national politics (Indian removal being an obvious exception). He or she was unlikely to be articulate about the imperfections of the nation to be left behind. At a conscious level, the foreign missionary accepted political affairs as they were. Perhaps the missionary experience itself encouraged political conservatism. By comparison with the alleged barbarities of the host country, American institutions seemed nearly perfect.

The ideal of personal self-sacrifice dominated foreign missionaries' thoughts. Mrs. E. H. Jones, upon leaving Calcutta for the Burmese interior, wrote that she intended to "pass away [her] earthly existence in a foreign, sultry clime, surrounded by Pagans who are destitute of the common feelings of humanity." Likewise, Henry Lyman, somewhat more benignly, dreamed at Andover, "I want to go off somewhere into some dark corner where I can have my Jesus, and my Bible, and there tell poor heathen that the blessed Saviour died for them, and wants them to love Him." In the manner of the steel engravings that graced the pages of missionary literature, Lyman imagined himself sitting beneath a palm tree with eager brown faces peering up at him, the white brother, reading from Scriptures. No theological uncertainties, no commercial bustle, no electioneering buncombe, no intrusive parents, no "gay associates" could disturb that idyll. The bit of New England carried off to the new site of evangelism would remain as remembered, no matter how drastically the flux of history altered the region left behind.[43]

42. William B. Weeks to Amos A. Phelps, June 15, 1829, June 14, August 19, 1830, all in Phelps Papers; Wright Journal, December 8, 1832, May 9, 11, December 3, 1833 (MS in Wright Papers, Houghton Library).

43. "Memoir of Mrs. E. H. Jones, Late Missionary to Burmah," *American Baptist Magazine*, XII (1832), 98; [Lyman], *The Martyr of Sumatra*, 72; see also Wright Journal, May 20, 1833 (MS in Wright Papers, Houghton Library).

Yet, missionaries had their own toughness. Their inner resources, gifts of restraint and endurance, even intractability—all aspects of their upbringing—equaled the qualities of the most outspoken root-and-branch reformer. So slight, in fact, were the secular considerations and so bold the desire for brave evangelism that some went abroad indifferent to the sins of the homeland and to the needs of family and friends as well. Dr. Asahel Grant, a young widower with children to care for and a medical practice in Connecticut, put his deepest feelings this way: "I stand ready to go, in the face of danger and death, to any part of the world under the dominion of the prince of darkness. What though I tear away from children and all the endearments of home, wear out life amid toil and suffering, and find a grave among strangers?" Relatives complained, but the divine call, Grant insisted, took precedence over domestic considerations.[44] Abolitionists shared Grant's willingness to experience danger and sacrifice. Yet, there was somehow a predisposition to seek spiritual answers for political and social dilemmas close to home.

As a result, the actual decision to become an abolitionist was almost a secular matter. The conversion cycle of juvenile religious identity and then, in young adulthood, of career choice did reappear in the antislavery decision, but only in some instances and seldom with much drama. Weld's Lane debates ritualized for seminarians the cause of the slave in much the same manner as Judson's efforts at Andover in behalf of foreign missions. But many reformers simply reacted in a variety of ways to the prospect of immediate emancipation. James G. Birney, one of Weld's most prominent converts, Lydia Maria Child, Gerrit Smith, Lewis Tappan, Charles Torrey, Wendell Phillips, Elijah Lovejoy, Henry Wright, Sarah Grimké, and others claimed to have heard an inspiring speech, read a particular pamphlet, reacted indignantly to some slaveholder's or Yankee's atrocity, all of which signified a sudden heartfelt change. The conversion rite rather demanded such specificity. It made a better story. From what limited records we have, however, it is clear that the process was much lengthier than the reformer cared to admit. Henry Wright

44. Thomas Laurie, *Dr. Grant and the Mountain Nestorians* (Boston, 1853), 27.

talked for many months, for instance, with various friends and critics of the cause—James Birney and the conservative revivalist Henry Blagden of Brighton, among others. Birney, then in Boston on antislavery business, convinced Wright that bringing the gospel to the heathen was impossible so long as slavery existed. Blagden, however, took the pietistic side. In his opinion, Wright noted in his journal, such causes as temperance and antislavery "lead men to make Religion consist in breaking off from *external sin. Seems to think it wrong to urge men to break off from external sins till their hearts are charged & the fountain is purified.*" Wright believed, though, that the best way "to conquer an evil propensity is to cease to indulge in it *outwardly.*" Works, as much as faith, he was implying, were necessary for salvation, a position with secular overtones, though one that evangelicals generally professed. Like most everybody else in the antislavery cause, Wright had had no flashes of revelation. He adopted antislavery for intellectual as well as emotional reasons. Over time, however, that commitment developed deep and abiding roots, at least for many antislavery leaders.[45]

Clearly, the process toward antislavery reform showed only a predisposition to do something in life for God and fellow beings. Events, not special psychological factors, led directly to antislavery; circumstances determined which branch of Christian mission was to be chosen. Furthermore, the very nature of the abolitionist cause all but precluded much uniformity. There were a few that managed, like Garrison, to make a genuine career of reform. In fact, Garrison was one of the first to offer the prospect of professional reformism. This sense of the vocation helps to explain his branching out in the late 1830s in a number of new fields of inquiry. Each of the areas that Garrison explored—feminism, peace, and anti-Sabbatarianism, for example—opened up the possibility of new reform careers, some of which were more promising than others.

Yet, the list of professionals in the movement was scanty. Here and there an antislavery press required an editor—thus the careers of Sydney Howard Gay, Gamaliel Bailey, Marius Robinson, and

45. Wright Journal, January, 1834–May 10, 1835, June 10, 1835 (quotation) (MS in Wright Papers, Houghton Library).

Oliver Johnson. Some, like Wendell Phillips, could make a modest living on the lecture circuit. These were exceptions. Besides, most reformers found that abolitionism was a young person's vocation. The high risks, low pay, and incessant travel were burdens that bachelors could bear. But many married men, as they watched their families grow, gradually left the antislavery career behind. Elizur Wright, Amos Phelps, Theodore Weld, Joshua Leavitt, Sydney Howard Gay, and David Lee Child all had to give up full-time antislavery employment eventually, some never to be heard from again. For many others, antislavery had always been a calling, but never a career at all. The Tappan brothers, merchants; William Jay, judge; N. I. Bowditch, physician, George B. Cheever, Gilbert Haven, and James A. Thome, clergymen; Gerrit Smith, landowner; and many others drew their livings from other sources.

In contrast, foreign mission labor was a salaried vocation with guarantees of full employment. Mission clergymen and physicians in the ranks of the American Board of Commissioners for Foreign Missions, most of them with families abroad, spent an average of fourteen years in service. In view of the hazards and the primitive living conditions, that figure (for the period 1809 to 1858) reflected a high rate of career stability. Lacking the institutional resources of the foreign mission field, abolitionism could not match that length of unbroken service. Instead of financial support, the cause of the slave ordinarily provided only the camaraderie of friends from whom to draw whatever strength was needed. Nevertheless, the two movements were comparable. There can be no doubt that the abolitionist and the missionary began at the same point of origin and later had, in many respects, similar experiences and points of view.

In summary, what the missionary and the abolitionist shared often included a common upbringing under strict, orthodox, evangelical parents; a conversion experience of rich personal meaning; a sense of special destiny, the product of compulsive application to study; a later subjection to pious, admired superiors and elder friends who stirred religious ambitions; and finally a decision to seek a risk-taking course for the sake of God and personal fulfillment. The sole distinction, aside from the obvious institutional differences between the causes, was in the matter of politics. One should not, however, overstress the discrepancy. During the 1840s and 1850s, the American Missionary Association, created by abolitionists, served the ambitions of politically minded young evangelicals in the foreign and domestic fields. These pious missionaries were keenly aware of domestic moral troubles, a contrast with the views of their missionary predecessors in the period from 1810 to 1830.

Quite clearly, political interest could well be combined with foreign mission work. The difference between the abolitionist and the foreign missionary might really have reflected only a question of timing and opportunity rather than psychological predisposition. In the years following the War of 1812, political matters were momentarily quiescent. Religious revivals and concerns, on the other hand, seized the public imagination. The brightest and most committed idealists of that era naturally turned to the grand adventure of foreign and domestic missions. The years from 1810 to 1830 were the high-water mark in foreign mission work. After that, however, it gradually became less a leap into the inspiring unknown. Though outstanding leaders—accomplished linguists, teachers, and physicians—continued to enter the mission field in the decades thereafter, the cause was becoming routine and, for some, even unpromising. Guilt for *not* joining fellow seminarians in the pledge to Christianize the heathen became easier to bear. At the same time, in the 1830s and 1840s, attention turned to domestic matters, especially antislavery. The talented, ambitious evangelical had a choice: to follow Adoniram Judson, Harriet Newell, and Henry Lyman or instead to join Theodore Weld, William Lloyd Garrison, and the Lane seminarians and brave the clamorous tribes at home. The eventual result was that the abolitionist became increasingly man-centered. It was the nature of the cause itself. The foreign missionary, on the other hand, remained God-centered.

In any case, the two causes of foreign missions and antislavery had the same sources of inspiration. Their advocates sought to bring order and healing freedom to those they believed prisoners of slavery, chaos, and blind ignorance. In this effort, discipline and freedom, conscience and career, hope and anxiety were uniquely blended for one generation. The results outweighed the defects. Their accomplishments endured. "No man can begin to mould himself on faith or an idea without rising to a higher order of experience: a principle of subordination, or self-mastery has been introduced into his nature; he is no longer a mere bundle of impressions, desires, and impulses," wrote George Eliot, who understood the evangelical mind so well. For all their many failings of credulity, regimentation, and unconquerable seriousness, the missionary and the abolitionist, both man and woman, knew there was "divine work to be done in life," as Eliot said, and set about to do it as best they could.[46]

46. Ian Bradley, *The Call to Seriousness: The Evangelical Impact on the Victorians* (New York, 1976), 202.

III

THE "FAMILY ARROW IN TIME":
An Evangelical Case History

LIKE ANY social organism, families express a thematic unity or collective purposefulness, one that influences personal motives and gives meaning to kinship. In a memorable phrase, the historian Natalie Z. Davis calls the long-range strategy the "family arrow in time."[1] Some families set the goal of property accumulation, the maintenance of a particular status or professional commitment, or the acquisition and retention of political power and service, local or national. With deep roots in Yankee soil, the Tappan clan represented an aspiration so firmly associated with that time and region: the fulfillment of Puritan spirituality. Residing in Northampton, Massachusetts, once the site of Jonathan Edwards' great ministry, the Tappans, as members of the First Church, found assurance that their goal was the noblest calling available to mankind. We know much about the early and late developments of New England pietism. Yet there have been relatively few attempts to explore the means by which parents passed on religious obligations. The interaction of place, personality, and social evolutions and the conflict of generations were bound to affect the standards and the quality of the religious experience itself. Not only was this the case within the Tappan

Previously published, in slightly different form, as "Three Generations of Yankee Parenthood: The Tappan Family," in *Illinois Quarterly*, XXXVIII (1975), 12–29. Used with permission.

1. Natalie Z. Davis, "Ghosts, Kin, and Progeny: Some Features of Family Life in Early Modern France," *Daedalus*, CVI (Spring, 1977), 97.

family, it was also true within other pious households, such as those of the missionaries described earlier.

As in any family, not all members of the Tappan clan respected the common drive. Nevertheless, even the dissenters and deviants had to respond to its demands. In reaction to the heavy press of religious and political orthodoxy, Benjamin Tappan, the eldest son, became a Jeffersonian Deist and a hard-boiled Democratic warhorse and senator from Ohio. It was a career and an allegiance that separated him from old Washingtonian and New England traditions. Yet he promoted his heretical ideas of religion and politics with evangelical fervor. William Tappan, a younger brother, sailed a different sea as well. He ended his impious days in drink and debt, degradations that perplexed but also provided grounds for self-congratulations for the rest of the family circle. The Tappans were scarcely alone in producing black sheep, despite or perhaps because of the intensity of their dreams for the future. The Garrison family also had its prodigal: James Holley, younger brother of William Lloyd. Like his father Abijah, James was an alcoholic, and his brother took care of him until he died of cancer in October, 1842. As Paul C. Nagel has shown, the still more illustrious Adams clan had its share of troublesome offspring.[2] In any event, the remaining early-nineteenth-century Tappans clung tenaciously to a familiar anchor, the family's Calvinistic heritage. Lewis Tappan, the youngest of the children and the most spiritually engaged of the sons, was also the most distinguished. On his pilgrimage he discovered wealth and even a degree of national prominence.

Something should be said of that career in order to place in historical context the family from which he came as well as the brood over which he was to preside. Although he was raised in a provincial community, Tappan as an adult was not at all parochial in religion or business. He contributed his wealth and, still more, his time to Christian causes of an interdenominational and global flavor. He took particular delight in advancing what he thought to be the moral and religious needs of the settlers moving west, the deprived classes

2. John L. Thomas, *The Liberator: William Lloyd Garrison, a Biography* (Boston, 1963), 282; Paul C. Nagel, *Descent from Glory: Four Generations of the John Adams Family* (New York, 1983).

close at hand in eastern cities, and the non-Christians of other continents. As leading participants in various evangelical organizations
and as wealthy New York merchants, Tappan and his brother Arthur
supported the Bible, temperance, Sunday school, tractarian, and foreign mission campaigns throughout the 1820s. Thereafter, however,
they gradually turned to the plight of the southern slaves. Long associated with British Evangelicals in the peace and emancipation
causes, Tappan undertook a vain mission to London in 1843 to enlist
British aid against the annexation of Texas. Hoping to bring educational and Christian light to frontier and backward regions, Lewis
and Arthur had in 1833 established Oberlin College in Ohio. For
these reasons, too, in 1846 they helped to create the American Missionary Association, both antislavery and evangelistic in purpose.
The places of darkness in need of Christian illumination included the
American South. All these efforts showed Tappan's wide-ranging fascination with Christian mission.

Even in business matters, Tappan was not small-minded. In the
operations of a prosperous silk store, Lewis and his equally devout
brother Arthur depended upon merchants and storekeepers—North,
South, and West—who sought goods and credit from the Manhattan
firm. In 1828 the Tappans, using a Mississippi family's former driver,
son of a West African king, as resident agent, had planned to operate
a shipping line to Liberia. The prince's death ended the Tappans' experiment in international trade. In 1841, when the brothers' partner-
ship was dissolved, Lewis established the Mercantile Agency, later
known as Dun & Bradstreet Company. This nationally oriented enterprise, Lewis Tappan insisted, did not merely exist to render a fair
return on investment, although in good Yankee fashion the various
branch offices did so. Instead, as he liked to repeat, he wished to "pu-
rify the mercantile air" throughout the country.

Divine anticipations are as complex and subtle as any other human motivation. Succeeding generations of Tappans tried to bequeath
ideals of godly experience, intact and unchanging. They aspired to
things unseen, but ones much affected by social transformations. For
all the surrounding perplexities, the intensity of the search was as
profound a commitment as ambition for political recognition was in

the descendants of President John Adams. How to impel a child to perceive the majesty of God vexed the Northampton family for more than one hundred years. A judgment upon their success enters the forbidding realm of metaphysics. If biographically visible results reflected the measure of inner spiritual progress, then the Tappans confronted severe disappointment. Even so, there was ample room for irony, about which more will later be suggested.

Sarah Homes Tappan, Lewis' mother, set the awesome criterion by which the family gauged spiritual resolve. Born in 1748 in Boston, Sarah was the daughter of William Homes, a goldsmith and justice of the peace. Homes's mother was Benjamin Franklin's younger sister Mary. Like his seventeenth-century forebears, but quite unlike his uncle, Homes was a loyal and cheerless predestinarian. He came by his faith naturally. His grandfather, a strict Sabbatarian of Chilmark, Martha's Vineyard, bore on his tombstone this inscription: "Reverent, Learned, Eminently Prudent and Pious, Mr. William Homes." According to family tradition, this William Homes, the first in America, had once refused to voyage out of harbor on a Sunday with his competitors. By waiting until Monday, he missed the storms that drove them off course and instead enjoyed a smooth and profitable trip. Reliance on God's Providence was always a leading virtue in the Homes family. During a cholera epidemic, a female relative suggested to William Homes, the Boston goldsmith, that baby Sarah should stay with her in a healthy part of town. Homes refused. Two youngsters had already died; several others were sick; but a change, he ruled, would tempt God's wrath.[3]

As one might expect, Homes believed in strict and physical punishment for moral instruction, so much so that Sarah "stood in awe of him and almost trembled when she heard his heavy tread on the entry." Once when she was twenty, her father boxed her ears for staying out past nine o'clock. Such parental behavior was customary and therefore somewhat less emotionally disturbing than it might seem at first. As Sarah wisely observed, it was the general practice then

3. Bertram Wyatt-Brown, *Lewis Tappan and the Evangelical War Against Slavery* (Cleveland, 1969); Terry Alford, *Prince Among Slaves* (New York, 1977); James R. McGovern, *Yankee Family* (New Orleans, 1975), 12.

for parents to "treat their children rather sternly [and] avoid familiarity with them." By natural stubbornness children were supposedly prone to rebellion against both father and God. The solution was not only aloofness on the one hand and deference on the other but also prompt attention to childish offenses. One method was to connect physical pain or its absence with the prospects of an afterlife. Hell was often described as "a terrible place, that is worse a thousand times than whipping." Heaven was simply where beatings never occurred. Given the high rate of mortality among the young, the child's sense of perdition or beatitude, as David Stannard has described, was immediate and literal indeed.[4]

Adding to the restrictive cast of Sarah's upbringing was the fact that her father William Homes also served in Boston as a tithingman. The post required that he prod malingerers to church and keep them awake and orderly during services. A heavy staff of office assisted him. Duties of this kind encouraged Homes to allow no cause for embarrassment to arise in his own house. The children were to set examples of godliness and obedience in the neighborhood. Yet Sarah was not crushed under the regimen. In fact, few Puritan children ever were. In all likelihood her upbringing was similar to that of Jonathan Edwards' children in Northampton. The great minister used to "attend" them at the first sign of "self-will and stubbornness [until] he had thoroughly subdued them, and brought them to submit." Formidable as he was, however, words of warning or a few strokes were enough. Moreover, Edwards knew how to enter "freely into the feelings and concerns" of his little ones. Homes was not so gifted with children as was his contemporary in western Massachusetts. Yet Sarah did not seem to doubt that her father loved her. Somehow, he as well as her mother Rebecca Dawes Homes, of whom she left no recollections at all, managed to convey a concern for her general

4. Lewis Tappan, *Memoir of Sarah Tappan* . . . (New York, 1834), 86, 87; Lewis Tappan, "My Forefathers" (MS in Lewis Tappan Papers, Library of Congress), 12; Lawrence Stone, *The Family, Sex and Marriage in England, 1500–1800* (New York, 1977), 164; Philip Greven, *The Protestant Temperament: Patterns of Child-Rearing, Religious Experience, and the Self in Early America* (New York, 1977); David Stannard, *The Puritan Way of Death: A Study in Religion, Culture, and Social Change* (New York, 1977), 141–61.

well-being, not just the state of her soul. About the latter, Sarah's father, a firm believer in youthful wickedness, had dire forebodings. Nevertheless, Sarah received no regular religious instruction. It simply did not occur to anybody that children should have specifically designed lessons. Attendance with the Homeses at Samuel Sewall's Old South Church sufficed. "They taught me the Assembly's Catechism," she recalled, "but I have no remembrance that it was ever explained to me."[5]

Certainly William Homes's periodic ear-boxings, demands for deference, and admonitions about the fate of willful children do not fully explain Sarah's peculiar yearning for divine truth. These were standard deterrents in mid-eighteenth-century Boston. Yet few contemporaries ever could have matched her driving ambition for redemption. Instead, the source lay at least partly in the miracle of her own survival. Out of sixteen children whom her mother bore, Sarah was one of five to reach full maturity. How taxing it must have been for a child to face constant reminders of mortality—the illness and death of brothers and sisters, playmates and rivals for familial attention. In fact, Homes's paternal stiffness was probably itself a result of these steady disappointments. According to some historians, one reason why parents of the early modern era were so insensitive about their children's needs and so harsh in their discipline was the tacit worry that any affection too freely lavished would be rewarded all too soon in dust and agonies of grief. Certainly laymen were so advised, as in Richard Baxter's words: "Prepare for the loss of children and friends. It is your unpreparedness that maketh it seem unsupportable." Yet, one hesitates to overstress the seemingly stunted feelings of past generations toward their children. Possibly, the self-protective feature worked both ways. A child rendered fatherless was perhaps better equipped to accept the loss and adjust to a new situation if the relationship had not been very close.[6]

5. Edwards quoted in Arthur Calhoun, *A Social History of the American Family: From Colonial Times to the Present* (2 vols.; New York, 1945), I, 114; see Lewis Tappan, "My Forefathers," *passim*; Sarah Tappan quoted in *Home Missionary*, I (November, 1828), 122.

6. Stone, *The Family, Sex and Marriage*, 213–15; Richard Baxter, *The Christian Directory*, vols. II–VI of *The Practical Works of Richard Baxter*, ed. William Orme (23 vols.; London, 1830), IV, 255.

Religion in New England was not just a comfort at the time of bereavement, it was almost a necessity. Faith offered the reward of an afterlife of painlessness and joy. Later, in her own adulthood, Sarah was to lose a beloved daughter quite unexpectedly. The eighteen-year-old had died in the night without warning of illness. Sarah prepared the family for Sunday meeting as usual, leaving the body as found. "I could never have done it," she later remarked, "if I had not been so raised above self by the overwhelming sense of the happiness of my departed child. My first thought when I saw her dead body was, 'Oh, what a beautiful morning this is to her,' and this went with me all day." Such restraint over feeling, such faith in God's will were bound to impress her children. Lewis spoke of the incident many times and always with awe.[7]

What made Sarah so brave in this instance was her own intimacy with death. As a child who survived in a house where death was a frequent visitor, she had learned how to behave in grief. Sarah also found how to reconcile fascination, terror, guilt, and joy in being alive when others fell away like leaves in autumn. The lesson was provided in the Christian message itself: Sarah knew that she must be worthy of the trust God had placed in her. Every threat to her life seemed a demonstration of God's power to take and to restore life. Three times, she claimed, she had fallen out of a moving chaise. Once when barely a toddler, she had slipped from "a chamber window," suffering a concussion that kept her in bed for three weeks. These perils and, by her account, two near-drownings "made a still deeper impression upon my mind, and I was led to reflect upon the power and goodness of God through my past life." That sense of God's special regard was born of her uniqueness: a survivor in a family that boasted so few.[8]

As a mother, Sarah showed uncommon gifts, losing only one baby, George Washington Tappan, last of the line, in 1793. Seven years old at the time, Arthur Tappan never forgot, said Lewis, "the solemn scenes; the christening, the death, the funeral, the long procession, the grave, the lowering of the coffin, the heavy sound upon it, and the toll-

7. Lewis Tappan, "My Forefathers," 31; Lewis Tappan, *The Life of Arthur Tappan* (New York, 1870), 17–18.
8. Lewis Tappan, *Memoir of Sarah Tappan*, 15, 16, 19.

ing of the dreadful bell." In the Tappan house, children were not spared the sights and rituals of death—far from it. Yet, Sarah had reversed the doleful pattern that her own parents had set: her children were healthy. Again, the meaning to her was clear. God intended that each of her offspring should accomplish great things in his name, but especially Lewis and Arthur. Moreover, her husband was prospering in the 1790s; he could afford to get the extra help his wife needed. There was more time for child-rearing, meditation, and reading, all of which suited the quiet but determined temperament of the boys' mother.

In accordance with late-eighteenth-century ideas of child-raising, Sarah did not rely so much upon the rod and fist to instruct her children in moral conduct and spiritual aims. Like most New England mothers who were earnestly devout, she recognized the imperative of developing the children's inner restraints. "Train them up in exact obedience to yourselves, and break them of their wills," commanded Richard Baxter, her favorite authority and one whom father Homes had no doubt revered. Baxter also said, "They must be ruled as rational creatures, that love themselves, and those that love them." The more affection shown them, he declared, the better their understanding of "severity when they commit a fault. For then they will see, that it is their fault only that displeaseth you, and not their persons." A close textual reader, Sarah Tappan saw the possible contradiction and the balance between strictness and love that Baxter tried to convey and her own father had not wholly achieved. As well as any pious mother of her time, she followed the advice to the very letter.[9]

As a result, there were special treats to reward good behavior. The children were always allowed to have pets, a favor that provided them with the experience of care and responsibility. Punishments were inevitable but they were undertaken almost by Baxter's prescription in *The Christian Directory*. Lewis was headstrong and stubborn: Baxter advised that the penalties be suited not just to the offense but to "the different tempers of your children." As he ordered, Sarah punished Lewis with both switch and biblical injunction. Her texts were ones that she had heard herself as a young girl. Taken from Proverbs and

9. Baxter, *The Christian Directory*, IV, 177.

other Old Testament sources, they served in *The Christian Directory* as a litany of penance to accompany the rhythms of the strokes. According to her son Lewis, Mrs. Tappan was accustomed to repeat these words: "'The rod and reproof give wisdom; but a child left to himself bringeth his mother to shame.' Prov. xxii, 15. 'Foolishness is bound in the heart of a child; but the rod of correction shall drive it far from him.'" These and other passages, Lewis later said, made him recoil from Scriptures as much as from the stripes.[10]

Arthur, on the other hand, was more submissive and introspective. "He had the good fortune," Lewis remembered, "to escape much chastisement either at home, or in school." A reason for this malleable disposition was that his mother impressed upon him how much he resembled her in the uncertainty of his hold on life. He, too, she often pointed out, was constantly in debt to God for particular miracles of survival. Once he had nearly smothered in a "press-bedstead" in the sitting room. Wielding an ax, his father had almost mistaken him for a piece of firewood in the woodshed, and on another occasion Arthur had come close to drowning after a skating accident. These incidents, driven home with Sarah's usual forcefulness, had more of an impact than could any birch rod on the reserved but conscientious boy.[11]

Whereas the source of discipline and moral instruction had been paternal during Sarah's rearing, it was she, not Benjamin, who administered the cold baths and the switchings. The father only performed the melancholy duty (though never on a Sunday) when she requested it. The transfer of authority, or at least its sharing, indicated that in the Tappan family at least, there was a rather efficient division of labor. Sarah made sure that neither she nor her husband fell to angry scoldings, boxing ears, and pulling hair. The older methods of abrupt response belonged to the less enlightened times when Homes had tried to humiliate his daughter upon her return after curfew. By such standards, Sarah Tappan was a modern woman.

Though successful in imparting desires for self-control through appeals to conscience, Sarah found that the deeper task of conveying

10. Lewis Tappan, "My Forefathers," *passim*; Lewis Tappan, *The Life of Arthur Tappan*, 19.
11. Lewis Tappan, *The Life of Arthur Tappan*, 19.

her sense of religious mystery was beyond her powers. She loved the meditative life, spending hours on her knees at night and finding daily respites for reading favorite theologians and Scripture. The writings of Philip Doddridge, Richard Baxter, Samuel Hopkins, David Tappan (of Harvard College), and Jonathan Edwards, all were carefully read and reread. In fact, she was considerably more knowledgeable and intellectual about such weighty matters than was the Reverend Solomon Williams, a pale reflection of his predecessor in the Northampton pulpit—the great Edwards himself. A child of the first Great Awakening, who had once thrilled to the voice of George Whitefield, she believed that "every action of my life [was] so wofully polluted by indwelling sin," only constant prayer, perseverance, and submissiveness could bring her close "to Jesus . . . my Prophet, Priest, and King." But with Arthur an exception, her children—robust and perhaps lucky—could not share her feelings of mingled wonder, guilt, and relief for just being alive. Their remorse, if ever it arose, had to spring from a failure to match her luminous inner life. "I love to acknowledge myself nothing, that God may be all," she rejoiced. It was not an easy proposition to inculcate in others.[12]

Perhaps the reason why neither Lewis nor Arthur underwent rites of conversion was related to the formidable spirituality of their mother. Besides, there simply was not much opportunity. Both teenage lads went off to Boston to start merchant apprenticeships before revivals had refreshed the Northampton church. Yet, Sarah had carefully nurtured them to fulfill the family purpose. In a most interesting and predictive way, Arthur Tappan referred to it in 1807, when he was just twenty-two. Then living in Montreal with a bankrupt merchant's family, Arthur expressed some dread of his speculative landlord's unhappy lot. "When I behold such a picture," he wrote nineteen-year-old Lewis, "my mind recoils at the view, and a resolution half escapes me, to avoid the possibility of ever sharing a similar fate." But to be overly cautious out of "apprehension of misfortunes which ten thousand chances to one never happen" was cowardly. "Should we not brand that person as an idiot, who refuses to buy an

12. Lewis Tappan, *Memoir of Sarah Tappan*, 20; Sarah Tappan to Arthur Tappan, June, 1807, in Lewis Tappan, *The Life of Arthur Tappan*, 44.

estate because it would increase his cares and subject him to greater losses, when the possession would extend his means of benevolence, and enable him, by giving happiness to others, to enlarge the bounds of his own." These ruminations, however, embarrassed the young clerk. He confided to Lewis, "But what am I writing? You will, I believe, be no less puzzled than myself to answer the question." What he said, however, foretold a lifetime: the amalgamating of Sarah's hopes for godliness and Benjamin's occupation of merchant, to which they were also ever faithful.[13]

Lewis Tappan was endowed with his mother's high intelligence, but he put it to different uses. However mightily he strove, meditation bored him. He loved society and the comfort of a crowd united for godly enterprise—in church or lecture hall. Following this inclination, Tappan joined with the popular William Ellery Channing's Unitarians as a young businessman in Boston. One might call the conversion a minor rebellion, for his mother agonized about the defection from orthodoxy to the day of her death in 1826. But really Tappan was responding to Channing's obvious spirituality, and Lewis' years at the Federal Street Church did seem a time of release from Sarah's religious preoccupations, and he concerned himself with chiefly human affections. In 1816, for instance, Tappan and his bride Susan Aspinwall suddenly lost their firstborn, a two-year-old named Susan. In his diary, Tappan wrote that the child's "affectionate mother & myself were enabled to feel a sweet composure & resignation. . . . She said, 'If it were not for submission to God's will her heart would break',—so persuaded was she that it was well with our little girl that 'she would not, if she could, wish her to return, even if she could run into the room as gaily as she used to do.' We are persuaded that . . . she is a sweet cherub in heaven; & that she may welcome us to heaven if we live the life of the righteous." The feelings behind these words evinced a poignancy that Tappan did not always sustain when he returned to the faith of his ancestors in 1828.[14]

The death of Tappan's mother, a series of calamitous business fail-

13. Arthur Tappan to Lewis Tappan, October 25, 1807, in Lewis Tappan, *The Life of Arthur Tappan*, 48.
14. Lewis Tappan Diary, October 27, 1816 (MS in Lewis Tappan Papers).

ures, and an offer to join Arthur's Pearl Street emporium in New York City (if Lewis arrived in an orthodox frame of mind) led Lewis Tappan to convince himself that his Unitarian course had been mistaken. Once more, he sang in Arthur's company the doxology, a hymn to the Triune God whom Sarah had worshipped. As if to suppress personal and indeed public doubt about his motivation, Tappan became almost a caricature of the Christian Achiever. By that term is meant one who measured convictions by the quantity of good deeds performed rather than by justifications by faith, his mother's spiritual preference. Whereas Sarah had conceived evangelism as a duty of familial instruction, Lewis thought in terms of preaching to the world. Religion took him out of the home, with consequent effects upon the atmosphere around the hearthside.

Children of extremely dynamic, intense parents may face special strains in the search for self-fulfillment, but none more so than those born to the first generation of nineteenth-century moralists. For his part, Lewis had grown up in a society that accepted Adamic sin as natural and inevitable. Sarah Tappan knew that evil acts and thoughts could never be wholly mastered. Evangelicals like her son preached otherwise. Once, for instance, she wrote Lewis that she had dreamed that he had gone awhoring after visiting a Boston theater and then had died from venereal disease and medical quackeries to cover the shame. The nightmare was vivid, and the recounting boldly graphic as only an eighteenth-century villager could be when contemplating the terrors of the city. Yet, it was the only time she mentioned the topic, a contrast to Lewis' admonitions to his own offspring. Sarah expected her sons to be sexually pure before marriage; she rejoiced that her children were "shielded from infamy" by the world's standards. Good Calvinist as she was, she paraphrased Baxter on the sinfulness of the young: "I know by woful experience, that by nature they are totally depraved." It did not occur to her to make a fuss about the "secret sin" of self-indulgence. The practice was, by her lights, probably no worse than any other form of alienation from God's mercy and love. However wrong it was to condone human wickedness, she believed, one should not be surprised when it appeared. Women were expected to exercise a self-mastery that men need not wholly imitate when sexual passion was aroused. Besides, as an eighteenth-century woman, there were limits even to mothers' authority, in intrusions upon male behavior.[15]

Tappan may never have entered a gambling house or a brothel, except to deliver a tract on moral reform, though he had been raised in a society of lower expectations for human improvement. The Tappan family had stressed internalized controls within the household, but in the larger arena in which Lewis and Arthur moved as children, habits and institutional controls were primitive and rustic. Even in pious, tranquil Northampton, the atmosphere was masculine and peasantlike. "The fathers," said Lewis, were accustomed to spend weeknights, even Sundays too, "at the public house" gossiping, card-playing, and drinking; at home "the mothers were engaged in sewing and knitting." Aside from the occasional tavern scuffle, crime was scarcely rampant. Yet, to overawe the populace in good English style, the five "shire justices" of western Massachusetts used to march through town on their twice-yearly visits "in platoon form, with cocked hats and powdered hair preceded by the high sheriff. . . . August sight!" Lewis recalled. Tappan later rejoiced that conscience, in the form of the penitentiary method of punishment, had replaced older means for correcting wrongdoing. In his youth, penalties were supposed to be visible, terrifying, and shaming, from the cropping of ears to the public hanging. On execution days, "the boys were let out of school, it being considered proper that the rising generation should, for their learning, see in the punishment inflicted, that 'every transgression and disobedience received a just recompense of reward.'" As a youth, he had seen boys imitate the cruelties of the law upon some unpopular playmate. These examples of sin and punishment served as rough-and-ready points of psychological reference in relation to what Mother and Father Tappan inculcated at home. Sarah had had to permit Lewis associations with the nonchurchgoing children at the common school; it was impossible to prevent some mixing: the boys were not necessarily bad but they were certainly tough. The result was that Lewis had a real sense of alternative ways of behaving, a

15. Sarah Tappan to Lewis Tappan, June [?], 1809, in Lewis Tappan, *Memoir of Sarah Tappan*, 64–65; Ellen K. Rothman, "Sex and Self-Control: Middle-Class Courtship in America, 1770–1870," *Journal of Social History*, XV (1982), 414.

knowledge later denied his own children. His adult struggles with sin—even sexual sin—were therefore healthy, dynamic, and genuinely valiant.[16]

Separated from his wife Susan during the summer months of 1828, he fell to temptation—partly out of sheer loneliness and distress as he took up new duties and tried to meet creditors' demands in New York City. The donor of the Tappan papers to the Library of Congress (by admission to the author in 1961) tore out two pages of her grandfather's diary before turning the documents over to the curator. She also erased some passages elsewhere; as faint tracings reveal, however, the sexual urge had overwhelmed him more than once. Not long afterward, Susan arrived from Boston.[17] Unhappily, Tappan's children were not permitted the luxury of even contemplating such acts. The gospel that their father espoused condemned deviations from man's perfectibility in thought and deed, even as it liberalized the sterner aspects of Sarah's old-fashioned Calvinism and brimstone.

Being the modern parent that he was, Tappan conjoined religious precept with medical admonitions, a new device for winning the final war against harmful bodily corruptions. "Physiological knowledge," Lewis publicly advised, and the "warning of scripture" could dispel childish ignorance of the dread "consequences of yielding . . . idiocy, insanity, disfigurement of body, and imbecility of mind [that] youthful lusts" produced. Such preachings on sexual matters replaced the switch altogether in the rearing of the Tappan children. Only once did Lewis' temper get out of control. Lucy Maria had eaten his strawberries, a favorite dish, and he switched her. The reliance upon daily sermons, family prayers, and withdrawal of privileges were ordinary means of inculcating discipline in the early Victorian home. They tended to place a great burden of guilt upon the developing moral resources of the child. Problems of a sexual nature were to be rather prominent in the lives of some of Lewis' offspring. Tappan's parental style did little to mitigate the side effects.[18]

16. Lewis Tappan, *The Life of Arthur Tappan*, 25–26.
17. Interview with Anna Hulett, October 24, 1961; see also Lewis Tappan Diary, March 16, September 18, October 4, 1828.
18. Lewis Tappan, *The Life of Arthur Tappan*, 121; Lewis Tappan Diary, October 21, 1836.

Growing up in the Tappan household was not an easy matter for a number of other reasons, too. Susan was a gentle, long-suffering soul. She provided a healthy measure of affection and evenhanded fairness in raising her children. But Lewis was very much the modern father. As his career in commerce, religion, and philanthropy showed, he was happiest when employed. Eight to ten hours were spent on business affairs in the city. He occupied his evenings with various benevolent activities—antislavery, a home for prostitutes, services, lecture duties, and special meetings, all of which were in behalf of a better arrangement of civilized living or a disarrangement of something deemed uncivilized. Also, he frequently undertook trips, mostly for religious or moral purposes, such as a tour in 1829 to demand Sunday post office closings or his trip to England in 1843 to prevent American annexation of slaveholding Texas.

Of course, Tappan felt homesick sometimes. Once, when he had remained in the city while the family departed for summer vacation, he remarked in his diary, "I miss my little children very much. No longer does Georgiana watch to open the door as I go home from the store, nor do I see little Ellen peeping behind the nursery door to catch a look of papa & then run away." But these thoughts were soon translated into matters of general, abstract application: "Does not our discontent arise chiefly from selfishness? If so, the secret of contentment & happiness is benevolence." In other words, he consoled himself with the thought that service to God in charitable ventures was more uplifting and ultimately brought more personal joy than a simple romp in the nursery with his children.[19]

When the whole family was in town together, Tappan spent the weekends passing out tracts, conducting Sunday schools, and visiting the pious sick and admonishing the impious poor. Even on holidays when he joined the others as circumstances permitted, Tappan could not refrain from well-doing in the neighborhood. This peripatetic running hither and yon was bound to leave some scars on the young. Not only was his absence sorely felt, his energy set an example hard to emulate.[20]

19. Lewis Tappan Diary, July 20, 1839.
20. Lewis Tappan Diary, August 6, 1841; Wyatt-Brown, *Lewis Tappan*, 98–99.

Another source of distress that the Tappan children faced was their father's unpopularity. In 1834, Susan and the little ones were alone when a mob of anti-abolitionists banged on the door, demanding Tappan's hide. Rushing from a special antislavery worship service, Lewis arrived before any harm was done. The next morning he moved the family to Harlem Village, but that evening all their furnishings and playthings were burned in the street—certainly a most difficult event for the children to understand. Sometimes, too, Lewis almost seemed to court public disfavor, admirable though his egalitarian principles were. On the summer vacation in 1836, he outraged a congregation in upstate New York by placing his family in pews reserved for black communicants. Such incidents would surely embarrass teenagers sensitive to public opinion and uncertain of their own courage for which the parent set so lofty a standard.

As one might anticipate, Lewis' two boys felt the effects rather intensely. Lewis Henry, the elder, exasperated his father by his poor performance in Sunday school. Moreover, he did not flourish at Oneida Institute, a manual labor boarding school, a type of work-and-study arrangement popular with all sorts of reformers. Worried that the boys would learn bad habits from city ruffians, Lewis had sent them to a school where the children of other evangelicals predominated. The atmosphere was rigorous, plain, and pious. Both Lewis Henry and William idolized the devout Theodore Weld, then a senior scholar at Oneida. Emulating the great reformer, they even enjoyed the appropriate and conventional religious outpouring expected of young people. The season of holy refreshment passed all too quickly to suit their father. After a few months, William and Lewis Henry lapsed into teenage indifference once more. Then, at sixteen, Lewis Henry came down with rheumatic fever and lay on his deathbed in 1838. "Do you ever think my dear child that you shall get well?" Tappan asked. "'I can't tell whether I shall or not'" was the reply. "'Do you wish to get well?'" Tappan queried. "'No.' 'Do you have delightful views of the future, of going to be X^t ?' 'Sometimes, & sometimes not so bright.'" Sorrowfully, Tappan recorded in his diary, "I have tried to engage him in some conversation about his spiritual interests, but in vain." Ten days later, Lewis Henry died, the state of his soul, Tappan feared, in serious doubt. Tappan's disappointment encouraged him to labor all the harder in the vineyards of New York City.[21]

William, too, presented his parents with difficulties. Beriah Green, president of Oneida Institute, wrote Tappan that son William kicked "Mr. Hough, the treasurer, & [spoke] abusively to him!" "Alas!" wrote the father, "how keen are the pangs of a parent in view of the wickedness of children." But he pleaded, on this as on many other occasions, "May this dear son be made to feel his guilt, repent & humble himself. . . . Oh! thou blessed Jesus—overrule this event to the everlasting good of my son—of myself, and of my dear family." William arrived in New York City shortly afterward in a filthy state, as Tappan reported. The runaway was promptly sent back to Oneida with a letter of apology to the insulted school official.[22]

Actually William possessed a sweet disposition when suitably treated. Theodore Weld at Oneida told Lewis Tappan that "Wm requires a teacher who will get into his heart & carry him along by love," but a Mr. Grant, his instructor, "is not such a man at all." Grant did leave much to be desired as an instructor. According to one report, he "'walked among the students like a speechless ghost'" and prepared none of the students for their compositions or declamations. Allegedly, he "'lay abed late in the mor[ning], drank tea and coffee stoutly and his manual labor consisted in journeying from his room to the backhouse.'" Whatever the teacher's faults may have been, though, William was as shy and frightened of public speaking as his grandfather Benjamin had been. As a result, he ran into trouble at Middlebury College in 1837. His refusal to deliver an oration before faculty and students, a general requirement, was so defiant that he alarmed the president. Summoned to the scene, Lewis Tappan had to bring the freshman home in dead of winter. The worried parents then placed him with a lawyer in Cherry Valley, New York. Lewis fretted that D. H. Little would be too easygoing, but under the attorney's guidance William recovered his stability. He did not, however, take to the law, in view of his forensic fears.[23]

---

21. Lewis Tappan Diary, July–August, 1838, July 27, 1838 (quotation).
22. Lewis Tappan Diary, July 24–26, 1836.
23. Robert Abzug, *Passionate Liberator: Theodore Dwight Weld and the Dilemma of Reform* (New York, 1980), 79; Lewis Tappan Diary, July 24, 1836, May 23, 1837, Novem-

For a while in the 1840s, William joined the Mercantile Agency in Hanover Square. Father-son relations were too strained for that occupation to work out satisfactorily. William abruptly quit and escaped to Concord, Massachusetts. There he became an intimate of Ralph Waldo Emerson, Henry Thoreau, and Caroline Stugis, a gifted member of the Transcendental circle, whom he shortly married. They had two daughters, but the couple was ill-matched and separated within three years. William then bought a property in the Berkshires which eventually was willed to the Boston Symphony Orchestra. The farm was known as Tanglewood.

Throughout these years, William's closest friend was Nathaniel Hawthorne, who seemed to enjoy his quiet, intellectual manner. Needless to say, Lewis Tappan was disappointed. In 1846 he had written, "I have been apprehensive that William's acquaintance with Mr. E[merson] would be disadvantageous to him. Let us pray that it may not be so & that God will add to Wm's many amiable qualities the riches of His grace." But William's spiritual and public contribution was not a signature on a temperance card or the management of an eleemosynary cause, his father's style. Instead, in his last years, he published a translation of Homer's epics—a heathenish choice, by Lewis Tappan's lights at least.[24]

The girls in the Tappan clan fared somewhat differently, none of them having a literary bent. Juliana, the eldest, was her mother's favorite. Indeed, Susan seemed to be rather possessive about Julia because she needed a companion while her husband was away. In 1846 she wrote her daughter, asking her to come home, "I do not wish to be selfish in monopolizing your time, [but] I need you to walk and talk with." Barred by evangelical restrictions, Julia had no occupation except helping about the house. Marriage apparently did not appeal. Then in 1853, Susan, her mother, died. Georgiana and Ellen, the two

ber 24, December 6, 8, 10, 1838, July 9, August 2, 1839; Lewis Tappan to D. H. Little, January 18, 1840, in letterbook, Lewis Tappan Papers.

24. Lewis Tappan to Mrs. John Bigelow, March 31, 1846, in letterbook, Lewis Tappan Papers; Louise Hall Tharp, *The Peabody Sisters of Salem* (Boston, 1950), 350–51; Leon Howard, *Herman Melville: A Biography* (Berkeley, 1958), 160; Randall Stewart (ed.), *The American Notebooks by Nathaniel Hawthorne* (New Haven, 1932), September 17, 1849, p. 129, September 4, 1850, p. 132, July 29, 1851, p. 217, August 5, 1851, p. 226, and pp. 305n, 329n.

youngest, were devastated by the loss. Uncle Arthur urged Lewis to spend free moments comforting them. Lewis admitted the necessity. "I think so to[o], but am in a dilemma about what is due from me to each [daughter] & whether, after devoting proper time to them I can be an efficient Sec. of the Soc. May God direct!"[25]

Apparently God's and Tappan's inclinations happily coincided. Antislavery duties triumphed over domestic concerns, but the girls managed to cope somehow. Actually Julia was the one to bear the harshest reaction. A spinster of thirty-six, she tried to become as useful to her father as she had been to her mother—serving as his secretary and housekeeper. A few months after Susan's death, Julia suffered a severe nervous breakdown. Torn with grief, guilt, loneliness, and feelings of uselessness, she accused the proprietor of a water-cure establishment of trying to seduce her. Lewis reacted to her telegram by taking a Sunday-morning train, contrary to his Sabbatarian principles. She knew her father's mind. If anything could ever have roused him from his reform labors, it was the thought of her sexual distress. Tappan administered to her needs insofar as he could, having ascertained that there was no reality to her claims of abuse. After a month with her father, Julia managed to pull herself together.[26]

The remaining daughters also struggled with feelings beyond their understanding, though the record is meager about the cause or consequences of their difficulties. Susan, named for the firstborn who had died in 1816, a common practice then, married well. Hiram Barney, her husband, served the New York bar, Abraham Lincoln's party, and the cause of God and Unionism. By him Susan had several children, but in 1864, in a single but ominous reference in a letter to an English friend, Tappan indicated that Susan had been confined in the Philadelphia Insane Asylum for over six months. Nothing more is known about the matter.[27]

25. Susan Aspinwall Tappan to Juliana Aspinwall Tappan, August 24, 1846 [copy, donated by the present writer], in Lewis Tappan Papers; Lewis Tappan Diary, April 21, 1853.

26. Lewis Tappan to Benjamin Tappan, August 11, 1853, in Benjamin Tappan Papers, Library of Congress; Lewis Tappan Diary, August 17, August 29–September 14, 1853.

27. Lewis Tappan to Mrs. Joseph Sturge, May 3, 1864, in letterbook, Lewis Tappan Papers; Lewis Tappan Diary, May 5, 1863.

In Lucy Maria's case, less is actually known than surmised. She too married successfully. Henry C. Bowen, a former clerk in the Pearl Street silk store, had one of New York's largest dry-goods businesses. A firm puritan and abolitionist, Bowen installed Henry Ward Beecher in the Plymouth Church in Brooklyn. Bowen held the church's mortgage, a princely investment, as Beecher invariably filled the pews. With a shrewd eye for business—and religious advance—Bowen also appointed Beecher as one of the editors of the *Independent*, Bowen's highly lucrative religious newspaper. Beecher's gratitude for these benefices took a singular form. Upon her deathbed in 1863, Lucy Maria confessed to her husband that for a number of years she had enjoyed sexual relations with the famous divine. Bowen was shocked. He supposedly did wring a confession from Beecher, but business interests and prudence required public silence. Some years later, Theodore Tilton, another editor, learned from his wife that she had likewise fallen prey to Beecher's prayerful charms during pastoral calls. Less circumspect and more hot-tempered, Tilton told Bowen of his marital woes. Bowen commiserated with the younger journalist by confessing his own situation. Eventually the sordid business resulted in two sensational court trials. They concluded with Tilton ruined and Beecher legally exonerated—all because Bowen refused on the witness stand to support Tilton's case. Beecher later took his revenge on Bowen for not vigorously supporting his defense. He saw to it that the elders excommunicated Bowen from the Plymouth Church, which Bowen himself had established.[28]

The scandal has taken us afield. The main point here is that Lucy Maria, a genuinely affectionate mother of nine children, had not found full satisfaction in her husband's company. One cannot blame her infidelity upon the misdirections of Lewis Tappan's parenthood. She was a responsible lady who knew the dictates of Victorian morality. Given the nature of the times and Lucy's particular upbringing, however, she did not gain much pleasure from her associations with Henry Ward Beecher. The final confession made that poignantly clear. She must have been a sad, distraught, and perhaps angry indi-

28. Wyatt-Brown, *Lewis Tappan*, 342; Altina L. Waller, *Reverend Beecher and Mrs. Tilton: Sex and Class in Victorian America* (Amherst, Mass., 1982), 9–10, 34, 75–76.

vidual to lay before her husband such a story which would always cloud his memory of her.

If Lewis Tappan's children did find that joyful fellowship with God that grandmother Sarah had promised would be theirs, the lives they led, though outwardly unblemished during life, give little reason for hope that they did. Of course, even for Sarah Tappan, the vision of Christ's riches often flickered and died out, only to rekindle her soul once more. Moments of contentment also came in Lewis Tappan's religious life, but not the ecstasy, clarity, and profundity that Sarah experienced. Lewis knew that all his good works could not bring him to that glory. Only once, in 1844, did he even dare, however, to admit the failing to someone else, a confession which nevertheless revealed his humanity and self-recognition. "Since abandoning the Unitarian church," he wrote an English friend, "I have not had that spirituality of mind, and benevolence of heart, that the Gospel of Christ requires. I have been zealous for the truth, anxious for the conversion of men, liberal in supporting the institutions of religion, but have not to the extent I should have done, had that love for fellow-Christians, and that compassion for sinners, that Jesus inculcated." [29]

One may only speculate, but William Tappan may well have possessed the inner spark that animated the life of his grandmother. The form it took was so alien to the evangelical precepts that Sarah and her dutiful son Lewis used as guides that neither one nor the other parent would ever have recognized it in William. In 1879, Julia Tappan visited her brother at his Berkshire farm, and she found him, as always, a congenial but quiet companion. "We had a few days of true brother and sister talk together," Julia wrote the aged Theodore Weld, "not so much in words, but in their unspoken sense." William so loved his solitude, his books and meditations, she continued, that whenever she went into the library, there he was in "grave study" and contemplation. [30] Indeed, William was a proper grandson of Sarah Tappan.

29. Lewis Tappan to Sophia Sturge, January 24, 1844, in letterbook, Lewis Tappan Papers.
30. Julia Tappan to Theodore Dwight Weld, [?], 1879, in Theodore Dwight Weld Papers, William L. Clements Library, Ann Arbor.

IV

JOHN BROWN'S
ANTINOMIAN WAR

JUST AS the Shakespearean critic must come to terms with Hamlet, the Civil War historian must face up to the enigma of John Brown. Given the vast literature, the interpretive possibilities for both figures seem inexhaustible. For Brown at least, the choice is narrow. One generation of critics concluded that he was a half-crazed fanatic whose actions triggered "paranoid" and "counterparanoid" reactions throughout the country. Others, particularly in recent times, have restored him to the pedestal he once occupied as a symbol of Unionist war aims. With some admitted blemishes that made him forgivably human, Brown's most enthusiastic biographers portray him as more rational than a nation that practiced and condoned the inhumanity of black bondage.[1]

Neither position, however, is entirely satisfying. Common sense tells us that he was not just a careworn old man who loathed that "rotten old whore slavery" and nobly decided to do something about it. Simplehearted he was, but old John Brown had more to him than that. In any event, something was odd about his character and be-

Previously published, in slightly different form, as "John Brown, Weathermen, and the Psychology of Antinomian Violence," in *Soundings*, LVIII (1975), 417–40. Used with permission.

1. An excellent summary of the literature on Brown may be found in Stephen B. Oates, "John Brown and His Judges: A Critique of the Historical Literature," *Civil War History*, XVII (1971), 5–24. A more directly Freudian approach than the one offered here is found in James West Davidson and Mark Hamilton Lytle, *After the Fact: The Art of Historical Detection* (New York, 1982), 139–68.

havior. The psychological factors cannot be casually dismissed; they need reexamination. On the other hand, the term *paranoia* condemns as much as it explains both him and the times. Psychiatric metaphors, no matter how sophisticated in definition, carry uncomfortable risks and limitations. Before the Civil War, religion more than psychology conveyed the language of the spirit. Therefore, to perceive him as an antinomian—a zealot with a special understanding of his relation to God and the cosmos—would be more fitting than to find an appropriate Freudian label. Moreover, it would help to explain why so troubled a soul made such an impact on his society. Like the Prince of Denmark, Brown was a procrastinating if not downright fumbling avenger, but great failings and noble virtues have never been incompatible.

A new approach to Brown gains encouragement from the aborted efforts of the insurrectionary American Left a few years ago. First, the activities of the underground revolutionary movement showed just how extraordinarily weak the tradition of antinomian violence was in this country. Americans are a violent people—our murder statistics testify to hopes for world leadership in that respect. Nevertheless, we have ordinarily adopted peaceful means in dissent. Anti-institutional objectives and heretical ideas have usually taken rhetorical, religious, and pacifistic forms. Roger Williams, Anne Hutchinson, Mother Ann Lee of the Shakers, and, in pre–Civil War times, John Humphrey Noyes of the Oneida community, Joseph Smith, the Mormon prophet, and other visionaries all claimed a special insight into God's intentions. In revealing the corruption of the world and preaching the best means for purifying mankind, none of them advocated the washing away of sins in the blood of the guilty. More often than not, American antinomians were victims, not perpetrators, of violence. The fate of Mary Dyer, hanged at Boston as a Quaker heretic, and Joseph Smith, killed in a lynch-mob affray, may serve as examples. Nevertheless, antinomian expression had so ordinarily offered a pacific road toward millennial fulfillment and spiritual wholeness that it has been almost legitimized within the American system—more so than anywhere else, according to Hannah Arendt.[2]

2. Anthony F. C. Wallace, "Revitalization Movements: Some Theoretical Considerations for Comparative Study," *American Anthropologist*, LVIII (1956), 277; Raymond

Therefore, the exceptional nature of the 1970s—Weathermen's "Days of Rage" (a trashing expedition in October, 1969, against Chicago store windows), sporadic, sometimes accidentally lethal bomb explosions, and the pathetic history of the Jonestown mass suicide in Guyana—merely accentuated the nonviolent style of antinomian dissent, both religious and secular. Not only were these efforts feeble and singularly inept, they did not seem indigenous. There was no tradition of conspiratorial anarchy upon which American radicals could build. It was almost as if violence were the monopoly of those seeking to conserve old bigotries. Thus, in any contest, the Klan or some other extremist gaggle on the Right could easily outmatch any leftist heritage for bloody proclivities.

The second insight which the outbreaks of the 1960s engendered was a vivid demonstration of the close relationship between secular protest and religious feelings, a connection that social scientists, particularly of the Weber and Durkheim schools, had analyzed long before. Theory, however, suddenly became fact, although journalistic hyperbole and faculty nervousness carried predictions of fanatical upheavals much farther than circumstances warranted. Nevertheless, the unrest during the Vietnam years—both in America and in Western Europe—provided an opportunity to social scientists to reformulate the apparent causes of what the noted anthropologist Anthony F. C. Wallace had called "revitalization movements."[3]

In *Natural Symbols*, Mary Douglas offered an interpretation that will help to explain the power and charismatic effect of John Brown, who, like the rebels of the 1960s, linked the rise of oppressed peoples with hopes for a New Kingdom. Douglas argued that a gradual disjunction between the rules governing a social group and the actual daily sense of how people ought to behave toward each other as members of that group creates a radical change in self-perception. Or-

---

Aron, *The Opium of the Intellectuals*, trans. Terrence Killmartin (Garden City, 1957), 265–94; Perry E. Gianakos, "New Left Millennialism and American Culture," *Thought*, LIX (1974), 397–418.

3. Daniel P. Moynihan, "Nirvana Now," *American Scholar*, XXXVI (1967), 539–48; Lewis Perry, "Freedom and Community," *Inquiry*, March 6, 1977, p. 23; Bertram Wyatt-Brown, "John Brown, Weathermen, and the Psychology of Antinomian Violence," *Soundings*, LVIII (1975), 438n1; Wallace, "Revitalization Movements," 264–81; see also Norman Cohn, *The Pursuit of the Millennium* (London, 1957).

dinarily, people know who they are by reference to the rituals and structures of the social order. When those rituals no longer reflect what society really cares about, when institutions seem mere shells of discarded tradition, the sensitive soul must look for assurance within himself. Security and sense of selfhood are not to be found in old externalities. Instead, they are discovered in the body and mind of the individual. Inward-looking of this kind, she believes, encourages hostility to old formulations and their replacement with new symbols—possibly vague, egoistic, totalistic, and sometimes violent. Leaders of such cultural upheavals, as Anthony Wallace has observed, may have suffered "from recognizable and admitted mental disorders" at some point in their lives. Nevertheless, they are by no means psychotic or incoherent because they are certain of both their identity and their divine mission. As Mary Douglas points out, however, the price of an impulsive desire for new and "expressive action" may well be a diminishing of the "sense of individual worth, human warmth, and spontaneity." A conservative, she did not see that some valuable gains in human affairs may emerge from the grim but romantic abstractionism of this process. Nevertheless, her attempt to link the individual's search for fulfillment with vast and kaleidoscopic changes in the social order has a bearing on the history of John Brown.[4]

No less pertinent was the work of Nathan Adler, a criminologist of Berkeley who identified a specifically "antinomian personality" based, he said, upon clinical observations of young people during the Vietnam period. Following the same theoretical lines as Mary Douglas and Anthony Wallace, Adler tried to relate the traits of this personality to particular moments in history. He deliberately attached a psychoanalytic dimension to the theological term. Adler's explanation was not particularly original. In fact, the deviant nature of the individual who claims a special relation to unseen forces and a severe alienation from ordinary ways and ideas was well recognized in literature long before social scientists Max Weber, Karl Mannheim, and Norman Cohn described it. Fyodor Dostoevsky in *Notes from Under-*

4. Mary Douglas, *Natural Symbols: Explorations in Cosmology* (New York, 1970), viii, 19, 40, 183; Wallace, "Revitalization Movements," 272.

ground and Joseph Conrad in *The Secret Agent* provide examples of the type. Nevertheless, Adler's theoretical sketch is useful. He maintained that at times of unusual social turmoil, when the values of society seem at war with routine customs and expectations, these psychic features become accentuated in people who have experienced childhood problems at home and difficulties of adjustment with the world outside.[5]

The antinomian, Adler observes, is one who places faith in his own intuition and physicality, but not in the institutions and practices of the society around him. According to psychoanalyst Karen Horney's tripartite "pride system," as she calls it, the contradictory expressions of personality include: (1) a desire to be humble, dependent, compliant, to repress anger and aggressiveness, to control anxiety by gaining outside approval, particularly from elders and authorities; (2) to demand mastery, not love, to insist that the world is hostile, to condemn softer feelings as manifestations of weakness, in oneself and in others; (3) to seek privacy and detachment, to solve problems by denying their existence, to subdue all personal temptations in ascetic denials, to disdain success of the ordinary kind, to take grim pleasure in the hardships of life. Moving from one to another of these strategies, the antinomian, as Adler identifies the style, enjoys only temporary feelings of wholeness, by idealizing himself or herself in each posture and attaching universal, divine meaning to the dominant mood of the moment. As Dostoevsky's Underground Man typically declares, "I was a terrible dreamer. I would dream for three months on end, tucked away in my corner. . . . I suddenly became a hero."[6]

Surrounded by a dread anarchy of social contradictions, the individual seeks a unity of purpose. Self-condemning, he or she searches for an inner salvation that transcends the restrictions of earthbound

5. Nathan Adler, *The Underground Stream: New Life Styles and the Antinomian Personality* (New York, 1970), and "The Antinomian Personality: The Hippie Character Type," *Psychiatry*, XXXI (1969), 326, 329, 330; Herbert Hendin, *The Age of Sensation* (New York, 1975), 285–308.
6. Karen Horney, *Our Inner Conflicts: A Constructive Theory of Neurosis* (New York, 1945), 68, 74–75; Bernard J. Paris, "*Notes from Underground*: A Horneyan Analysis," *PMLA*, LXXXVIII (1973), 513; Fyodor Dostoevsky, *Notes from Underground* (New York, 1960), 26–27.

life. Convinced that God orders every thought and action contemplated, the individual denies responsibility for consequences. Although drawn to causes requiring cooperative action, the antinomian remains a private, introspective, and self-regarding individual.

Adler identified the periods when the antinomian impulse appeared most acutely: the third century A.D., when the Roman Empire rocked in the tumult of Gnosticism, Donatism, and other mystical schisms; the Reformation, with its pantheon of Martin Luther, Johann of Muenster, and the English Levellers; the Romantic era during and after the French Revolution; and the 1960s. One may doubt the comparability of the last decade with the earlier, more cataclysmic times. In any event, the Romantic epoch (commonly referred to as the Jacksonian period in America) shared many of the antinomian characteristics. Owing to the rapid expansions of population, economic opportunities, and means of communication and expression, the 1830s in America exhibited a number of the concerns that Adler used for his typology: the radical challenge to old religious orthodoxies; the yearning for simplicity, bodily purity, restraint, asceticism, and rustic living; the desperate advocacy of individualism because men and women needed fresh assurances of their individuality in mass society; and a tendency toward deep introspection, romantic apocalypticism, and a mystical demand for a perfect order to arise from the ashes of a dying world.[7]

Within the abolitionist movement, these characteristics of antinomian thought were evident. In some respects, however, antinomianism was itself traditional, that is, deeply rooted in Quaker ideology. This quietistic source of anti-institutional thought somewhat modified the charismatic aspect of abolitionist immediatism. Nevertheless, Quakerism supplied such leaders as John Greenleaf Whittier, Lucretia Mott, and Isaac T. Hopper. The Friends' hostility to oath-swearing, luxury, and militarism and violence profoundly influenced reformers such as Garrison. In addition, as Lewis Perry has observed, a vigorous anarchistic movement developed within antislavery

7. Adler, *The Underground Stream*, 26–54; Ronald G. Walters, *American Reformers, 1815–1860* (New York, 1978); John L. Thomas, "Romantic Reform in America, 1815–1865," *American Quarterly*, XVII (1965), 656–81.

circles, whereby purely human government was eventually supposed to be replaced by "the moral government of God." This emphasis upon pacifism and Christian, romantic anarchy helped to prevent the doctrine of immediate emancipation from becoming a call to arms. Perhaps there was always a latent possibility of violence in the very stridency with which abolitionists denounced slaveholding sinfulness. Further, the clamor of the 1850s encouraged defensive belligerence against the South, even among abolitionists. Yet only John Brown actually brought insurrectionary action and antinomian ideals together as a conscious, aggressive, and dynamic part of the abolitionist movement.[8]

Of the white emancipationists John Brown was by far the most psychologically complex and personally wayward—hostile and gentle, authoritarian and self-humiliating, patriarchal and childlike, sensitive and sometimes benumbed. His hatred of slavery and slaveholders, his willingness to sacrifice himself for black freedom, his anger over his fate as child, father, and sinner were all intertwined in a way that helps to distinguish this violent antinomian from other reformers of his day.

In 1857, John Brown wrote a young boy about his own upbringing. This account of his emotions in recollection is moving and oddly disturbing. It should be said at once that the letter does not simply bear upon the actualities of his early years. It also reflects his feelings at the time of its composition. Brown was trying to explain his own history to himself as well as offer a child some idea of how heroes must suffer to be glorious. The letter will not be quoted in full, but as the best record of his early years, it is the basis for much of the interpretation to follow, supplemented, however, by other information. Brown was not in the best of health at the time he wrote Henry Stearns, son of one of his wealthy New England patrons. "I am much confused in mind and cannot remember what I wish to write," Brown

8. Lewis Perry, "The Panorama and the Mills: A Review of *The Letters of John Greenleaf Whittier*," *Civil War History*, XXII (1976), 236–53, and *Radical Abolitionism: Anarchy and the Government of God in Antislavery Thought* (Ithaca, 1973); Bertram Wyatt-Brown, "William Lloyd Garrison and Antislavery Unity: A Reappraisal," *Civil War History*, XIII (1967), 5–24.

had told his wife only two months earlier.[9] His plans for antislavery warfare were then in some disarray. He was also suffering from malarial fever—the ague, as it was called. What he wrote to the Massachusetts boy must be seen in two ways: what Brown in 1857 considered most important in the course of his early life, a process of selection that revealed present concerns as well as past ones; and what those concerns may genuinely have meant in his psychological development. The two matters cannot be separated: the letter showed a child and man deeply at war with himself and his surroundings. Throughout, Brown spoke of himself in the third person, as if he sought a special detachment and objectivity in this remarkably candid and joyless document.

Brown's father Owen, an orthodox Congregationalist and a tanner by trade, transplanted his family from rural Connecticut to Ohio when John was five years old. The trip itself was so filled with adventure that it compensated for the uprooting. The little boy quickly adjusted to the wilds of Hudson, Ohio, a crude settlement on the Western Reserve in northeastern Ohio. Then on December 9, 1808, Owen Brown lost his wife Ruth and a daughter in childbirth. In less than a year, Owen, then thirty-nine, took an eighteen-year-old bride named Sally Root. These events occurred when Brown was eight and nine. To be sure, the experience was common enough in those days, and John Brown was less vulnerable to such difficulties than if he had been either much younger and unable to articulate his feelings or on the threshold of the always difficult adolescent years. The loss of his mother and her quick replacement nevertheless left the boy with an acute sense of bewilderment and rage, a state of mind that psychologists and common sense tell us has a permanent, marked, and alienating effect unless promptly and properly handled.[10]

Whatever its source, John Brown's early and easily aroused anger found a convenient outlet in a hatred of his stepmother. The boy and

9. John Brown to My Dear Wife & Children Everyone, May 27, 1857, in Oswald Garrison Villard Collection, Loeb Library, Columbia University, New York.

10. John Brown to Henry L. Stearns, July 15, 1857, in Oswald Garrison Villard, *John Brown, 1800–1859: A Biography Fifty Years After* (Boston, 1910), 1–2. On how this letter came to be written, see George L. Stearns File, Villard Collection. On childhood bereavement, see John Bowlby, *Separation, Anxiety and Anger* (New York, 1973), 273.

Levi Blakeslee made their displeasure known early, often, and unmistakably. (Levi was John's brother by adoption.) As late as five
years after Sally had joined Owen's household, the two boys, by then
in their teens, fashioned a crude bomb of gunpowder and tried to
blow her up in an outhouse. The device failed to explode. Undaunted,
they removed some planks from a hayloft flooring. Hunting eggs in
the barn, she fell, but was more frightened by the meaning of the incident than seriously hurt. Dumbfounded, Owen broke his religious
scruples against flogging. Christian Cackler, a neighbor and some-
time hired hand at the tannery, recalled that John stuffed a sheep-
skin in his pants and howled with appropriate conviction as the
blows fell.[11]

In writing Henry Stearns, John Brown did not recollect these serious intimidations of his stepmother. Instead, he remarked that
Sally Root was "a very estimable woman." Yet, he admitted, "he [that
is, John Brown] *never adopted her in feeling*; but continued to pine
after his own Mother for years. This opperated [*sic*] very unfavorably
uppon him; as he was both naturally fond of females; &, withall, extremely diffident; & deprived him of a suitable connecting link between the different sexes; the want of which might under some circumstances, have proved his ruin." Somehow the death of his mother
and the arrival of an inexperienced but decent young girl were tied to
his general attitude about women.[12]

Brown was by no means as confused in his sexual role as the statement seemed to suggest. There was certainly no evidence of ambivalence in his relationship to women. Indeed, as an adult, Brown enjoyed feminine company, and they thought him most appealing,
though he tended to swagger. Whereas his sons were later to find his
absences from home a welcome relief, his daughters always missed
him. A man of great inner resolve and complexity, he reflected both

11. Katherine Mayo, interviews with Benjamin Kent Waite, December 26, 1908,
with Christian Cackler, December 24, 1908, both in Villard Collection; Christian
Cackler, *Recollections of an Old Settler* . . . (1874; rpr. Kent, Ohio, 1904), 54, 55; Clarence S. Gee (ed.), "Owen Brown's Autobiography" (MS in Clarence S. Gee Collection,
Hudson Library and Historical Society, Hudson, Ohio); compare Villard, *John Brown*,
16.
12. Brown to Stearns, July 15, 1857, in Villard, *John Brown*, 3–4 (italics are
Brown's).

bitterness over his early childhood loss and strong signs of gentleness, love, and concern. Salmon Brown, his son, remarked that at times "the suffering of others," especially of those dear to him, "brought out the woman in him, [for he] was ever the nurse in sickness, watchful, tireless, tender, allowing no one to lift the burden of the night watch from him." These were contrasting attributes that were as much a part of this antinomian hero as were his inflexibility and rages.[13]

In the days after Ruth's death and Sally's appearance, young Brown's feelings of loneliness and deprivation were at first uppermost. The letter to Henry Stearns revealed his state of mind. Brown spoke with intensity about the nonhuman possessions he had acquired as the focus of his affections. One example is worth quoting: "About this period, he was placed in the School of *adversity*, which was . . . a most necessary part of his early training. You may *laugh* when you come to read about it; but these were *sore trials* to John: whose earthly treasures were very *few & small*. . . . A poor *Indian boy* gave him a *Yellow Marble* the first he had ever seen. This he thought a great deal of; & kept it a good while; but at last *he lost it* beyond recovery. *It took years to heal the wound* & I *think* he cried at times about it." Other toys and little animals were cherished and then mourned when they disappeared. According to Brown, these losses occurred before his mother's death, but the memory of them was no doubt indelibly etched on his mind when his mother, his greatest possession, died.[14]

Brown tended to place his faith in things that he could *totally* possess. His father was no tyrant, but he could hardly have unraveled the tangled emotions of his boy. Given the nature of the evangelical conscience and given the impression the young have that all the world revolves about their doings, John probably felt that he, by his

13. John Brown to Theodore Parker, March 7, 1858, in Franklin B. Sanborn, *The Life and Letters of John Brown, Liberator of Kansas, and Martyr of Virginia* (Boston, 1885), 449; Katherine Mayo, interview with Mrs. Thomas Russell, reprinted from New York *Evening Post*, October 23, 1909, in Louis Ruchames (ed.), *John Brown: The Making of a Revolutionary* (New York, 1969), 242–48; Richard O. Boyer, *The Legend of John Brown: A Biography and History* (New York, 1973), 6, 7, 63, 448; Brown to Stearns, July 15, 1857, in Villard, *John Brown*, 3–4; Salmon Brown, "My Father, John Brown," *Outlook*, January 25, 1913, p. 215.

14. Brown to Stearns, July 15, 1857, in Villard, *John Brown*, 2–3.

sinfulness against parents and God, was implicated in his mother's death. The very impermanence of his possessions distressed him long after time should have healed his disappointment over broken playthings and dying pets. Like his real mother, they too were gone forever. It was perplexing for a grieving child to comprehend death. Perhaps the losses, especially that of his mother, signified God's displeasure. Young John sensed that he had done something or felt something so vile that divine justice required the further meting out of chastening woes. When in later years he lost some of his very young children (one was accidentally scalded), he found it hard to endure "smarting under the rod of our Heavenly Father," he wrote. It became clear to him that "Divine Providence has been cutting me loose from one Cord after another" so that ties to earthly existence would not be constraining. These sentiments marked his special burden. "I expect nothing but to endure hardness," he said. The bitterness and, one suspects, a degree of unvoiced satisfaction were characteristic of John Brown. Yet he was as tough as the hides upon which he labored, and his devoutness was no less enduring. Brown's expressions of unworthiness and self-abasement were scarcely unusual in someone accustomed to Calvinistic rhetoric and thought. Nevertheless, his depressions were sometimes a little more extreme than those of other evangelicals, even those who experienced Byronic *angst* in their early twenties. "I felt for a number of years in earlier life a steady strong desire to die," he wrote at a contrastingly happy but brief period in 1858.[15]

Brown's alienation was evident soon after he reached school age. He was a lonely and rather terrifying boy. He learned how to compensate for a feeling of rejection—he bullied others. Milton Lusk, later his brother-in-law, remembered that Brown had led a Federalist band to victory over a Jeffersonian crowd of snowball-throwing schoolboys. "He did not seem angry, but there was such force and mastery in everything he did," Lusk said, "that everything gave way before

15. Brown to Owen Brown [his father], August 11, 1832, in Villard, *John Brown*, 8; John Brown to Dear Children [Ruth and Henry Thompson], January 23, 1852, in Ruchames (ed.), *John Brown*, 87; John Brown to Franklin B. Sanborn, February 24, 1858, in Sanborn, *The Life and Letters of John Brown*, 444–45.

him." In his letter to Henry Stearns, Brown confessed that he "was *excessively* fond of the *hardest & roughest* kind of plays; & could *never get enough* [of] them. Indeed when for a short time he was sometimes sent to School the opportunity it afforded to wrestle & Snow ball & run & jump & knock off old seedy Wool hats; offered to him almost the only compensation for the confinement, & restraints of school." Much of his time was devoted to chores at home by himself. The result of his truancy was evinced in his poor spelling and incompetent ciphering, a circumstance he always regretted but was never able to overcome with adult study. Yet, at age ten, "an old friend induced him to read a little history" and introduced him to "a good library." His taste for reading, he later recalled, "diverted him in a great measure from bad company."[16]

The isolation, although it conformed with evangelical ideas about the usefulness of education as a deterrent to evil, was not altogether beneficial. It became a way to shield himself from the criticism of elders. Brown liked to think that his withdrawal even from "good" company signified self-reliance. In a way it did, but escape from companionship was also involved. At twelve, Brown, with his father's permission, took a large herd of cattle a distance of one hundred miles through Indian wilderness. John was rightly proud of the responsibility. He boasted to Henry Stearns that if anyone had insisted upon escorting him, he would have disdained the offer. Friendship meant little to him; independence from others and solitude meant much more.

Another way to avoid showing any signs of vulnerability or dependency was to lie, "a verry *bad & foolish* habbit to which John was somewhat addicted," he told Henry Stearns. The purpose was "to screen himself from blame; or from punishment. He could not well endure being reproached; & I now think had he been oftener encouraged to be entirely frank; *by making frankness a kind of atonement* for some of his faults; he would not have been so often guilty in after life of this fault; nor have been obliged to struggle *so long* with *so mean* a habit." Brown's cure for himself, he implied, would have more

16. Lusk quoted in Sanborn, *The Life and Letters of John Brown*, 33; Brown to Stearns, July 15, 1857, in Villard, *John Brown*, 3–4.

beatings from his father Owen. A rather kindly soul, for all his worries about the hereafter, Owen was not the whipping kind. To some extent he must have recognized the effect of Ruth's death on the boy and made allowances. In any case, Brown was harder on himself than anyone else was. Yet he tried to hide his mistakes out of pride and fear, motives that simply increased a sense of guilt.[17]

The "lies" of which he spoke to Henry Stearns reflected an active fantasy life. Brown did not mention what thoughts crossed his mind during his lonely walks in the woods and solitary work on the farm and at the tannery. He did, however, intimate that he dreamed of a kind of special glory and seldom gave up once he had formed "*some deffinite plan*" in his mind. Tenacity and optimism were signs of strength. Unfortunately, though, he was unable to combine them with a requisite ability to work with others or feel comfortable with those of his own age, male or female. With boys, he had to be in command entirely; with girls, he was diffident and shy, although he overcame the handicap in later life. He did enjoy the praise of older men for his solemnity, attention to duty, and hard-mindedness. "This was so much the case," John told his young correspondent, "that he came forward to manhood quite full of self-conceit . . . notwithstanding his *extreme* bashfulness. . . . The Habit . . . of being obeyed rendered him in after life too much disposed to speak in an imperious or dictating way." According to Brown, his younger brother Salmon (who had died in 1833) used to complain of him as "'A King against whom there is no rising up.'" Even by Brown's lights, he was not a pleasant fellow to know. Like his father Owen, he had a sense of humor, but he did not care to exercise it much. He preferred a grimmer, more defensive public face.[18]

However, Brown was no deviant whose delusions set him wholly apart from the community and its standards. Many traits were ones that his Yankee society honored. If he was out of full touch with his inmost feelings, the problem arose in part from the common re-

17. Brown to Stearns, July 15, 1857, in Villard, *John Brown*, 3; Gee (ed.), "Owen Brown's Autobiography"; Katherine Mayo, interview with Robert W. Thompson, December 20, 1908, in Villard Collection.
18. Brown to Stearns, July 15, 1857, in Villard, *John Brown*, 5–6.

straints of conscience and inducements of anxiety that evangelical parents thought useful for young people to have. If he was "very early in life [supremely] ambitious to excel in doing anything he undertook," he was simply conforming to the mores of his religion. The question was, however, the spirit in which he sought to meet conventional standards. Was he reasonably happy with his own performance and moral life? About these matters, John Brown himself said, "He found much trouble with some bad habits I have mentioned & with some I have not told you of: his conscience urging him forward with great power in this matter." Rigid in his orthodoxy, he found it especially grueling when he transgressed. To exercise what little control he had over excitability, he checked spontaneity as much as possible. When he laughed, an acquaintance recalled, "he made not the slightest sound, not even a whisper, or an intake of breath, but he shook all over and laughed violently. It was the most curious thing imaginable to see him, in utter silence, rock and quake with mirth."[19]

Anger was more difficult to restrain and it arose more often than laughter. As boy and man, John Brown gave vent to rage but left the impression that his actions expressed only a portion of his wrath. A "haughty obstinate temper"—a maternal legacy according to family tradition—made others fearful of still greater explosions. As John Brown's son Watson remarked shortly before being killed at the siege of Harpers Ferry, "The trouble is, you want your boys to be brave as tigers, and still afraid of you." So it was in many of Brown's relations with contemporaries and with those beneath him. He liked to rule by fear, and manliness was a virtue that he cherished almost as much as he loved piety.[20]

Like other juveniles of the era, Brown underwent the spiritual regeneration required by his church and culture. In fact, at age sixteen, he even proposed to enter the ministry. Preparing for eventual col-

19. *Ibid.*, 4–5; Katherine Mayo, interview with Mrs. Thomas Russell, January 11, 1909, in Villard Collection, also in New York *Evening Post*, October 23, 1909, and reprinted in Ruchames (ed). *John Brown*, 242–48; see also Stephen B. Oates, *To Purge This Land with Blood: A Biography of John Brown* (New York, 1970), 202–203.

20. Brown to Stearns, July 15, 1857, in Villard, *John Brown*, 6; Watson Brown quoted in *ibid.*, 20.

lege entrance at Amherst, Brown suffered from low morale and poor health. Severe inflammation of his eyes from overstudy and a hesitancy to compete for honors with younger and better-trained students at the two eastern schools that he attended broke his resolve. In 1817 he returned from Morris Academy in Massachusetts to Hudson, never to mention again his sole attempt at professional life.[21] Many young men of the era similarly gave up college and its rigors because of a nervous condition, physical ailment, or some other signal of distress. If Brown's life had continued on a serene and successful course, the painful memories of childhood and the failings at schoolwork could well have healed with few scars. He would simply have become known as a good tanner, a fine burgher in Hudson, and a firmly orthodox churchman who might even have graced a pulpit had circumstances favored his prospects. Actually, Brown was remarkably kindhearted when, on several occasions, he apprehended thieves in the neighborhood. Like most towns then, Hudson had its rough elements, and Brown was steadfast in upholding the peace. It would be completely unjust to picture Brown as merely the sum of his faults and aberrations. Without them, however, he would not have had any impact upon his times at all. His very divergence from the routines and orthodoxies of American life was the source of his ultimate significance. Besides, he took pride himself in his differentness.

Between 1820 when he married Dianthe Lusk and 1832 when she died, Brown was as close to conventional ways and perhaps to happiness—material well-being, at least—as one of his passionate temperament ever could be. Curiously enough, most of the stories of his abusiveness toward his own children came from this period. It seemed as if his violent tendencies had no other means of expression than the flogging of his young ones—though these assaults only occurred when the children had crossed his strict ideas of proper behavior. He was not an arbitrary, unpredictable disciplinarian, but his severity cannot be merely attributed to Calvinistic culture or frontier insensitivity. He was "a sharp character, none of your soft fellow," said a Hudson neighbor. Although he was gentle with those who were

21. Sanborn, *The Life and Letters of John Brown*, 591n; Boyer, *The Legend of John Brown*, 202–205.

suffering, Brown could be unfeeling, too. A member of the Perkins family of Summit County, Ohio, recalled that "Cousin Anna" and other relatives "all abhorred him. When one of his babies died, he did not call a doctor nor a minister but simply put the little body in a rough wooden box" and buried it in the yard.[22]

Son Jason reminisced that for some weeks at age four in 1827 he had been away from home at a neighboring farm, receiving early schooling. Just before returning, Jason recalled, "I dreamed that by the corn crib I found a beautiful little baby coon," which became a pet. Wanting to express his joy at being reunited with his mother and to catch her attention, Jason excitedly told her the dream as if it had really happened. Dianthe stopped churning butter. She plied him with questions. Was the story true? she persisted. "I tried to discriminate between the reality & the vision. Finally I said: 'No—I guess not.' 'I'm afraid, then, that you have told me a wicked lie.'" Dianthe reported the miscreant to John Brown. At once he cut "a 'limber persuader' as grandfather Brown used to call them." Without a word of explanation, Brown stripped down the child's trousers—"no one wore drawers in those days," Jason added. "He took both my hands in his and held me up in the air and thrashed me. How I danced! How it cut! I was only four. *But Father had tears in his eyes while he did it*, and mother was crying. That was the kind of hard heart he had. He would tell us to do a thing *once*, without any threat. *Next time*, came the 'limber persuader.'"[23]

One must suspect that the next illustration of Brown's behavior as father was an exercise not in moral instruction alone but also in self-chastisement. In physical terms, it paralleled what he often felt in mental anguish. John Brown, Jr., his eldest son, recalled that in 1831 his father had summoned him to the tannery-shed to present the ten-year-old with a written statement of his misdemeanors. The father had listed the particulars in the form of a moral ledger. The son remi-

22. Jacob Bishop Perkins to Ralph Perkins [reminiscence of Simon Perkins family], n.d., [#75, folder 3], Simon Perkins Collection, Western Reserve Historical Society, Cleveland; compare, though, Ruth Thompson, reminiscence, in Sanborn, *The Life and Letters of John Brown*, 94–95; Boyer, *The Legend of John Brown*, 210–11, 229, 236–37.
23. Katherine Mayo, interview with Jason Brown, n.d. [1908], in Villard Collection. Mayo's italics indicate Jason's emphases in speech.

nisced that the document "exhibited a fearful footing up of *debits*," in fact, so many that if he had received all the strokes demanded he would scarcely have survived the beating. The old man, once again tearful in dismay and concentrating on some inner agony, gave him some strokes. Then he suddenly stopped. Brown stripped off his own shirt and sat on a block. Peremptorily he ordered his son to lay on the remainder with a blue-beech switch. Throughout the ordeal, the father urged his son to strike "harder, harder, harder!" until John, Jr., could see "small drops of blood [that] showed on his back."[24]

John, Jr., claimed that this was his first lesson in the meaning of Christ's atonement. In other words, the son was supposed to represent sinful mankind; his father symbolized the Christ who died on the cross to bear away the sins of the world. It is a strange story. It showed how Brown objectified the ordinary afflictions and personalities of human beings so that they could be reduced to symbols of some abstraction. Religion, punishment, countinghouse terminology, tears of fatherly rage, masochistic pleasure from the giving and receiving of blows—all these elements in the drama create an impression of a man whose impulses were too powerful for him to understand or control. Indeed, on another occasion, neighbors recalled, John Brown squeezed one of the little boys nearly to death for refusing to repeat a word as the father wished. After some reluctance, Salmon Brown, another son, admitted in his old age that he was that very frightened child. At the same time, these sessions with the formidable father were often accompanied by tears of anger. The most illustrative example was the scene that Jason had described when Brown punished him for lying. The fault was one that Brown despised so greatly in himself. He would have flogged or squeezed the sin out of any youngster who might otherwise have inherited his own "verry *bad & foolish* habbit." Not many fathers in that day sobbed over the misdeeds of their children as they whipped them or reversed the roles of father and son as John Brown had done. Not many sought to impress their children with their adult sorrows and self-contempt, an intrusion upon their young worlds as intimidating as the beatings

24. John Brown, Jr., quoted in Sanborn, *The Life and Letters of John Brown*, 91–93.

themselves. Obviously Brown's harshness was directed inwardly though expressed against others. The compulsion to punish far exceeded the requirements of the religion that he had inherited from his father Owen.[25]

During these years, the state of Dianthe's mental health was so precarious that it undoubtedly added much to her husband's already overburdened temper. Although a brother-in-law and some other neighbors later claimed that Brown was a "tyrant" to her and contributed to her madness, the testimony is not altogether convincing. Others spoke well of their relationship. Besides, Dianthe's family was predisposed to emotional disorder; two sisters suffered from some sort of mental affliction. By one account, Dianthe once threw John Brown, Jr., then newly born, into the hearth. John Brown was luckily close enough to rescue the infant. Only the clothes were singed. Ordinarily, she was not dangerous, but overly passive.[26]

Brown's tenuous hold on his own feelings gave way entirely with the unexpected death of Dianthe, victim of "Child bed fever," said her distraught husband. If he had felt any responsibility for her illness, if guilt were a factor in his grief, one might conjecture that the loss affected his future actions more than any written record could ever prove. So overwhelming were his feelings, comparable in intensity to those that his own mother's death had aroused, he literally went numb—"a dead calm," he said. Such a condition is often a sign of acute depression. He did not know what to make of his own mood at the time. Writing his partner in the tanning trade, Brown declared, "Such is the state of my health (& of my mind in consequence), for I am unwilling to ascribe it to any other cause, that I have felt my loss,

25. Katherine Mayo, interviews with Ransom M. Sanford, December 20, 1908, with Salmon Brown, October 11–13, 1908, with Jason Brown, n.d. [1908], all in Villard Collection.

26. Katherine Mayo, interviews with Mrs. Darnley Hobart, December 2, 1908, with Ransom M. Sanford, December 20, 1908, with Abner Caldwell, December 28, 1908, with Benjamin Kent Waite, December 26, 1908, with Jason Brown, n.d. [1908], with Mrs. Annie Brown Adams, October 2–3, 1908, with Mrs. Henry Pettengill, December 20, 1908; John Brown, Jr., told Mrs. Pettengill that "'Father was never good to my mother,'" or so Katherine Mayo reported Mrs. Pettengill to have told her. All interviews are in the Villard Collection.

but verry little & can think or write about her, or about disposing of my little children, with as little emotion as of the most common subject." Unable to weep, he surprised himself, he said, "for I loved my wife." So distracted was he that the neighbors quietly removed the five children from the house. "I find I am still getting more & more unfit for every thing," he wrote his partner. "I have been growing numb for a good while."[27] Reactions of this kind often signify the fact that earlier feelings about death, loss, and displacement have not been resolved.

Brown was resilient: he recovered from the temporary breakdown after three months. Soon he was back at the tanning business. As if duplicating his father's experience with a second bride half his age, John Brown married a girl of seventeen when he was thirty-three. The second Mrs. Brown (Mary Ann Day) was "a curiously crude woman who clung to the few religious ideas to which she had been educated with all the strength of a crude mind." She suited Brown's temperament ideally. Yet, his attitudes toward life changed rather dramatically in this period. As if to challenge a Providence that heartlessly seized those whom he loved, Brown fiercely determined to lay up earthly riches. Although it is true that speculations were also driving others to wild enthusiasms during the mid-1830s, Brown's exuberance was ill-advised. Moreover, when the financial crash of 1837 finally sobered almost everybody else, Brown's folly continued unchecked. His risk-taking revealed faulty judgment and bad management. Nor could he learn much from previous experience or from the advice of others. His lively inner world shut out words of caution and other unpleasantries. When he chose to blame himself, he did so strictly on his own terms, just as he had when he was a child. The old habit of lying cropped up in business matters, much to Brown's own chagrin. Some Ohio neighbors thought him dishonest. He lacked, said the Reverend Andrew Wilson rather pompously, "any proper manly sense of responsibility." Brown had loyal defenders, too, but

27. John Brown to Seth Thompson, August 13, 1832, in Boyer, *The Legend of John Brown*, 249–50; compare John Brown to Owen Brown, August 11, 1832, in Ruchames (ed.), *John Brown*, 49–50.

others complained that his integrity did not match that of his popular father, Owen.[28]

The problem was erratic rather than devious behavior in land, cattle, and wool enterprises. The cycle began with ill-conceived plans and ran through ridiculous expectations, gloomy overreactions, poor decisions, and further confusion, relieved by the prospect of another adventure, also doomed. One historian has estimated that Brown plunged into twenty undertakings in no less than six states. He must have often wondered how others succeeded when he could not, despite the necessity he felt to provide for his large and growing family. (He had twenty children, with as many as twelve to care for at any one time.) At some moments he dreamed of wealth and honor. At other times he aimed to be a distinguished philanthropist, serving others and not himself. In 1837, he, like Wendell Phillips, was so outraged by the killing of Elijah P. Lovejoy, the antislavery martyr of Alton, Illinois, that he pledged to devote his life "to increasing hostility toward Slavery." But business debts constantly interfered. The mission itself, which faded out of mind under the onslaught of debts, law suits, failures, and humiliations, would be revived a decade later.[29]

Brown was eccentric not only as a businessman but as a man of religion as well. Historians have long pictured him as a typical fire-and-brimstone Calvinist of the day. Actually, his religious beliefs and practices were strictly his own. As his son Salmon said, he had "a cranky sort of piety!" When he taught Sunday school, a Hudson pupil later recalled, he told the children that one "man's opinion was as good as another provided he is naturally as smart a man. This principle [helped him to] establish his own title to interpret," declared his former student. "He didn't want anyone to explain Scripture to

28. Ian C. Emery, "The Hero of Harpers Ferry," *Nichell Magazine*, VII (June, 1897), 323–35; Katherine Mayo, interview with Andrew Wilson [Universalist minister in Ravenna, Ohio], December 24, 1908, in Villard Collection; see also her interviews with Ransom M. Sanford, December 20, 1908, and with John Whedon, [December, 1908–January, 1909?].

29. C. Vann Woodward, *The Burden of Southern History* (Baton Rouge, 1960), 41; Boyer, *The Legend of John Brown*, 440; quotation from Lora Case's reminiscences, in Emily E. Metcalf, "Historical Papers," September 4, 1904 [copy], in Villard Collection, also Case quoted in Oates, *To Purge This Land with Blood*, 369n11.

him." Thus, the antinomian found what he wanted in the Testaments, Old and New, and made them suit his disposition without the intervention of preacher, scholar, or church dogma. Such license was not altogether popular in the conforming atmosphere of the Western Reserve. Traditional predestinarian Calvinists in Hudson were followers of the conservative David Hudson, wealthy landholder and founder of Western Reserve College there. By dismissing some faculty members, David Hudson had preserved the school from antislavery contamination. Already a Garrisonian in 1833, Owen Brown resigned from the Board of Trustees in protest over Hudson's attitude. Thereafter Owen Brown associated himself with Oberlin College, a rival school and an oasis of abolitionism about twenty miles away. By the standards of the time, Oberlin was theologically as well as racially liberal. Antislavery and notions of free will, human perfection, and other anti-Calvinist doctrines were logically compatible. But as a man who gloried in an ability to withstand suffering and pain, John Brown read the Bible with greater anguish than did the Oberlinites. Yet, his racial egalitarianism and his disgust with slavery were also part of his charismatic faith. He was by no means a stranger to the "unsearchable riches" of the New Testament. Struggling so hard and often vainly to overcome personal weaknesses, he nevertheless did not have that joyfulness and optimism about human possibilities which were tenets of belief among most other abolitionists. The Old Testament appealed to him with the same force as the agony of the Crucifixion, but the balm of redemption seemed out of reach.[30]

In 1850 he called his first band of black fighters, quite fittingly, the League of Gileadites (an Old Testament reference). By that time, Brown was cooperating with Gerrit Smith, a wealthy abolitionist and landowner, and with Smith's black tenants settled on a tract near

30. Mayo, interviews with Salmon Brown, October 11–13, 1908, and with Benjamin Kent Waite, December 26–27, 1908; Robert S. Fletcher, *A History of Oberlin College from Its Foundation Through the Civil War* (2 vols.; Oberlin, Ohio, 1943), I, 155; Frederick C. Waite, *Western Reserve University: The Hudson Era* (Cleveland, 1943), 44–45; Mary Land, "John Brown's Ohio Environment," *Ohio Archeological and Historical Quarterly*, LVII (1948), 30–32; John S. Duncan, "John Brown in Pennsylvania," *Western Pennsylvania Historical Magazine*, XI (1928), 50; Ernest C. Miller, "John Brown's Ten Years in Northwestern Pennsylvania," *Pennsylvania History*, XV (1948), 25–26; Boyer, *The Legend of John Brown*, 257–59.

North Elba, New York. The league could accomplish little except help fugitives heading for Canada, but it set a healthy example of black consciousness. Brown's labors for black freedom, spasmodic as they had to be from 1835 to 1855, must be understood as part of his Christian conscientiousness. Nonetheless, his religious perspective was unorthodox in its very quaintness.[31]

Urged in 1855 by his sons to join them in a move to the plains of Kansas to fight the proslavery Border Ruffians, Brown made a last, fateful effort to advance the cause and achieve greatness. Although he was physically ill and emotionally drained, he could finally claim to have found the calling for which God had prepared him in His "school of adversity." He became a religious revolutionary. All the frustrations of a hard, ill-fated life without purpose or meaning, without stability or rootedness, burst forth in his savage midnight attack in 1856 on some unarmed proslavery farmers near Lawrence—the Pottawatomie Massacre.

To an antinomian like Brown, the massacre was just, necessary, and God-inspired. In that respect, it was similar to the acts of vengeance that the slave Will and others in the Nat Turner insurrection committed against men, women, and children of Southampton County in 1831. The Virginia rebels and John Brown both found authority in a direct relation between the prophet and God, who sanctified their deeds. Unlike Turner, Brown did not, however, claim to have seen visions or heard voices commanding insurrection. The Yankee Calvinist was not prone to mysticism and instead found sufficient authority in the Bible. Yet, Jason Brown, his son whose nonviolent scruples held him back from participation, later remarked, "I wish Father had been well, & his mind entirely clear." Perhaps, as Brown's most sophisticated biographer has declared, the old man watched the atrocities "in a kind of trance." By surviving accounts, not Brown but Salmon and Owen performed the bloody deeds in front of their father's eyes. Before the party moved off to commit two other murders, the boys cut down the Doyles, father and twenty-year-old son, and William Drury, field hand, with finely sharpened broadswords. But

31. Villard, *John Brown*, 50–53; Oates, "John Brown and His Judges," 20n55.

John Brown's role may have been an active one, for in old age, his son Salmon admitted that he had been lying for years about the events of that night. By implication at least, he suggested that Brown shot Doyle *before* the sword work, not afterward.[32] However, the truth of the matter can never be resolved.

Although known as the "family coward," son Jason showed greater courage than any of the others by confronting the old man about his role. "'I did not do it,'" Brown lied, "'but I approved of it.'" Distraught, Jason declared, "'I think it was an uncalled for, wicked act.'" Brown's retort was "'God is my judge; and the people will yet justify my course.'" Later, Brown gave a more expansive justification, based upon a singular interpretation of the Bible: each of the men killed, he said, had "committed murder in his heart and according to the Scriptures they were guilty of murder and I felt justified in having them killed." If so, then, as one of Brown's most charitable biographers has declared, "we must decide that John Brown believed planning murder to be worse than murder itself. We have here an extraordinary confusion of ethics and morals." Nothing except an antinomian view of God's will could reconcile his actions with Christian precept. Indeed, true to the peculiar intimacy which Brown enjoyed with the Deity, he argued that the slaughter had been "decreed by Almighty God, ordained from eternity." Besides, Border Ruffians had killed six antislavery supporters in cold blood not long before. Brown's rationale was attuned to Calvinistic predestinarianism, to currently popular ideas about a "higher law" of freedom beyond human instruments like the proslavery Constitution, to the indigenous American tradition of the lynch law, and to the justifications of the antinomian and revolutionary spirit of justice in the name of oppressed people.[33]

There was a close connection between Brown's antinomian posture and his committing these atrocities. Moreover, questions natu-

32. Mayo, interview with Jason Brown, n.d. [1908], in Jason Brown file, Villard Collection; Oates, *To Purge This Land with Blood*, 135; Mayo, interview with Salmon Brown, October 13, 1908; see also Salmon Brown File, Villard Collection, which contains information from Salmon Brown's daughter in Portland, Oreg.; Villard, *John Brown*, 158–60.

33. Jason Brown, in Lawrence (Kans.) *Journal*, clipping, February 12, 1880 [copy], Jason Brown to F. G. Adams, April 2, 1884 [copy], both in Villard Collection; Villard, *John Brown*, 179; Oates, *To Purge This Land with Blood*, 147.

rally arise regarding the mental state of the man who directed them. To be sure, one must admit that the evidence of familial instability is not wholly convincing, because affidavits attesting to such problems were submitted by kinspeople and friends later in an effort to save Brown's life after his capture and trial in 1859. However exaggerated the reports were, they should not be totally dismissed. Oswald Garrison Villard, one of Brown's staunchest defenders, reviewed these documents, which stated that

> Brown's grandmother on the maternal side, after lingering six years in hopeless insanity, had died insane; that of his grandmother's children, Brown's uncles and aunts, two sons and two daughters were intermittently insane, while a third daughter had died hopelessly lunatic; that Brown's only sister, her daughter and one of his brothers were at intervals deranged; and that of six first cousins, two were occasionally mad, two had been discharged from the state lunatic asylum after repeated commitments, while two more were at the time in close restraint, one of these being a hopeless case. This is a fearful record.

Needless to say, the unpleasant family statistics proved nothing at all by themselves, except as they indicated a melancholy streak that Brown himself evinced in his own confessions and behavior.[34]

The mental record of John Brown's sons also suggests that whatever had caused the familial troubles in earlier generations persisted in the descendants. Moreover, Brown's own handling of the boys had not ameliorated the tendency toward mental instability. Son Frederick suffered from frequent disorders. Shortly before the move to Kansas, he tried to castrate himself with a knife. John Brown said of this "most dreadful surgical operation [that it] well might have cost him his life." (The historian Stephen Oates suggests, however, that Frederick might have suffered from a brain tumor or epilepsy.) John Brown, Jr., went temporarily insane upon learning of the Pottawatomie atrocity. Owen, though never deranged, later became a morose, reclusive bachelor, not a little eccentric. Salmon showed no ill effects from participating in the massacre. At eighty-five, however, sick, despondent, and lonely, he shot himself to death.[35]

34. Oates, "John Brown and His Judges," 8, 21; Villard, *John Brown*, 508–509.
35. Villard, *John Brown*, 166; Boyer, *The Legend of John Brown*, 455; Oates, *To Purge This Land with Blood,* 332; Mayo, interview with Jason Brown, n.d. [1908], Mayo to Villard, November 4, 1908; Charles Wesley Moffat, in Topeka (Kans.) *Daily Capital,*

Certainly there seemed to be a psychological connection between Brown's preoccupations with personal, self-thwarted ambition and his scheme to arm the slaves with guns from the Harpers Ferry arsenal. One of the great curiosities of history was the nature of his intentions. Certainly the policy of guerrilla warfare was feasible if the leadership were adequate, the tactics and strategy carefully mapped out, and the training well planned. Unluckily, Brown was no Garibaldi. In the same year, 1859, the Italian revolutionary met reverses but succeeded in 1860 in the guerrilla conquest of Sicily. So poorly arranged were matters, so muddled were Brown's tactics that according to C. Vann Woodward, he "cut himself off from his base of supplies, failed to keep open his only avenues of retreat, dispersed his small force, and bottled the bulk of them up in a trap where defeat was inevitable." Either John Brown, Jr., or his father was so disoriented that the son did not know when the raid was to take place and therefore failed to send on additional forces. The contrast with modern examples of rural guerrilla warfare or with urban terrorism reveals just how hopeless Brown was as an underground fighter.[36]

Years later, Salmon Brown said that he thought that the old man was doomed to fail: "I did not want to go to Harpers Ferry very much. I said to the boys before they left: 'You know Father. You know he will *dally* till he is trapped.'" Procrastination is the ultimate sin in terrorist activity. If Brown had seized the necessary firearms at the arsenal and left at once for the hills, he could have begun a war of attrition. His New England backers understood that such were his intentions. As Salmon observed, however, he "had a peculiarity of insisting on *order*." He had a ritualistic compulsion to control his surroundings. It was a family joke to "egg strangers on to offer to help" him pack for a trip. The courtesy thoroughly "'stirred him up.'"

October 24, 1892, clipping in James H. Holmes Diary [copy], in Frederick Brown File; L. R. Witherall, "Old John Brown," Davenport (Iowa) *Gazette*, clipping, November 3, 1877; Jason Brown, in Lawrence (Kans.) *Journal*, clipping, February 12, 1880 [copy]; [Richard J. Hinton], "Old John Brown and the Men of Harpers Ferry," *Time* (July, 1880), 733; Jason Brown to Brother, Sister, and All Dear Friends at Home, June 28, 1856 [copy], Jason Brown File; Lawrence, Kans., newspaper clipping, May 19, [?], in Salmon Brown File, Villard Collection.

36. Woodward, *The Burden of Southern History*, 45; David M. Potter, *The South and the Sectional Conflict* (Baton Rouge, 1968), 201–219, esp. 212.

Salmon had worried that "'Father . . . would insist on getting everything arranged just to suit him before he would consent to make a move.'" The quirk, however, was more serious than Salmon intimated. Brown was in some kind of confused reverie at the height of the clamor and excitement. John Henry Kagi, a young intellectual in the band, kept urging him to move out quickly. Instead, Brown delayed so long in the firehouse headquarters with his hostages and his sobbing, mortally wounded son Watson, he was surrounded, rushed, and captured. By sheer luck (or divine intervention) Brown was not killed in the final minutes, but only wounded.[37]

After his capture, however, Brown once again discovered himself. He made himself a symbol, one representing an atonement to his wrathful God and sacrificed Christ for his failures. His new role was, as it seemed, a capital investment in future, immortal glory. Sublime sacrifice would extinguish the many debits and sins of his career. Writing his wife after the expedition had failed so disastrously, he declared, "I have been *whiped* [sic] as the saying *is*; but am sure I can recover all the lost capital occasioned by that disaster; by only hanging a few moments by the neck; & I feel quite determined to make the utmost possible out of a defeat." The mission for which he was certain the Lord had called him was at last fulfilled. Just how conscious Brown was of achieving a punishing end to his life in order to free himself of the passions that dominated his inner life, one will never know. In his last days on earth he genuinely did achieve a more tender vision of Christ the Redeemer. Brown became kinder to his fellow men than he had ever been when he was a free man. Like a suicide who has resolved past confusions by preparing for the final act, Brown set his affairs in order with resignation, indeed with "all joy," he said as the hours of the deathly triumph approached. Like Mary Dyer and other antinomians of the pacifistic tradition, he could die for the sins of others, not for his own.[38]

37. Mayo, interview with Salmon Brown, October 11–13, 1908; Richard J. Hinton, *John Brown and His Men* . . . (New York, 1894), 298, 300, 302–305; Allan Keller, *Thunder at Harper's Ferry* (Boston, 1958), 123–28; Oates, *To Purge This Land with Blood*, 294; Osborne P. Anderson, *A Voice from Harper's Ferry* (Boston, 1861), 35–37; Villard, *John Brown*, 438.

38. John Brown to Mary Ann [Day] Brown, November 10, 1859, in Villard, *John Brown*, 540–41; Oates, "John Brown and His Judges," 20n55.

Salmon Brown later said that his father's intention all along was "to strike terror—to make agitation. He believed that in the excited feeling resultant from such an agitation, the South would secede, that the Government would whip the South back into the Union, & that in the war Slavery would be abolished. He had a clear insight into the future. *He wanted to bring on the war.*" Brown's son was obviously boasting of his father's allegedly superhuman clairvoyance. Brown was indeed carrying out exactly the sort of testamentary, symbolic act of which Mary Douglas had spoken and which present-day European and Near Eastern and Iranian terrorist leaders have used so effectively to dramatize their cause and humiliate the enemy. In America, where such acts have been rare, the Russian immigrant Alexander Berkman, who tried to assassinate Henry Clay Frick, a prominent steel executive, during the Homestead strike, provided a similar example of the *attentat.* These actions were supposed to cast doubt on the power of established institutions and raise the morale and consciousness of the oppressed. Yet most acts of terror seldom achieve the final objective: the overthrow of a regime. Appropriately, Abraham Lincoln questioned the importance of Brown's antinomian zeal: "An enthusiast broods over the oppression of a people," he told a Republican crowd at Cooper Institute in New York, "till he fancies himself commissioned by Heaven to liberate them." It was not the American way, he continued. Brown's effort and Orsini's attempt on the life of Louis Napoleon (to hasten Italian independence) "were, in their philosophy, precisely the same." By all objective criteria, Lincoln's view was correct. Moreover, Brown had violated a long-standing abolitionist tradition: the "higher law" of moral suasion over "carnal weapons," the association of John Humphrey Noyes and William Lloyd Garrison's antinomian perfections with antislavery nonviolence. Repudiation and ridicule should have been the consequence. Instead, no antinomian rebel was ever more successful than he was. He knew exactly how to play upon the religious and social ideals of the country.[39]

Historians have sometimes attributed the excited reaction to

39. Mayo, interview with Salmon Brown, October 11–13, 1908; Roy P. Basler (ed.), *Abraham Lincoln, His Speeches and Writings* (New York, 1962), 531.

Brown's raid and execution to the wildly delusional fears of the Great Slave Power and the threat of abolitionist-inspired slave rebellion. Such anxieties simply reflected the basic struggle for power in which the sections were engaged. Brown aroused positive as well as defensive emotions. For instance, he excited Yankee adulation because his actions were *manly*, Christian, and oddly nostalgic. He helped to clarify what it meant to be a man and a northerner. For years, abolitionist leaders had been subjected to proslavery ridicule: their unmanliness. The Baltimore *Patriot*, for instance, sneered that the antislavery leaders on lecture tours had to be flanked by "a life-guard of elderly ladies, and protected by a rampart of whale-bones and cotton-padding." At last, "Captain" Brown, whose demeanor and actions were unmistakably masculine, offered them a champion, someone to represent Yankee honor. Even Governor Wise of Virginia recognized his "courage, fortitude and simple ingeniousness," fanatical though Brown was. The governor saw great dangers in the new spirit that Brown had roused in northern minds.[40]

There was a yearning for saintly heroes in an age of vulgar preoccupations, moral complacencies, and worrisome effeteness as urban conveniences replaced rural hardships. Theodore Parker, Ralph Waldo Emerson, Henry Thoreau, and Thomas Wentworth Higginson, among many other New England luminaries who had secretly backed or had later come to admire him, perceived the grizzled Kansas warrior as the ultimate expression of romantic Christian hardihood. Men of philosophic temperament may be especially sensitive to the charge that they are cowards and merely reflect the "pink of modernity [that] bites no longer," to borrow Friedrich Nietzsche's phrase. The life of the mind could be too seductive; the quest for glory and righteous manhood too uncouth and sweaty.

Brown's message was a reminder that even as American institutions became more solidified, more powerful than ever, testamentary and violent drama revealed their underlying weakness. As Mary Douglas explains, institutions that do not embody the ideals and

40. Baltimore *Patriot*, quoted in Boston *Liberator*, June 2, 1854; Wise quoted in Craig Simpson, "John Brown and Governor Wise: A New Perspective on Harpers Ferry," *Biography*, I (1978), 17 (see also 15–38).

faith of citizens must adjust to new conditions or lose their constituencies. Thus, in spite of the many years of abolitionist nonresistance, John Brown reanimated the spirit of Yankee idealism by violence. He endowed antislavery with a virility that its long association with Sunday school ethics, missions to the "heathen," women's causes of temperance and equality, and New England "priestcraft" had seemed to deny. A degree of nostalgia was also involved. The decade of the 1850s was a rather conservative era. Abolitionism had settled into a routine response, and the political implications of slavery concerned brute sectional power more than humanitarian righteousness, a romantic impulse that had thrived in the early, Transcendental days of the abolition cause.

Thus, Brown's insurrectionary plot was in a sense a recollection of a fading religious tradition and an attempt to find assurance from self-doubt. Predestination and election were dead concepts, yet there was still worry about repudiating the faith of the fathers. Brown reminded the apostates, most especially his immediate abolitionist friends, how far they had strayed. According to Jeffrey Rossbach's study, the aging reformer Samuel Gridley Howe, one of the "Secret Six" who backed the Harpers Ferry mission, had been looking "for a cause that would help him throw off a crisis of confidence that engulfed him in the late 1850s." Other New England intellectuals only partially identified with antislavery zeal also responded to Brown's example of self-sacrifice. Emerson, for instance, remarked that our fathers were "orthodox Calvinists, mighty in Scriptures," and from them Brown had developed his "romantic character," hatred of luxury, undeviating honesty, and other virtues. According to the recollections of Mrs. Thomas Russell, widow of an abolitionist judge in Massachusetts, it delighted many to see Brown as "'the Old Covenanter,' 'the border chieftain,' 'the Roundhead hero,'" all virile, Christian, and basically sentimental labels. So too was his softer side seen in retrospective fashion: the patriarchal figure "quiet and gentle as a child in the house," said Emerson. Referring to the popular engraving of Brown's departure for his moment of reckoning, Thoreau remarked, "*Who* placed the slave-woman and her child, whom he stooped to kiss for a symbol, between his prison and the gallows?"

Home, love, children—these sentimental themes—wreathed the popular remembrance of the hanging at Charlestown, Virginia.[41]

Even the Yankee anti-abolitionists had to give him his due, however grudgingly. James Gordon Bennett, the shrill voice of anti-intellectualism, stopped denouncing "white-coated philosophers" who pranced about in behalf of one outrageous cause or another, long enough to remark, "Truly there is as much difference between the manly heart and the politician's gizzard, as physically between the massive form of the Abolitionist and the insignificant figure [of a political time-server]. Would not a Southern gentleman respect the former far more than the latter?" Bennett, like most of his kind, cared nothing at all for racial freedom. Nevertheless, manly duty— honor—which even a "crazy scoundrel" like John Brown represented in Bennett's opinion, deserved some acknowledgment.[42]

The issue of black emancipation mattered less to most people, in both the North and the South, than what the slavery question meant in terms of regional self-regard. It was Brown's shrewdness and theatricality that helped to clarify the matter. The antinomian deeds made starkly obvious the fact that men had to stand for *something* or not call themselves men. The language of the dialogue was set in terms of slavery and freedom. Few southerners really worshipped slavery, however much they accepted it, but most of them felt no obligation to love black bondage before defending the South against the likes of Brown. Similarly, few Yankees believed in emancipation, but insults to northern masculinity had to be met in kind. As Theodore Parker, one of Brown's secret patrons, observed, "Young lads say, 'I wish that heaven would make me such a man.'"[43]

41. Jeffrey Rossbach, *Ambivalent Conspirators: John Brown, the Secret Six, and a Theory of Slave Violence* (Philadelphia, 1982), 272. As Rossbach shows, though, the "Secret Six"—Samuel Gridley Howe, Gerrit Smith, Franklin B. Sanborn, Theodore Parker, George L. Stearns, and Thomas Wentworth Higginson—were ambivalent not only about the efficacy of violence but also about Brown's competence and judgment. Katherine Mayo, interview with Mrs. Thomas Russell, Emerson, and Thoreau quoted in Ruchames (ed.), *John Brown*, 242, 270, 277.

42. Bennett quoted in Bertram Wyatt-Brown, "The Abolitionist Controversy," in Howard Quint and Milton Cantor (eds.), *Men, Women, and Issues* (2 vols.; Homewood, Ill., 1980), I, 248.

43. Theodore Parker to Francis Jackson, November 24, 1859, in Ruchames (ed.), *John Brown*, 258.

Likewise, as will be explained later, the purpose of southern diatribes was to dramatize the Yankee insult to southern honor, to justify community outrage, and to provide the same kind of community consensus as slave-insurrection scares and lynchings had. Throughout the South, alleged plotters and other scapegoats, white and black, felt the agonies of reprisal. Historians have stressed southern fear, but there was also plain anger, born of self-confidence and conviction in the rightness of the southern cause. Moreover, southerners like Christopher Memminger of South Carolina felt hurt that "our institutions [were regarded as] sinful" and that Brown's actions were supposed to be excusable on those grounds.[44] It was easier to know who one was by identifications of the enemy, and Brown provided southerners the means to understand what mattered most to them. Perhaps that was the very quality which so distinguished the greatest abolitionist of them all, latecomer though he was. Brown was very much himself—so queerly simple, so extraordinarily complex. But he was so very much alive, even in death. In Mary Douglas' terms, he performed a ritual of purification in the view of northerners and of defilement in the view of southerners. His timing was accurate, and he became exactly what he wished to be: a Christlike figure for the North and an avenging angel for the South.

44. Memminger quoted in Steven A. Channing, *Crisis of Fear: Secession in South Carolina* (New York, 1970), 123.

PART TWO

SOUTHERN SINNERS

V

W. J. CASH AND
SOUTHERN CULTURE

C VANN WOODWARD once observed, with Wilbur J. Cash specifically in mind, "In America, historians, like politicians, are out as soon as they are down. There is no comfortable back bench, no House of Lords for them." Woodward's sentiment well applies to the famous North Carolina journalist and author of *The Mind of the South*, published in 1941. Cash was once a thinker to be reckoned with. For laymen he continues to be popular, but among leading southern scholars his work has been largely regarded as a period piece, like the 1930s Southern Agrarians' *I'll Take My Stand*, or else it has been ignored. When Eugene D. Genovese wrote his thoughtful essay "Yeomen Farmers in a Slaveholders' Democracy," he referred to *The Mind of the South* not at all. Yet his own perceptions of white class structure reflected Cash's influence. Condescension is the prevailing mood whenever his name does appear. Sheldon Hackney has called him "the South's foremost mythmaker," a dubious compliment for one who had hoped to dispel, not create, illusions. In *The Crucible of Race*, Joel Williamson finds the book a hopelessly dated "artifact" whose survival rested on the fact that "there was no one to challenge it," rather than on its insights. No less condescending is the view of

Michael O'Brien, another distinguished intellectual historian, who declared, "One may not be able to save the book as a primer to students of the southern past, but one can learn a little from its declining prestige."[1]

Cash offered, however, a set of interpretations with a vitality and resonance no longer recognized. He insisted that the South was a separate—peculiarly separate—cultural entity in the larger American framework. An intractable will to rule the blacks, a slowness of population growth, especially the absence of large towns, a primitive economy of cash-crop and subsistence farming, a distrust of education, ideas, and strangers, a common experience of war and colonial exploitation in Reconstruction and afterward—these and other factors, he said, arrested change. As a result, the ethic of the South remained backward, crude, and far from the myths of cavalier graciousness behind which the South had so long hidden its mediocrity. These notions southerners had come to expect from such outsiders as H. L. Mencken of the *American Mercury*. Cash, though, was a southerner; he had to be taken seriously. Moreover, Cash committed suicide in the same year the book appeared. The reasons were not known, but his early death added piquancy to his words. *The Mind of the South* became the legacy to the region he both loved and hated. As Woodward has suggested, so eloquent an epitaph was very hard to criticize. Whatever its faults, students of southern history and general readers enjoyed its crisp prose and memorable insights. The book not only helped to explain a South that was disappearing in the prosperous years after World War II, but in demolishing old regional legends, it hastened that transformation as well.

1. C. Vann Woodward, "W. J. Cash Reconsidered," *New York Review of Books*, December 4, 1969, p. 34; Eugene D. Genovese, "Yeomen Farmers in a Slaveholders' Democracy," *Agricultural History*, XLIX (1975), 331–42. Although the essay was expanded when republished, the author did not relate his theme to Cash's approach. See Elizabeth Fox-Genovese and Eugene D. Genovese, *Fruits of Merchant Capital: Slavery and Bourgeois Property in the Rise and Expansion of Capitalism* (New York, 1983), 249–64. Sheldon Hackney, "*Origins of the New South* in Retrospect," *Journal of Southern History*, XXXVIII (1972), 201; Joel Williamson, *The Crucible of Race: Black/White Relations in the American South Since Emancipation* (New York, 1984), 3; Michael O'Brien, "W. J. Cash, Hegel and the South," *Journal of Southern History*, XLIV (1978), 381, 379–98, and see also O'Brien's restatement of the point in his *The Idea of the American South, 1920–1941* (Baltimore, 1979), 213–27.

Perhaps the explanation for Cash's present ill repute lies in his former popularity, as Woodward's comment implies. In fact, among scholars his ideas have been so thoroughly carved up, chewed, and digested that serious review is no longer possible. As Woodward aptly pointed out, Cash's vivid language has entered common parlance: the "Proto-Dorian" consensus that bound whites in the common subjection of blacks; the "Man at the Center," Cash's typical, ill-educated Southerner; the "lily-pure maid of Astolat," a rendering of the mythical southern belle. Indeed the style was catching. Woodward, Cash's leading critic in recent years, added his own tags to the storehouse of southernisms that Cash had begun: "Bulldozer Revolution," the "Man on the Cliff," "Jim Crow," forever unsegregatable from a "Strange Career," and the alliterative "Reunion and Reaction." "Irony," "Burden," and "Forgotten Alternatives" are vintage Woodward, but they belong to the same genre as "Savage Ideal" and "hell-of-a-fellow" complex, terms of Cash's minting. Like William Faulkner and C. Vann Woodward himself, Cash is simply part of a southern scholar's intellectual frame of reference. He can no more be expelled from memory, conscious or otherwise, than the author of *The Sound and the Fury* or the biographer of Tom Watson can be. They all belong to a great tradition in southern letters, one that began in the 1920s and is only now coming to a close.[2]

Unfortunately, as Sigmund Freud explained long ago, such indebtedness does not inspire gratitude. It is discomfiting to find out later that one's most cherished thoughts were not so novel after all. Something from Woodward's *Tom Watson* or Cash's *The Mind of the South* stirred a fresh line of inquiry or possibly a fierce reaction—the ultimate compliment. Harold Bloom, the literary critic, claims that formidable precursors in poetry so deeply affect younger artists that the latter can create only by repudiating them. The principle in question is "the anxiety of influence," the fear of being artistically overwhelmed. "In every work of genius we recognize our own rejected

2. C. Vann Woodward, "The Elusive Mind of the South," in his *American Counterpoint: Slavery and Racism in the North-South Dialogue* (Boston, 1971), 262. On Cash's style, see Michael P. Dean, "W. J. Cash's *The Mind of the South*: Southern History, Southern Style," *Southern Studies*, XX (1981), 297–302.

thoughts—they come back to us with a certain alienated majesty,"
Bloom remarks.[3] As his comment implies, there are dangers in pay-
ing too much homage to predecessors. The present eclipse of the
work, however, makes the task of reexamination both easier and
more necessary than ever before. The South that Cash described is
past resurrection, but *The Mind of the South* offered valid proposi-
tions about southern conduct not fully appreciated.

The book was admired from the start, yet in many ways it was not
altogether understood or accepted. Some critics reacted in an ambivalent or hostile way even upon its first appearance. Donald Davidson,
a major literary critic and professor at Vanderbilt University, greeted
the work with a review that made all later criticisms seem polite by
comparison. Rhetorically Davidson invited Cash to be the object of a
lynching party, fit penalty for one who had traduced southern character. Davidson, a conservative and former member of the Agrarian
school of southern intellectuals, meant no genuine harm. He dispersed the mob before harm came to Cash in his unfortunate little
parody, which he closed with the admonition: "Stonewall, don't forget
you left that jug in the hollow beech-tree." If Cash had not taken his
own life, the review might have been a minor classic in the art of re-
viewing. (Stricken by the news of Cash's death, Davidson tried to
withdraw the essay from the *Southern Review*, but it was too late.)
Despite his later regret, Davidson clearly bristled at Cash's portrait
of a primitive, anti-intellectual South, but he somehow exemplified,
even in his satire, what Cash had called the "Savage Ideal"—that
touchiness and celebration of gut feeling so typical of the section.[4]

Even Cash's fellow southern liberals were not wholly convinced by
the book, though most praised him highly. In an otherwise appre-
ciative review (1941), C. Vann Woodward, already recognized as the
South's most promising young historian, pointed out that Cash had
"chosen a literary and imaginative rather than a scholarly approach.
He has not attempted to write intellectual history, and must be for-

3. Harold Bloom, *The Anxiety of Influence: A Theory of Poetry* (New York, 1970), 30.
4. Donald Davidson, "Mr. Cash and the Proto-Dorian South," *Southern Review*, VII
(1941), 4–5, 20, also available in his *Still Rebels, Still Yankees and Other Essays* (Baton
Rouge, 1972), 191–212; C. Vann Woodward, Review of W. J. Cash's *The Mind of the
South*, in *Journal of Southern History*, VII (1941), 400.

given for ignoring some of the South's most important minds in writing about the mind of the South." The fault was apparently forgiven but not forgotten. Although Woodward recognized the typological character of the work—the use of such a "simple generic figure as 'the basic Southerner' or 'the man at the center'"—he did not wholly approve even then. Cash's approach was unsettling. It was indeed unusual for a work on the southern past to forget the usual genuflections toward Monticello and Mount Vernon. Not even wrongheaded geniuses like John C. Calhoun and George Fitzhugh received the attention customarily due their standing. As if to defy the cloister, the Tarheel journalist supplied neither bibliography nor a single footnote. If mentioned at all, academicians and historians like John Spencer Bassett appeared only to illustrate southern persecutions of independent minds, not to back a particular piece of information or interpretation.[5]

Cash was not, though, at all divorced from academic sources. He was greatly swayed by Howard W. Odum, the dynamic sociologist at Chapel Hill. Yet Odum's friend and disciple did not place himself firmly in the European behaviorist tradition, which Odum had introduced to southern social science. He might well have done so. At the start he made clear that he was undertaking the kind of analysis that Max Weber had employed in *The Protestant Ethic and the Spirit of Capitalism*, a typological style that sought out the essentials of social behavior, the connections between ideals and collective activity in a past community. Probably Cash knew little or nothing directly of academic, European sociology—Emile Durkheim, Weber, and others who proposed generalized rules of custom and social development. He nevertheless spoke with authority when he announced his intentions in the preface. He planned to describe, he said, "a fairly definite mental pattern, associated with a fairly definite social pattern—a complex of established relationships and habits of thought, sentiments, prejudices, standards and values, and associations of ideas, which, if it is not common strictly to every group of white people in the South, is still common in one appreciable measure or another, and in some

5. Woodward, Review of Cash's *The Mind of the South*, 400.

part or another, to all but relatively negligible ones." Thus he emphasized the consensual and the durable in southern ethical life and social intercourse. Although American, this "one South" stood apart. Cash was clearly opposed to the moral texture of southern habits, even to the point of a "muffled bitterness" just below the surface. His literary approach was directed toward description, not, however, toward demoralization. To some degree he veiled his biases and rather successfully took the value-free stance in accordance with the mode that Weber offered as a guide. Neither his method nor his style of presentation was familiar to most professional historians. As late as 1961, Dewey Grantham expressed what had been a long-standing intellectual problem when he chided Cash for not making "known to the reader the historical rubric or conceptual framework out of which he wrote." Cash, however, was innocent of the academic obligation. The amenities went unobserved.[6]

When history advisors spurred their graduate students toward promising historical subjects, none used *The Mind of the South* as a point of departure. Issues that suggested the durable contexts and solidarity of southern life went begging even when Cash's influence was allegedly so great. Except for John Hope Franklin's valuable survey of violence, Cash's Savage Ideal and its outcroppings gained little attention. Not even a first-rate study of southern lynching appeared, nor has it yet. Clement Eaton dealt (1940) with antebellum anti-intellectualism, but not as a part of a larger cultural pattern. Perhaps nobody wanted to be accused of supporting H. L. Mencken's old sarcasms about moonshine and boobery.[7]

One reason for the neglect was Cash's dissent from a contemporary academic romance with southern farmer stock. In regard to the antebellum yeomanry, Frank Owsley of Vanderbilt took his romantic inspiration from Frederick Jackson Turner. On the other hand, Cash

6. W. J. Cash, *The Mind of the South* (New York, 1941), viii; Edwin M. Yoder, Jr., "W. J. Cash After a Quarter Century," in Willie Morris (ed.), *The South Today: 100 Years After Appomattox* (New York, 1965), 90; Dewey W. Grantham, Jr., "Mr. Cash Writes a Book," *Progressive*, XXV (1961), 41.

7. John Hope Franklin, *The Militant South, 1800–1861* (Cambridge, Mass., 1956); Clement Eaton, *The Freedom-of-Thought Struggle in the Old South* (rev. ed.; Durham, 1964).

depicted widespread yeoman deference to planter leadership and a troubling agrarian resistance to education and other useful notions. Likewise, when others were praising Populists as forerunners of modern social reform, Cash voiced a different opinion. Although they had genuine grievances, the Populists were unable to inspire "an overt and realized class awareness in the South." To claim otherwise, he continued, presupposed "a whole new habitus of thought and a new complexity of mind" that yeoman and mill villager simply did not have. Southern Populist studies did not take these views into account. Woodward's *Tom Watson: Agrarian Rebel* (1938) swept these academic honors with ease. In 1955, however, Richard Hofstadter brusquely challenged the liberal historians' sympathies for the plight of farmers in their long struggles against banks, robber barons, and southern elitists. Hofstadter labeled the Plains Populists as backward thinking, socially dislocated nativists. Whatever its merits, the assault unleashed a fearsome pack of dissertation writers in dissent. By contrast, Cash's criticisms, which were in fact at least as intriguing as Hofstadter's, inspired not a single monograph pro or con. Only in the last few years have historians taken the yeomanry seriously— and on the latter's own terms.[8]

If, as some claimed, Cash had overstressed upcountry folk to the neglect of the old planter elite, few young scholars shared the preference. Indeed, research still focused in conventional ways on large-scale slaveholders and their locales—the Blue Grass, Chesapeake, Black Belt, Gulf, and Delta. In sum, Cash did not affect the way history was written. Southern scholars preferred themes of discontinuity and class conflict. They proposed a divided South, not a region with strong cultural and ethical uniformities. They did not venture into cross-disciplinary approaches, despite Cash's having perhaps set some kind of example, muted though it was. Perhaps the situation was for the best: southern history flourished handsomely.

Cash, however, did not carry the weight sometimes attributed to

8. Richard Hofstadter, *Age of Reform: From Bryan to F.D.R.* (New York, 1955); compare C. Vann Woodward, "The Populist Heritage and the Intellectual," in his *The Burden of Southern History* (Baton Rouge, 1960), 141–66; Steven H. Hahn, *The Roots of Southern Populism: Yeoman Farmers and the Transformation of the Georgia Upcountry, 1850–1890* (New York, 1983); Cash, *The Mind of the South*, 165, 166.

him. Unhappily he added to the problem with a seemingly misleading title that opened him to the charge of trying to prove southern "mindlessness," irrationality, and intellectual barrenness rather than fulfill the promise of the title. Compounding the problem was the fact that Perry Miller, his contemporary, had used the term in a more conventional way in *The New England Mind*. The contrast between the rigorous cerebrations of Miller's Puritan divines and Cash's parvenu planters was, to some southern intellectuals, unnecessarily demeaning. Indeed, the South had its religious thinkers, but especially its gallery of political theorists. Cash did underestimate both influential groups in southern life, even on the terms he had set himself. Such difficulties finally led Woodward to contend that "if he were convinced that the Southerner had a 'temperament' but no 'mind,' that he 'felt' but did not 'think,' he might have more accurately entitled his book, 'The Temperament of the South,' 'The Feelings of the South,' or more literally, 'The Mindlessness of the South.'"[9]

This view was inadvertently encouraged by the language of the work. Cash sought a large audience that could only be reached through a popular, journalistic style. Unburdening himself to Howard Odum as early as 1929, Cash remarked, "I have sometimes hesitated over writing the book at all just because of the fear that the literary demand for simplification might result in a wholly inadequate representation of the South." A colloquial, slapdash breathlessness was the result. The cavalier exaggerations and passionate statements also reflected Cash's own southernness. Nevertheless, as literary historian Richard King has observed, *The Mind of the South* "fused a southern capacity for irony and satire." But such embellishments have never been the fashion among professional scholars. Undoubtedly, the style betrayed the author's own nervousness about dissenting from southern orthodoxies, ones that his parents, mentors, and neighbors very much shared. Smashing household gods, as Cash himself often repeated, was not the role of the southern intellectual

9. Woodward, *American Counterpoint*, 263, 265; O'Brien, "Cash, Hegel and the South," 379; Woodward, Review of Cash's *The Mind of the South*, 400–401; Perry Miller, *The New England Mind: The Seventeenth Century* (New York, 1939).

at any time. Yet he, like Faulkner and Woodward, could not escape the necessity. Whereas Woodward mediated his own sense of southern tragedy in a skillful use of irony, Cash resorted to a breeziness that sometimes overshadowed the profundities of his work, as King has also indicated. Cash thought his fiercest critics would be fellow southern readers, but as it happened in later years, his sternest reviewers came out of the faculty common room, not the county courthouse.[10]

Like other liberal intellectuals of the era, Cash eagerly punctured a number of southern myths, but he did not join them in the assault on the venerable minor deity, the Solid South. Trenchantly, Davidson, as early as 1941, noted the discrepancy between Cash's perspective and the insistence upon the "many Souths [that] Southern liberals," as he put it, delineated to crack the walls of conservatism. Kenneth Stampp, C. Vann Woodward, and many others refurbished a host of southern dissenters who had defied the conventions of their day: southern-born abolitionists, wartime Unionists, scalawags, Populists, and others of once unsavory reputation. In contrast, Cash was oblivious to the political strength of men like abolitionist Cassius Clay and Populist leader Tom Watson. Whenever reformers did appear in *The Mind of the South*, Cash introduced them to show how quickly a white consensus drove them into exile, silence, or repudiation of former radical hopes.[11]

For scholars anticipating the Civil War Centennial, Cash's belittling of the conflict's disruptive and revolutionary effects was irrelevant. Rather than confront the record of disloyalty and demoralization behind Rebel lines, Cash stressed the unifying effect of war

10. Wilbur J. Cash to Howard W. Odum, November 22, 1929, in Howard W. Odum Papers, Southern Historical Collection, University of North Carolina Library, Chapel Hill; Joseph L. Morrison, *W. J. Cash, Southern Prophet: A Biography and a Reader* (New York, 1967), 49; Richard H. King, *A Southern Renaissance: The Cultural Awakening of the American South* (New York, 1980), 149; see also Daniel J. Singal, *The War Within: From Victorian to Modernist Thought in the South, 1919–1945* (Chapel Hill, 1982), 373–75.
11. Davidson, "Cash and the Proto-Dorian South," 1; Cash, *The Mind of the South*, 92, 250, 253; Kenneth M. Stampp, "The Fate of the Southern Antislavery Movement," *Journal of Negro History*, XXVIII (1943), 10–22; C. Vann Woodward, *Tom Watson: Agrarian Rebel* (New York, 1938).

experience. High and low, rich and poor, men learned, Cash said, "more and more to say and think the same things, giving them common memories" and harmonizing "local patriotisms" into a sense of regional brotherhood. Virginian and Texan, Creole and sandhiller shared bitter hatreds of Yankees. Cash's point was well taken. Over 90 percent of the Democratic congressmen from the South serving in the last quarter-century were former Rebel officers, according to Carl V. Harris. The myth of the lost cause had concrete results. Some historians did treat the notion of political and cultural continuity intensified by wartime loyalties, William B. Hesseltine and Clement Eaton in particular. Nevertheless, the Great Divide of the Civil War, separating Old South from New in historical periodizations, remained for the most part as unspanned as ever. Likewise, Cash's view of Reconstruction and Redemption scarcely matched postwar trends in historiography. He explored the desolation of white defeats, not the promise of new beginnings, which scholars in the 1960s thought the right perspective.[12]

No matter how well meaning Yankee interventions were supposed to be, Cash had nothing good to say about the whole period. Most of all, he stressed the South's colonial thralldom. Once co-equal, the region had slipped to peripheral significance. The process had begun much earlier, and secession had been proposed as the cure. Reconstruction chaos as well as wartime losses threw the region back to near wilderness. Yankee meddling, taxes, and subsidies to fatten northern industry at southern expense made matters worse. A sterner peace that might have arisen did not cross Cash's mind, but that remedy, as later historians would propose it, would have offered no blessing, by his lights. White southerners were sullen enough as it was.

Actually, the phenomenon that Cash briefly sketched resembled the tribulations of subregions undergoing European consolidation.

12. Cash, *The Mind of the South*, 106; Carl V. Harris, "Right Fork or Left Fork? The Section-Party Alignment of Southern Democrats in Congress, 1873–1897," *Journal of Southern History*, XLII (1976), 471; William B. Hesseltine, *Confederate Leaders in the New South* (Baton Rouge, 1950); Clement Eaton, *The Waning of the Old South Civilization* (Athens, Ga., 1968). Political continuities are well explained in Carl N. Degler, *Place Over Time: The Continuity of Southern Distinctiveness* (Baton Rouge, 1977), 104–114.

Both the "Celtic Fringe" in Great Britain and the people of southern Italy after the *Risorgimento* underwent similar subjugations. The nineteenth-century southerner would have felt a sympathy for the Scotsman, Irishman, Sicilian, and Neapolitan. Internal colonialism, whereby a rich, industrializing section reduces its backward, agrarian outlands to dependencies, received brilliant illustration in Woodward's *Origins of the New South*. In contrast to Woodward's economic approach, Cash concentrated on the high psychological costs of colonial status. From the Yankee occupation and into the early twentieth century, southerners, Cash declared, fed on destructive recriminations, impossible dreams of might-have-beens, and pathetic attempts at self-flattery to dress regional backwardness in the flashy apparel of New South rhetoric. As Woodward and others have justly observed, Cash himself fell victim to the myth of black Reconstruction, whereas he should have recognized that the stories of corruption and horror were part of that colonial mentality itself. As a result, he mixed insight with bathos when he observed, "Not Ireland nor Poland, nor Finland nor Bohemia, not one of the countries which prove the truth that there is no more sure way to make a nation than the brutal oppression of an honorably defeated and disarmed people—not one of these . . . ever developed so much of fear, of indignation and resentment, or self-consciousness and patriotic passion."[13]

Cash obviously could not wholly forsake the southern vice of nostalgia and romance that he himself vigorously denounced. What can be rescued from his conventional ideas about Reconstruction, however, is the perception that race supremacy and regional autonomy were durable, constant objectives that scholars of the 1950s either muted or firmly denied. In *The Strange Career of Jim Crow*, for instance, Woodward questioned southern immutability about race. As if addressing Cash in person, Woodward declared: "Lacking the tradition of historical continuity possessed by their fellow countrymen, Southerners have less reason to expect the indefinite duration of any set of social institutions." Emancipation, he argued, opened up vari-

13. Cash, *The Mind of the South*, 105–108; Michael Hechter, *Internal Colonialism: The Celtic Fringe in British National Development, 1536–1966* (London, 1975); C. Vann Woodward, *Origins of the New South, 1877–1913* (Baton Rouge, 1953), 291–320.

141

ous approaches to race relations, so that whites in Reconstructed states were less united on the status of blacks than has been thought. Likewise, Grady McWhiney discovered a redeemable South. The whites, he announced, were willing in early Reconstruction "to accept a large measure of democratization, including a goodly dose of colorblind democracy" for the sake of moving down "the progress road." According to scholars of the postwar generation, race repression a hundred years before was not a foundation of southern culture itself, but rather a device to be hauled out or shelved as politicians or special interests found appropriate. To Cash, as to historian Ulrich B. Phillips before him, the "central theme" of southern history was white dominance, but since to say so implied an endorsement, historians sought other ways of identifying southernness.[14]

Cash was totally unaware of the pliable, possibly benign nature of Rebel feelings after Appomattox that others discerned. If anything, Cash believed, race oppression grew worse as terrorism and lynching mounted. Moreover, unlike the postwar historians, he detected no dramatic shift in postbellum leadership. If Snopeses joined the Sartoris crowd to restore home and white rule, such accommodation of newcomers to the upper ranks had always been the southern way. Under Woodward's leadership, however, the generation of academicians who followed Cash reported that after the Civil War, former Whigs replaced Democrats, capitalists swept aside cavaliers, and town dwellers put country folk firmly in their social place. On the contrary, Cash insisted that nothing had really altered very much: continuity of leadership assured the perpetuation of plantation paternalism in the world of factories. Such scholars as Jonathan M. Wiener, Dwight B. Billings, and James T. Moore support Cash's insights.[15]

14. Grady McWhiney, "Reconstruction: Index to Americanism," in Charles G. Sellers, Jr. (ed.), *The Southerner as American* (Chapel Hill, 1960), 95; Ulrich B. Phillips, "The Central Theme of Southern History," *American Historical Review*, XXXIV (1928), 30–43; C. Vann Woodward, *The Strange Career of Jim Crow* (3rd rev. ed.; New York, 1974), 8–9.

15. Jonathan M. Wiener, *Social Origins of the New South: Alabama, 1860–1885* (Baton Rouge, 1978); Dwight B. Billings, *Planters and the Making of a "New South": Class, Politics, and Development in North Carolina, 1865–1900* (Chapel Hill, 1979); James T. Moore, "Redeemers Reconsidered: Change and Continuity in the Democratic

Quite apart from the untimeliness of Cash's views on particular events, there was his depressing and increasingly outdated refrain about changelessness. Clearly, the classic South of Cash's description had come to a close after World War II, if not even as Cash was preparing his manuscript during the New Deal era. There was an upbeat in southern affairs, despite Gene Talmadge, Theodore Bilbo, then "massive resistance," George Wallace (in his segregationist period), and other signs of old continuities in new guises. Whereas other writers, in the Methodist strain, found hope for fallen sinners in the record of a discontinuous and disunited South, Cash hewed to the Calvinist line. Like Fernand Braudel, the French historian, he seemed to believe that "man's whole life is restricted by an upper limit," some kind of boundary "always difficult to reach and still more difficult to cross." Cash expressed it in his most sarcastic moment when he noted the implausibility of skyscrapers in small southern towns that had "little more use for them than a hog has for a morning coat." The contrast of skyscraper and ground-scraper in hog-human form was his metaphor for how outward shows of modernity could hide age-old savagery, hedonism, and stupidity. The analogy seemed a trifle farfetched, excusable only perhaps as evidence that the author, as Davidson had said in 1941, was "writing poetically and should be answered poetically."[16]

In the way customary among historians, present prospects prompted congenial views of the past during the civil rights era of the 1950s and early 1960s. The South, most everyone agreed, had to break the chains of racial and sectional parochialism. Thus, in 1960, history was made to conform to the moment. The historian Charles G. Sellers, Jr., declared: "The traditional emphasis on the South's

---

South, 1870–1900," *Journal of Southern History*, XLIV (1978), 357–78; John V. Mering, "Persistent Whiggery in the Confederate South: A Reconsideration," *South Atlantic Quarterly*, LXIX (1970), 124–43; Harris, "Right Fork or Left Fork?" 471–506; Michael O'Brien, "C. Vann Woodward and the Burden of Southern Liberalism," *American Historical Review*, LXXVIII (1973), 589–605.

16. Braudel quoted in James A. Henretta, "Social History as Lived and Written: Structure, Problematic and Action" (Mimeo, Newberry Papers, No. 774-F, 1977), 8; Joseph L. Morrison, "W. J. Cash: The Summing Up," *South Atlantic Quarterly*, LXXVI (1977), 508; Davidson, "Cash and the Proto-Dorian South," 14.

differentness . . . is wrong historically," making it all the "harder for the South to understand both its Southernism and its Americanism, and hence escape the defensiveness, prejudice, and belligerence of its regional self-preoccupation." Likewise, Kenneth Stampp detected a yearning for national conformity beneath the call to arms in 1861. With equal moral fervor, historian William R. Taylor in *Cavalier and Yankee* self-confidently dismissed the previous generation of writers, including Cash, who had traced the Mason-Dixon Line in heavy black. "This idea of a divided culture has died a slow death," but, Taylor proclaimed, the concept was at last ready for interment. Americans had too much in common—speech, religion, ethnic roots, ethical principles, and law—to be divided in cultural ways, he argued. Stanley Elkins also described sectional uniformities: both Yankee entrepreneur and slave master were bourgeois, capitalistic, suspicious of institutions, and devoted to an individualism that bordered on megalomania.[17]

Further divergences from Cash's position appeared even on a topic about which there was supposed to be agreement: the sense of guilt over slaveholding. Cash explained that southerners well knew both the innate brutality and worldwide infamy of American slavery. In uneasy conscience—"social schizophrenia"—he argued, they reacted with such "defense-mechanisms [as the] banjo-playing, heel-flinging, hi-yi-ing happy jack of the levees" and the formal proslavery logic to "prettify the institution [and] boast of its own Great Heart." In the 1960s, however, guilt took on different meaning. The "travail of slavery," Charles Sellers and others argued, weighed heavily on white souls. It was a therapeutic release when the white man's yoke of slavery finally lifted in 1865. The argument hinted at romantic wishful thinking. Eugene D. Genovese was the first to detect and denounce the sentimentalism. Quite unfairly, Genovese accused Cash of conjuring up the myth. Actually Cash linked guilt more closely to fantasy than to remorse. The fictions of Sambo and Old Black Joe aroused,

17. Sellers (ed.), *The Southerner as American*, v–vi; Kenneth M. Stampp, "The Southern Road to Appomattox," in his *The Imperiled Union: Essays on the Background of the Civil War* (New York, 1980), 246–69; William R. Taylor, *Cavalier and Yankee: The Old South and American National Character* (New York, 1961), 15; Stanley M. Elkins, *Slavery: A Problem in American Institutional and Intellectual Life* (Chicago, 1959).

he said, "mawkish tears [and] mawkish laughter." In short, Cash thought that southern discomfiture over bondage lay not behind the region's most sensitive and cheering features but behind its worst: intolerance, violence, sexual anxieties, and sentimentality.[18]

Nevertheless, Genovese's point was well taken. Perhaps because of an intellectual distress with the blunt expressiveness that power seems to stimulate, liberal scholars overly inflated southern penitence and regret for slaveholding. The myth afforded comfort, though, to those anticipating a tolerant southern reaction to racial advances in the militant decade of the 1960s. By the time of Genovese's attack upon Cash, the long-standing silence on the vulnerability of *The Mind of the South* was broken. By then, too, an entire mode of writing, that is, what came to be called American Studies, had come into question. Cash's book had been one of the earliest examples of the genre.

For nearly a quarter century following the appearance of *The Mind of the South* in 1941, scholars had developed similar typological schemes for explaining American characteristics. None claimed indebtedness to Cash. Nevertheless, his best-selling work contributed to the acceptability of American Studies. These authors were most creative in their definitions of enduring features of American life: Louis Hartz on American liberalism; David Potter on the influence of abundance; David Riesman on the question of conformity; Henry Nash Smith on the frontier as symbol and myth. There were many others as well.[19]

Southern subjects also emerged: Elkins on southern anti-institutionalism and the archetypal Sambo; William R. Taylor on the unities beneath sectional image-making; C. Vann Woodward on the con-

18. Cash, *The Mind of the South*, 63, 86; Charles G. Sellers, Jr., "The Travail of Slavery," in Sellers (ed.), *The Southerner as American*, 40–71; see also James M. McPherson, "Slavery and Race," *Perspectives in American History*, III (1969), 460–73, and Fred Hobson, *Tell About the South: The Southern Rage to Explain* (Baton Rouge, 1983), 259; Eugene D. Genovese, *The World the Slaveholders Made: Two Essays in Interpretation* (New York, 1969), 134, 143–50.

19. See Robert F. Berkhofer, Jr., "Clio and the Culture Concept: Some Impressions of a Changing Relationship in American Historiography," in Louis Schneider and Charles M. Bonjean (eds.), *The Idea of Culture in the Social Sciences* (Cambridge, Eng., 1973), 77–100.

tinuity, as it were, of southern defeats, race and class confusions, and broken hopes, all of which held the South historically apart, though the region was otherwise American in its strengths and weaknesses. Despite their challenge to Cash's viewpoint, Taylor in *Cavalier and Yankee* and Woodward in *The Burden of Southern History* wrote in the literary genre that Cash had helped to initiate twenty years before. Based chiefly upon literary and cultural sources, these studies concerned the realm of aspiration and myth.

Myth was a slippery word indeed, and its meaning changed over time. Cash believed that romance and mythmaking were an integral part of the belief system and moral order of the South. He contended that there was too much fantasy, too little imagination in the southern "mind." Later practitioners of the American Studies genre, however, construed systems of belief in a way that made them seem false, artificial, and therefore manipulative. For instance, Woodward in *The Burden of Southern History* treats the myths that once defined the South—plantation legend, lost cause, white supremacy—as historical deceptions. They were always that. More important, they were ritual beliefs and rationales of custom by which individual and collective decisions were guided. Thus myth and reality became one. Nor could they ever be separated from the South's history or regional identity. Cash was close enough to the myths themselves to know their vitality. Later writers in the American Studies mode were not. Aside from that distinction, however, Cash and his successors had much in common. All were preoccupied with the moral durabilities of the American experiment.

Despite the pertinence of the questions raised and the inevitable ironies and paradoxes of the answers that these gifted authors provided, the fortunes of cultural topics of this kind fell dramatically in the mid-1960s. Fine-tuning on ethical matters gave way to belligerent certainties. Cash and American Studies were out; Marx and Malcolm X were in. Slavery and race became the sole preoccupations of the leading scholars whenever they looked southward. Eugene D. Genovese epitomized the mood of the decade when he announced that antebellum slavery had created "an organic relationship so complex and ambivalent that neither [white nor black] could express the simplest human feelings without reference to the other." Cash could not have anticipated these changes of emphasis. As Woodward correctly observed in 1967, "In view of the enormous impact slavery had on the mind of both whites and blacks, he cannot be excused for brushing over the Peculiar Institution as lightly as he did." Yet, as Fred Hobson observes, Cash was only slightly guilty of "mistakes in interpretation that many professional historians could, and did, make in the 1930s." Although his misreadings should be pointed out, it would be unfair to establish a criterion of historical accuracy that no one else of his day could meet.[20] Cash, however, focused on a prime issue: white supremacy. What form it took—slavery, Ku Klux, Jim Crow—mattered much less than the symbols, gestures, and habits to vouchsafe black submission and white rule. Men might even differ about the finer points of control, but not about the ultimate social objective.

As an exercise in social analysis, Cash's work proposed three major elements as the foundation of the southern ethic or *mentalité*. The first was the persistence of frontier conditions and attitudes; second, the agrarian style of lack of class consciousness; and third, race hierarchy as a sacrosanct principle. None was peculiar to Cash's vision alone; his insight was to trace the organic interrelationships of these elements.

In regard to the first issue, there is a tendency to mistake Cash's frontier for that of the Turnerians, who romantically described the blessings of democracy, good cheer, and neighborliness. Southern individualism, Cash maintained, was hardy, but not necessarily healthy. Whereas Frederick Jackson Turner and his disciples conceived of natural abundance as a source of character-building and self-reliance, Cash detected grounds for skepticism. In fact, ethnic origins, he claimed, had as much to do with southern habit as did the availability of land. The "man at the center," as Cash identified his typical settler, "had much in common with the half-wild Scotch and Irish clansmen of the seventeenth and eighteenth centuries whose blood

20. Eugene D. Genovese, *Roll, Jordan, Roll: The World the Slaves Made* (New York, 1974), 4; C. Vann Woodward, "White Man, White Mind," *New Republic*, December 9, 1967, p. 29; Hobson, *Tell About the South*, 164.

he so often shared, and from whom . . . he mainly drew his tradition." Curiously, we now accept the notion that there were unsuspected continuities in African and black American culture, but are less willing to see such persistences in the oral, primitive, and traditionalistic patterns of southern whites. He did not mean that an immutable folk memory linked southerners with old Celtic habits. Instead, Cash argued that the environment *preserved* but did not create the customs of the past. In almost Faulknerian prose, he observed that the frontiersman's "way of life was his . . . not because he himself or his ancestors or his class had deliberately chosen it as against something else, not even because it had been tested through the centuries and found to be good, but because, given his origins, it was the most natural outcome of the conditions in which he found himself."[21]

On this score Cash and Genovese agree. Both writers have interpreted the South as an organic, primordial society in the midst of dynamic, worldwide change. For both of them, too, the transatlantic community and the North offered an implied, but not specific, contrast. Their vision was completely at odds with the popular academic notion of a profit-making, bourgeois planter class. The chief difference between Genovese and Cash was Genovese's admiration for the self-confidence, commitment, and integrity of the slaveholding rulers. "It is rather hard to assert that class responsibility is the highest test of morality," said Genovese in rebuttal to the Old South's liberal critics, "and then to condemn as immoral those who behave responsibly toward their class instead of someone else's." On the other hand, Cash, like Allen Tate in *The Fathers*, thought there was something incomplete about the southern white male, a grievous simplicity or innocence that was much more dangerous and self-destructive than outright evil. But the two writers recognized that there was nothing hypocritical or manipulative in the manner by which white leaders assumed command, won the loyalty of the lower class, and exercised power. Like Genovese, Cash described a hegemonic relationship between leader and follower. Even after long years of settlement, that primal, institutionless sense of communal oneness called democracy

21. Cash, *The Mind of the South*, 30, 31.

endured, Cash asserted. The bonds lasted because the growth of cities, a disciplined educational system, a commanding church order, and a vast flow of alien peoples did not develop in the slave states, to disrupt "a world in which horses, dogs, guns, not books, and ideas and art"—and cotton and slaves—were "the normal and absorbing interests."[22]

The decision to open the analysis in the Jacksonian epoch was also a result of Cash's time: the current romance about the "common man," American virtue, and libertarianism of the New Deal days. Once again, however, Cash proved no sentimentalist. He reconciled a contradiction that Turnerians and others refused to admit: the apparent discrepancy between frontier individualism and the demands for a general social conformity. In Cash's view, southern individualism was not directed toward civic ends, that is, toward the building of community, the humanizing of social relations, the founding of powerful institutions. Such goals would have destroyed the elemental character of the society itself. Instead, individualism was most often synonymous with manliness. The ability to defend oneself received public applause. The "habitus" of masculinity contrasted with the impulse for other kinds of self-assertion—literary accomplishment, spiritual fulfillment, scientific discovery. Cash did not deny the existence of individuals who did so aspire—Matthew Fontaine Maury, Langdon Cheves, William Gilmore Simms—"and beneath these were others: occasional planters, lawyers, doctors, country schoolmasters, parsons, who, on a more humble scale, sincerely cared for intellectual and aesthetic values and served them as well they might." The trouble was that they were lost in a wilderness of mediocrity. Instead, the cultural aims were embodied in the "chip on the shoulder swagger and brag of a boy," the boast that the possessor could "knock hell out of whoever dared to cross him."[23]

Whereas Turnerians found frontier ideals praiseworthy, Cash detected backwardness, a luxuriating in the needlessness of mental

22. Eugene D. Genovese, *Red and Black: Marxian Explorations in Southern and Afro-American History* (New York, 1972), 342; Allen Tate, *The Fathers* (Chicago, 1938); Cash, *The Mind of the South*, 99.
23. Cash, *The Mind of the South*, 44, 97.

exertion. The Savage Ideal of manly aggression discouraged other activities. Those few who were cursed with intellectual gifts, he noted sympathetically, had to suffer alone, even those in his own literary generation. In reference to Faulkner, Wolfe, and Caldwell, he said, "They hated [the South] with the exasperated hate of a lover who cannot persuade the object of his affections to his desire." With rare insight, he elaborated, "Their hate and anger against the South was both a defense-mechanism against the inner uneasiness created by that conflict and a sort of reverse embodiment of the old sentimentality itself." The anti-intellectuality of the region revealed that in strictly utilitarian terms the society had "little need or desire" for heavy cerebral toil. Not only was the general public indifferent to the pronouncements of its intellectual tyros and sages, there was a sensitivity to even the breath of criticism, from home or abroad. Cash did not rejoice in southern hedonism, and he accused his southern literary contemporaries, the contributors to *I'll Take My Stand*, for taking too little notice of "the underdog proper, the tenants and sharecroppers, industrial labor, and the Negroes as a group." But the dismal record, he thought, could not be denied by forever hauling out the Founding Fathers, Carolina belletrists, and *Uncle Remus*.[24]

The Savage Ideal of frontier derivation with its anti-intellectual results was closely connected with Cash's second major theme, the relative absence of class consciousness. On this issue, Genovese has been Cash's most savage critic. Cash did confuse *gentility* as a social ideal with aristocracy as a class designation. It does not, however, illuminate the issue to say that Cash had, according to Genovese, "a pathetic fascination with the romance of aristocracy." The effort to break free of such long-standing ideals might seem "pathetic" a score of years after Cash's suicide, but his creativity, in fact the creativity of his literary generation in the South, owed much to just that wrenching away from the paternal grasp of old doctrine.[25]

The ultimate triumph for an author severely handled is to have his perceptions adopted even by his critics. Thus, Genovese in 1975,

24. *Ibid.*, 386–87, 147, 392.
25. Genovese, *The World the Slaveholders Made*, 140; see Cash, *The Mind of the South*, 3–102.

some years after the publication of his original complaints, reintroduced Cash's interpretation of class bondings, though he did not mention Cash's name or book. Genovese even peopled his account with Cash-derived archetypes: Josh Venable, the poor, independent-minded, forty-acre cousin of Jefferson Venable, his condescending but helpful neighbor at the Big House, with broad acres and well-populated slave cabins. Cash's parallel figure, Cousin Wash Venable, would feel right at home in the world Genovese made, sharing, as he does, the same patronymic. In short, Genovese repackages what Cash had explained a quarter century before. Ironically, Genovese's "Yeomen Farmers in a Slaveholders' Democracy" is among his most convincing short pieces, especially in its revised form.[26]

Cash's penetration, however, went beyond the simplicities of some sort of frontier democracy. Unfortunately, he called the style "paternal." Even so, he recognized the inadequacy of the designation. "I call the term [paternalism] inaccurate," said he, "because its almost inevitable connotation is the relationship of Roman *patron* and *client*; it suggests with a force that has led to much confusion, that there existed on the one hand an essential dependence, and on the other a prescriptive right—that it operated through command . . . and rested . . . on compulsion." Such was not the case. Cousin Wash or the "man at the center" expected and received respect for his individuality and resented any infringement upon his independence, his honor, or his desires. Yet, he accorded deference to those whose power awed him, so long as some mutuality of personal exchange existed.[27]

On this point, Cash and Faulkner shared the same vision of historical reality. Take, for example, Thomas Sutpen and Wash Jones in

26. Genovese, "Yeomen Farmers in a Slaveholders' Democracy," in Genovese and Genovese, *Fruits of Merchant Capital*, 249–64; Cash, *The Mind of the South*, 28–29.
27. Cash, *The Mind of the South*, 54. Patron and client relations in ancient Rome might not have been analogous to the southern situation, as Cash averred, but that concept, thoroughly explored in the anthropological literature, does have a bearing on southern class tensions and cooperations yet to be thoroughly examined. See, for instance, Steffen W. Schmidt *et al.* (eds.), *Friends, Followers, and Factions: A Reader in Political Clientelism* (Berkeley and Los Angeles, 1977); Ernest Gellner and John Waterbury (eds.), *Patrons and Clients in Mediterranean Societies* (London, 1977); S. N. Eisenstadt and René Lemarchand (eds.), *Political Clientelism, Patronage and Development* (Beverly Hills, Calif., 1981).

Absalom, Absalom!, John Sartoris (and then son Bayard) and George Wyatt in *The Unvanquished*, or, when matters did go sour, Major De Spain and Abner Snopes. Cash explained that there was no contradiction between the primitive individualism he had sketched and a required subordination to leaders publicly invested with the mystique of power. This preference for charismatic chieftains was based upon the commoner's assumption that the men who gained command could never, said Cash, "run counter to his aims and desires."[28] When that expectation was betrayed, however, the result was utter fury, as if a backlog of jealousies, malice, guilts, and grievances had erupted all at once. Cash, like Genovese, never quite penetrated the nature of the power still vested in the followers. The unspoken rules of conduct so easily overstepped, the dangers of pressing elitist innovations too hard, the helplessness of the rich when the ordinary folk assailed their slaves during alleged insurrectionary panics, the petty harassments of lawsuits brought by poorer neighbors—these were also part of the social structure. They did not destroy consensus, but they helped to make acts of violence, both great and small, a means of enforcing the ways of the "people out of doors," as it were, upon the wealthy. Neither Cash nor Genovese moved his argument about upper-class hegemony into these rather uncharted areas of social experience. Nevertheless, Cash provided an excellent starting point.

In connection with the feelings of the disreputable toward their social betters, as Cash outlined them, one could do no better than recall the example of Faulkner's Colonel Thomas Sutpen and Wash Jones. In his remorseless determination to found a dynasty, Sutpen seduces Milly, daughter of the useless Wash, caretaker of Sutpen's Hundred. After the end of the war, Milly gives birth in the stable straw to a daughter, not the son that Sutpen so desperately sought to immortalize himself. In his disappointment and callousness, Sutpen tells her, "Well, Milly; too bad you're not a mare too. Then I could give you a decent stall in the stable." By community standards, Wash Jones is poor-white trash, friendless, only marginally independent. Inwardly he knows his position, too. But the colonel has never forced him to confront his worthlessness, has never driven him to self-

28. Cash, *The Mind of the South*, 115.

humiliation before. The brutish remark shows how matters really stand. In mad reprisal Jones seizes a scythe and decapitates his chief. Then he sits passively to await the inevitable arrest.[29]

The scene dramatizes Cash's point almost precisely. Social interchanges between gentry and yeoman, sometimes even between those connected by blood or marriage, included such primitive and violent events. Moreover, it should be recalled that Sutpen himself rose out of the same obscurity and shiftlessness in which Wash Jones lived. Born poor and despised in the Virginia uplands, Sutpen was determined to be a master to whom the likes of Wash Jones would have to defer. Yet as Faulkner, and Cash as well, make clear, those who hold power must meet their obligations according to subtle rules of gentility that Sutpen failed to learn.

Finally on matters of race, Cash proposed the Proto-Dorian Convention. In a highly sophisticated way it has reappeared as *herrenvolk democracy*, a term of George M. Fredrickson's coining. As Genovese has forcefully observed, nonslaveholders were seldom "political marshmallows," easily gulled with talk of racial threats to their standing. Cash did not make this error. But his Proto-Dorian theme was a cornerstone of southern "fraternalism," that mixture of democracy and hierarchy which was so organic to the regional style. Fear of the contamination of blood lineage was not a sexual fear but a dread of loss of race command, the nightmare of impotence both physical and social. As a result, Cash observed, "any assertion of any kind on the part of the Negro constituted in a perfectly real manner an attack on Southern Woman." This imperative, a brother must defend his sister's purity, found expression in "would you have your sister marry one?" The query was not rhetorical but overloaded with the most visceral of emotions. Fraternalism, then, not only bonded white men together, it also made whites brothers in the guarding of female "perfection."[30]

As it turned out, Cash wrote just at the closing of what could be

29. William Faulkner, *Absalom, Absalom!* (1936; rpr. New York, 1972), 286.
30. George M. Fredrickson, *The Black Image in the White Mind: The Debate on Afro-American Character and Destiny, 1817–1914* (New York, 1971); Cash, *The Mind of the South*, 119.

called the classic South. Had he lived into the era of sweeping Supreme Court interventions, Martin Luther King, and the Voting Rights Act, had he watched the progress of a "Bulldozer Revolution" with an accompaniment of fried-chicken stands, and freedom, at last, from cotton if not from sin, he would have been tempted to tinker with the text. Cash suspected, but he did not know for certain, that the triptych of frontier traits, democratic hierarchy or fraternalism, and white supremacy was soon to fall. As it was, he wrote when it was still possible to puncture the hedonistic pretentiousness of Atlanta's lofty skyline over the clay hills of north Georgia: "Softly, do you not hear behind that the gallop of Jeb Stuart's cavalrymen?" Faulkner, too, was a child of that transitional period when the Confederate past was still remembered but distant enough to permit a newfound detachment. Harold Bloom's "anxiety of influence" stirred these writers to demolish the paternal myth, but the power of legend drove them forward. In Faulkner's *Intruder in the Dust* (1948), Charles Mallison, fourteen years old, could still relive the dusty afternoon "when Pickett himself is looking up the hill waiting for Longstreet to give the word and it's all in the balance" on that slope near Gettysburg.[31]

The metaphor of legendary hoofbeats ringing against the concrete walls of Atlanta's modernity may require a leap of imagination today. On the far side of the greatest of all southern fault-lines, the Second World War, it took much less insight to grasp Cash's meaning. How ludicrously, Cash was saying, southerners held to outworn beliefs and incorporated them in a world of shifting values and innovation. After all, Gene Talmadge was governor of Georgia then. With rhetoric and galluses ablaze, Talmadge kept alive the politics of nostalgia, even as his cracker constituency hankered after the good things. Tacky romanticism, violence, shouts against the wind—matters that Cash had so well depicted and mourned—were still part of a durable South. Only lately, in the last quarter-century, has it receded beyond easy recognition. We have Cash's study to thank for describing a fast disappearing southern way that *The Mind of the South* helped to speed on its unregretted departure.

31. Cash, *The Mind of the South*, 224, 225; William Faulkner, *Intruder in the Dust* (New York, 1948), 194.

VI

FROM PIETY TO FANTASY:
Proslavery's Troubled Evolution

IRONICALLY, post-1830 proslavery defenses owed much to the same source as abolitionism. Their common influence was the evangelical experience. It was itself part of a general humanitarian impulse that had transformed moral perceptions of the human condition during the eighteenth and nineteenth centuries. Vigorous attempts to reform manners and reduce suffering reflected a growing respect for human and natural life and a sense that events could be mastered by personal and collective effort. Both a cause and a result of the new determination to overcome ancient ills in the Western world, evangelical religion in Great Britain and America not only spread Christian faith but also set new standards of human sensibility. It was based upon individual conscience and appeals to empathy for the dependent, the unlucky, and the downtrodden.

From an attempted suppression of alcohol and its depredations to a disapproval of shaming rites—the stocks, branding iron, and village charivari—the religion of action instead of ritual was a vital part of the vast and still not well understood humanitarian movement. Why, after centuries, Western man should have perceived in a dramatically different light such evils as the maiming of animals and men, the selling of Africans into bondage, the disfiguring of crimi-

Modified from "Modernizing Southern Slavery: The Proslavery Argument Reinterpreted," in *Region, Race and Reconstruction: Essays in Honor of C. Vann Woodward,* edited by J. Morgan Kousser and James M. McPherson. Copyright © 1982 by Oxford University Press, Inc. Reprinted by permission.

nals, and the popular humiliating of social deviants remains a topic much discussed. There can be no doubt, however, that evangelicalism, by denying resignation to the depravities of men and institutions, played a major part in the transformation.[1]

Far from being a static and crankish exercise, the proslavery argument was evolving new strategies throughout the antebellum period. The point of departure was the conservative tradition that southerners had long espoused. Dickson Bruce explains it as a deep faith in human imperfection, a conviction that order was problematical, a certainty that civilization itself depended upon maintaining those inequalities of station and wealth that God had wisely sanctioned. As late as the Virginia Debates over slavery and constitutional change (1829–1830), these views underlay the arguments of Tidewater planters whose rule had been challenged by settlers in the western part of the state. But reasoning from ancient assumptions and common-law property rights was not congruent with the new American mood of progress and humanitarian concern. The South had to prove that its way of life was not retrogressive but carried forward the best principles known. After the abolitionists began in the 1830s to condemn slavery on biblical grounds, the southern clergy "surprised" even themselves, related David Benedict, a Baptist leader, when they discovered "from the sacred word" how easy it was to defend the institution. The quickly fashioned credo of Christian slaveholding probably meant little to nonchurchgoing southerners. But the general idea of slavery as a form of progress, David B. Davis concludes, was "a variant" on standard British and American notions of "historic mission," a Christianizing and ameliorative enterprise. In fact, he argues, "both white and black abolitionists discovered [that] emancipation could be even more effectively blocked by men who believed in progress than by those who fatalistically resigned themselves to the sins of this world." The optimistic evangelical creed that replaced old-fashioned pessimism, as Donald G. Mathews has noted,

1. David B. Davis, *Slavery and Human Progress* (New York, 1984); Keith Thomas, *Man and the Natural World: A History of the Modern Sensibility* (New York, 1983); James Walvin, "The Rise of British Popular Sentiment for Abolition, 1787–1832," in Christine Bolt and Seymour Drescher (eds.), *Anti-Slavery, Religion and Reform: Essays in Memory of Roger Anstey* (Folkstone, Eng., and Hamden, Conn., 1980), 149–51.

was "adaptable to different classes and conditions" and could be as well applied within as against slaveholding.[2]

For a time at least, the pro- and antislavery forces seemed fairly matched in the battle for the allegiance of American Christendom. Despite antislavery religious assaults, the discrepancies between the northern and southern evangelical perspectives were muted at first. In the 1830s, Yankee conservative churchmen applauded their southern brethren's "Mission to the Slaves," a widespread and successful effort of Christianization. Upon this basis, the pious proslavery defenders built their arguments, and despite the abolitionists' assaults within the northern churches, the national bodies did not affront their southern members.

As the tide turned against southern claims for benevolence, particularly in the 1850s, a strident romanticism appeared in proslavery literature. It paralleled abolitionist perfectionism and disunion. To a degree, it also replaced the more modest and Bible-based explanations for slavery's utility and benignity. The darkening mood showed a perilous inner turmoil born of desperation as the signs of northern disengagement from complicity with slaveholding mounted. Southern proslavery writers turned away from theological concerns and tried to use theories of political economy. The secularizing trend did little to halt the growing sectional divisions, even though the southern authors issued "dire warnings," as Elizabeth Fox-Genovese and Eugene Genovese observe, "that the bourgeoisie would rue the day it destroyed the landed classes and with them, a great bulwark against lower-class radicalism." The arguments of Edmund Ruffin, George Fitzhugh, and Henry Hughes, who denounced "wage slavery" in northern factories and posed an organic and utopian relationship of capital and labor in the South, were preparatory to the retreat into the Confederacy, war, and death.[3]

2. Dickson D. Bruce, Jr., *The Rhetoric of Conservatism: The Virginia Convention of 1829–30 and the Conservative Tradition in the South* (San Marino, Calif., 1982), 175–93; Benedict quoted in Anne C. Loveland, *Southern Evangelicals and the Social Order, 1800–1860* (Baton Rouge, 1980), 200; Davis, *Slavery and Human Progress*, 154, 235; Donald G. Mathews, "Religion and Slavery—The Case of the American South," in Bolt and Drescher (eds.), *Anti-Slavery, Religion and Reform*, 207.

3. Elizabeth Fox-Genovese and Eugene D. Genovese, *Fruits of Merchant Capital: Slavery and Bourgeois Property in the Rise and Expansion of Capitalism* (New York, 1983), 398.

The evolution of proslavery thought, from the sacred to the secular, from the classical to the romantic, should not obscure the defenders' high hopes at the start of their enterprise in the 1830s and 1840s. Their program was clear: the efficacy of Christian masterhood. The audience, too, was reasonably well defined: the Christian reading public of England and the free states. Moreover, the abolitionists were scarcely popular anywhere in the 1830s (except in selected quarters of middle-class English ranks). Yet they had to be countered at once with sound argument to check further inroads. It was vitally important for the integrity of the slaveholding states that antislavery zealots were given the lie. After all, reasoned their southern opponents, Garrison and company were representatives of chaos, godlessness, and materialism, tendencies that prevented, rather than stimulated, human advance. But equally important, the proslavery argument had to be proclaimed at home as well. It was unnecessary to convince slaveholders that their motives were free of venality and their race control good and God-ordained. Such views were thought to be self-evident. But planters had to be persuaded to improve their own chances for redemption and security by helping their benighted slaves, an effort that would save slavery for generations to come.[4]

Although southern Methodists, Presbyterians, and Baptists had earlier condemned slaveholding as a moral evil, by the 1830s they had come to rely on the doctrine of Christian stewardship. Left to themselves, the reasoning went, blacks would be wayward and dangerous. With Christian masters to guide them, however, slaves fulfilled their appointed roles to the benefit of civilization. As the system became more benign, world opinion would become enlightened. Abolitionists would be seen as the pariahs they really were. Moreover, these self-improvements in masterhood would encourage a much-needed clarity of thought about the institution. Proslavery argumentation could relieve the sense of intellectual inferiority that plagued the region. Therefore, declared Henry Hughes of Missis-

4. Robert E. Shalhope, "Race, Class, and the Antebellum Southern Mind," *Journal of Southern History*, XXXVII (1971), 557–74; David Donald, "The Proslavery Argument Reconsidered," *Journal of Southern History*, XXXVII (1971), 3–18; Drew G. Faust, *A Sacred Circle: The Dilemma of the Intellectual in the Old South, 1840–1860* (Baltimore, 1977).

sippi, "the young men [must be] taught to reason the matter. They must learn why our home system is *not* wrong: why it *is* right; and be able to give the reasons for it."[5]

For these reasons, as well as for the sake of the bondsmen's well-being, southern social and intellectual leaders set out to improve the "home system." They urged planters to fulfill Christian duty toward their slaves. In their minds no dichotomy existed between the old traditions of southern plantation life and a policy of moving forward with the age toward greater human charitableness. All depended, though, upon the quality of individual masters. The reliance, they thought, was compatible with tendencies toward individualism in society. "Moral suasion" of churchgoers and the "wise and good" was the southern watchword as much as it was for the antislavery cause. John S. Preston, congressman of South Carolina and a leading Episcopalian layman, in 1860 addressed a gathering in Tennessee. The ceremony was to establish a "University of the South" where the ideals of pious gentility would be the guiding principles. He declared that every planter was "relegated almost entirely to his own resources for the moral tone and the intellectual store which saves him from vice and soothes his way of life." With firm control and smiling condescension (then a virtue), he had to perform "dread responsibilities" of ownership or perish. "You cannot maintain this order of things . . . without elevating your minds and hearts by precisely that nutriment which the University proposes to furnish." Gentility might be on the defensive, but its survival was not just a southern necessity, he insisted. It was a problem facing the whole of the Christian world.[6]

Hearing this plea, southerners were keenly aware that they need not stand alone. Social and moral leaders elsewhere mourned a decline in old values, the rise of middle-class hedonism, and the economic distress of the lower orders. British self-criticism, as Marcus

5. Henry Hughes, "New Duties of the South," *Southern Reveille* (Port Gibson, Miss.), November 18, 1854, clipping, in Henry Hughes Scrapbook, Henry Hughes Papers, Mississippi Department of Archives and History, Jackson.
6. Preston quoted in *Reprints of Documents and Proceedings of the Board of Trustees of the University of the South Prior to 1860*, ed. Telfair Hodgson (Sewanee, Tenn., 1888), 55.

Cunliffe has noted, supplied them with ample means to catalog the wrongs of industrialization. Thomas Carlyle, Charles Kingsley, Sir Walter Scott, and other luminaries whom southern literati admired offered the same kinds of ambivalent responses to the new industrial order and the overthrow of ancient custom that they themselves had. In fact, Scott's popularity extended far beyond his romantic *Waverly* novels, with their sentimentality and derring-do in battle regalia. For Scott, as for most of his southern readers, there existed side by side a revulsion against the primitivism of warrior honor (duels were constantly, if ineffectually, deplored on every hand) and a hatred of the impersonality of modern trends. "[Scott's] elegy on the passing of the old Highland order comes not from a sitter-on-the-fence," one critic has noted, "but from the fair-minded man who knows that history cannot stand still, that there can be no change, even for the better without loss, suffering, and waste." Since many southerners were themselves of Celtic ancestry, they found in Scott the spokesman for the world that they were glad to lose, even as they gloried in its alleged strengths of intense family life, intimacy with wild nature, and simple if bloody principles and passions.[7]

However much defiance of Yankeedom masked inner vulnerabilities, southern intellectuals sought to combine the best of two worlds rather than merely storm ineffectually in the manner of Don Quixote. Without relinquishing the supposed virtues of their forefathers, whether Celtic, English, or Revolutionary American, they were determined to move forward. In 1911, looking back to the motives of pious planters, the Reverend James H. McNeilly of the Southern Methodist Church deplored the "*New* South's pretentious magnanimity" about the "relic of barbarism" from which war and defeat had freed the region. These advocates of post–Civil War industrialism ought to remember, he chided, how far their fathers and grandfathers had moved away from earlier cruelties and indifference. "It must be

7. Marcus Cunliffe, *Chattel Slavery and Wage Slavery: The Anglo-American Context, 1830–1860* (Athens, Ga., 1979); Robin Mayhead, *Walter Scott* (Cambridge, Eng., 1973), 43; see also David Daiches, "Scott's Achievement as a Novelist," in D. D. Devlin (ed.), *Walter Scott: Modern Judgements* (Nashville and London, 1970), 37; "Portrait of Sir Walter Scott, By Geo. W. Curtis of Putnam's Magazine," *Southern Literary Messenger*, XXII (April, 1856), 291–94.

understood, too, that the majority of earnest, sincere, upright Southerners who studied the subject believed that the relation of master
and slave was not in itself sinful, but that it was . . . sanctioned by
the Word of God." They insisted that "it could be so administered as
to foster and develop some of the noblest traits of character, such as
protecting care and wise direction of the weaker race by the master,
such devoted loyalty and honest service in the slaves." Although
clearly imperfect as an institution—what agencies were not so
flawed?— slavery had been, McNeilly argued, "a benefit to the slave,
as well as profitable to the master." His comments reflected neither
the actual circumstances of slave management nor the true feelings
of slaves, but they accurately portrayed the attitudes of churchgoing
slaveholders. They were implacably certain that each year progress
was being made under the auspices of the Lord himself. The "home"
institution was ill-suited to other sections of the country perhaps, but
in the South it was thought the *only* way, the *right* way.[8]

Thus, literary justifications of slavery were not just hymns of
praise for a changeless primordial society, but a stirring appeal to
place the South firmly in the context of contemporary national life.
The effort to justify themselves and their ways required a new regional pride and self-consciousness as well as concrete demonstrations of just, humane, and morally uplifting techniques of patriarchal control.[9]

The basis of this effort lay in the evolutionary nature of the institution itself. Slavery changed as society changed. In a crude way,
one may trace a progression from the beginning to the end of slavery.
Three ways existed whereby masters could perceive the system: as
crude chattel bondage, wherein slaves were more or less beasts of
burden to meet the possessors' needs and whims; as familial pro-
prietorship, in which reciprocal, parent-child obligations and affections gave meaning to those involved, a view that required a deeper

8. James H. McNeilly, *Religion and Slavery: A Vindication of the Southern Churches*
(Nashville, 1911), 7, 13; see also "Harper on Slavery," in *The Pro-Slavery Argument, As
Maintained by the Most Distinguished Writers of the Southern States* . . . (Philadelphia,
1853), 1–2; James H. Hammond, "Slavery in the Light of Political Science," in E. N.
Elliott (ed.), *Cotton is King* . . . (Augusta, Ga., 1860), 647.
9. Edward J. Pringle, *Slavery in the Southern States* (Cambridge, Mass., 1853), 43.

appreciation of the psychology and wants of the dependent class, although those beneath were still required to give in love and service more than those who ruled should reciprocate in kind; as state racial regulation, a civil interposition between white and black, setting limits upon proprietary powers and strictly defining proper racial boundaries. None of these perspectives was ever exclusive to one era or another. Roughly speaking, however, chattel bondage was rather characteristic of colonial thralldom. Although part of the household and its possessions, slaves were not often regarded as intimate family members. Stage two, the familial concept, became increasingly prominent in the early national years, largely as an outgrowth of Christian evangelicalism. Slaveholding benevolence never achieved more than spotty success. Yet the ideal of Christian slave stewardship was established as a way to distinguish respectability from churlishness. Stage three, state interposition, based on the growing use of civil bureaucracies and legal professionalization, had made only limited progress prior to 1861.

Sketchy though this description is, it helps to explain the point from which proslavery vindicators departed and the direction in which they were heading. Willie Lee Rose, one of our most perceptive southern scholars, observes a common tendency among historians to treat slavery—250 years old in America—as though it were "the same institution from start to finish." Proslavery authors did not make that mistake. They repudiated chattel bondage, but extolled the merits of patriarchal or "Bible slavery," as one apologist called it. James L. Petigru, a lawyer and planter in South Carolina, for instance, recognized the distinction in 1835 when he boasted, "The only thing to flatter my vanity as a proprietor is the evident and striking improvement in the moral and physical conditions of the negroes since they have been under my administration. When I took them, they were naked and destitute, now, there is hardly one that has not a pig at least." His Christian bounty left something to be desired. Yet, like most planters of the benevolent persuasion, Petigru judged his peformance against that of his forefathers and unenlightened neighbors. Robert Fogel and Stanley Engerman may have exaggerated the universality of Squire Allworthys like Petigru, but it stands to reason that advances in wealth and human sensibilities ameliorated plantation conditions, if only because the large slaveholders were becoming mindful of the comforts of general tidiness.[10]

The proslavery argument was largely based upon the familial solicitudes which Petigru serves to represent. A complementary development, stage three, was also emerging. State legislators passed laws that intervened in the personal relationships of master and subject. To safeguard the public against insurrection, masters lost the discretionary right to train slaves in literacy, to permit autonomous black assembly, even to use their property as clerks in stores.[11] Setting boundaries around various work specialties, excluding blacks, bond and free, from public places, and other forms of racial discrimination were already appearing on statute books long before 1865. At the same time, some slave states were enacting protective laws for the slave criminal and the slave victim of white crime as well.[12] These efforts at rationalizing the racial system not only conferred protections upon slaves and took away privileges from them, too. They also infringed upon the traditional options which chattel bondage had granted masters.

Likewise in jurisprudence, judges and lawyers sought to formalize the standards of admissible evidence, procedures, and resorts to appeal. Moreover, the penalties assigned to both white and black criminals were becoming more uniform and suasional rather than discretionary and corporal. This transition may have influenced plantation justice, though hardly enough to signify much. The Rever-

10. Willie Lee Rose, *Slavery and Freedom* (New York, 1982), 20; R. G. Grundy, "Thoughts for the People—No. 9," Memphis *Bulletin*, October 19, 1862; James L. Petigru to his daughter Jane North, December 24, 1835 [transcription], in James L. Petigru Papers, Library of Congress; see also William R. Taylor, *Cavalier and Yankee: The Old South and American National Character* (New York, 1961), 285–94; Robert W. Fogel and Stanley L. Engerman, *Time on the Cross: The Economics of American Negro Slavery* (2 vols.; Boston, 1974).

11. John C. Hurd, *The Law of Freedom and Bondage in the United States* (2 vols.; Boston, 1862), II, 94, 98, 107; Rosser H. Taylor, "Humanizing the Slave Code of North Carolina," *North Carolina Historical Review*, II (1925), 323–31.

12. Dale A. Somers, "Black and White in New Orleans: A Study in Urban Race Relations, 1865–1900," *Journal of Southern History*, XL (1974), 19; Hurd, *The Law of Freedom and Bondage*, II, 85, 91, 104, 106–107; Ivan E. McDougle, *Slavery in Kentucky, 1792–1865* (Lancaster, Pa., 1918), 36; Eugene D. Genovese, *Roll, Jordan, Roll: The World the Slaves Made* (New York, 1974), 37–39, 42.

end Charles C. Jones, an earnestly Christian master, was not a typical planter. Yet in 1859 he turned over to Georgia authorities a case of thievery, an offense usually handled at an owner's discretion. For lack of sufficient evidence, the case was dismissed. Jones was delighted. "It is my impression," he said, "that if owners would more frequently refer criminal acts of their servants to the decision of the courts, they would aid in establishing different kinds of crimes committed by Negroes, give better support to their own authority, and restrain the vices of the Negroes themselves." His son, a forward-looking lawyer, naturally and with pleasure agreed.[13]

The point of stressing the evolutionary character of slave culture is not to argue that the system would have died peacefully in a gush of Victorian sentiment, but for Yankee intervention and war. Far from it. Establishing the ideal of Christian masterhood and strengthening state controls fell short of genuine black autonomy of any kind. The evolutionary process was not toward freedom but rather toward more refined means of perpetuating black dependency, either through acts of personal benefaction or through state regulations which also reinforced white rule. One could argue that in fact intrusive patriarchal slavery was more psychically damaging in fashioning the Sambo personality than was haphazard chattel bondage. Under the latter formula, there was no reason to penetrate the slave's soul. The aim was not to save it, only to extract his labor. In any case, the evolution of slavery—"the domestication of domestic slavery," as Willie Rose calls it—was the chief point of departure for southern antebellum polemics. There is little need to explain the attractiveness of the domestic analogy. Not only was it an obvious contrast to the chattel servitude associated with the squalid foreign slave trade, outlawed since 1808, but it also was intimately connected with evangelical and indeed scriptural reverence for familial governance. As Frank Vandiver bluntly stated, "God counted in Dixie," especially

13. Daniel J. Flanigan, "Criminal Procedure in Slave Trials in the Antebellum South," *Journal of Southern History*, XL (1974), 537–64; Mark Tushnet, *The American Law of Slavery, 1810–1860: Considerations of Humanity and Interest* (Princeton, 1981); Charles C. Jones to Charles C. Jones, Jr., December 10, 1859, Jones, Jr., to Jones, December 12, 1859, both in Robert Manson Myers (ed.), *Children of Pride: A True Story of Georgia and the Civil War* (New Haven, 1972), 545, 546.

when it came to defending southern arrangements. The ordinary slaveholder, seldom a reading man, appreciated the domestic imagery and paternal authoritarianism that he heard from the pulpit.[14]

According to southern church fathers, slavery was a *condition*, not a moral evil.[15] As such it resembled the family, civil government, and hierarchies, all elements of social organization with which God had forever equipped his fallen, self-seeking creatures. To be sure, some proslavery advocates, mostly politicians, called the institution a "positive good," but the southern preacher generally claimed that it was only potentially so, according to the moral fiber of those involved. Like the southern lawyers, the professional clergy admired uniformity and rational objectives, in the evangelical assumption that what was truly practical and profitable was also divinely blessed. Therefore they championed a form of slaveholding that extended the protective authority of a loving father over the entire household of whites and blacks. Self-disciplined reciprocations of loyalty and duty bound the organic plantation community. Thus, in a vigorous attack on abolitionist "disorganization," Lucy Kenny, a Virginia churchwoman, declared, "It is in the interest of the master to observe to his slave that kind of love which makes [the slave rejoice] to serve and obey his master; not with eye-service," but with heartfelt, Christian "willingness." To live up to the Christian proposition, however, was quite another matter, and the clergy, aware of human depravity, knew it.[16]

14. Bertram Wyatt-Brown, "The Ideal Typology and Ante-Bellum Southern History: A Testing of a New Approach," *Societas*, V (Winter, 1975), 16–22; Rose, *Slavery and Freedom*, 18–36; Frank E. Vandiver, "The Southerner as Extremist," in Vandiver (ed.), *The Idea of the South: Pursuit of a Central Theme* (Chicago, 1964), 45.

15. McNeilly, *Religion and Slavery*, 12–14; Natchez *Courier*, September 3, 1835; Albert G. Seal (ed.), "Notes and Documents: Letters from the South, a Mississippian's Defense of Slavery," *Journal of Mississippi History*, II (October, 1940), 212–31.

16. B. M. Palmer quoted in William S. Jenkins, *Pro-Slavery Thought in the Old South* (Chapel Hill, 1935), 216; David Ewart, *A Scriptural View of the Moral Relations of African Slavery* (Charleston, S.C., 1859), 9, 11; James H. Thornwell, *The Rights and Duties of Masters* (Charleston, S.C., 1850), 31; Charles C. Jones, *Religious Instruction of the Negroes in the United States* (Savannah, 1842), 227; "A Lady of Fredericksburg, Virginia" [Lucy Kenny], *A Death Blow to the Principles of Abolition* (Washington, D.C., 183?), 4; Pringle, *Slavery in the Southern States*, 17; Patricia Hickin, "'Situation Ethics' and Antislavery Attitudes in the Virginia Churches," in John B. Boles (ed.), *America: The Middle Period; Essays in Honor of Bernard Mayo* (Charlottesville, 1973), 188–215.

Religious simplicities not only established Abrahamic ideals of the slaveholding father, they also implicitly defined what was ungodly, disreputable. Without the domestic feature, declared one pious writer, "Negroes are herded on the plantation and propagate as mere animals." In contrast to unfeeling masterhood, Christopher Memminger, a Charleston layman, offered the ideal which steadily became the most popular rendering of regional self-congratulation: "The Slave Institution at the South increases her tendency to dignify the family. Each planter in fact is a Patriarch—his position compels him to be a ruler in his household," guiding children, female dependents, and slaves alike with steady hand and loving voice. Like the image of the southern lady, gracious and ethereal, the model of the Christian slaveholder was a stereotype that served a cultural function. It celebrated the alleged disappearance of old barbarisms and offered a standard of behavior to which respectable folk were to aspire. The lines between what was and what ought to be were hopelessly blurred, but the instructional function remained.[17]

Just as there was an outpouring of advice literature to parents and young people, so too advice on Christian masterhood flowed from busy southern pens. The duty of religious instruction to slaves was a chief concern. Particularly revealing was an emphasis upon the need for setting slaves on moral paths by internal mechanisms of control. Godly writers urged owners to reach for the Bible, not the lash. Like northern reformers, southern thinkers had begun to question old-fashioned corporal penalties in the handling of prisoners, schoolchildren, and youngsters in the home. Application to slave management was not surprising.[18]

The transition symbolized a growing awareness of new psychological techniques that encouraged self-discipline, inner moral conscious-

17. Grundy, "Thoughts for the People," Memphis *Bulletin*, October 19, 1862; Christopher G. Memminger, *Lecture Delivered Before the Young Men's Library Association of Augusta, April 10th, 1851* (Augusta, Ga., 1851), 14; Jones, *Religious Instruction*, 241–42.

18. William G. Simms, "The Morals of Slavery," in *The Pro-Slavery Argument*, 275; Calvin H. Wiley, "The Art of Governing," a chapter in "The Christian Duty of Masters" (MS in Calvin H. Wiley Papers, Southern Historical Collection, University of North Carolina Library, Chapel Hill); Ralph T. Parkinson, "The Religious Instruction of Slaves, 1820–1860" (M.A. thesis, University of North Carolina, 1948), 13–15.

ness, and a sense of individual dignity. Thomas S. Clay of Bryan County, Georgia, and Calvin Wiley, a noted advocate of white common schools in North Carolina, both advised masters to apply rational systems of rewards and nonphysical punishments to uplift slave morality. They and other such leaders as the Reverend Charles C. Jones also stressed that every proprietor should know his slaves as individuals and select those disciplinary means suited to the abilities and characters of each. Moreover, the Christian planter was supposed to follow scriptural injunctions about the material wants of his people, provisions for decent housing, clothing, food, and sense of privacy that would promote the moral welfare of the whole plantation. This humanitarian advice, though seldom followed in its totality, embraced these attributes of Victorian modernity: self-control, rationality, and practical consistency. One might agree with Kenneth Stampp that this missionary effort to masters was largely designed to make slave property more efficient and secure. So it was. But the aim was also to achieve the Christian order—conceived in the revival style of personal, immediate religion—that proslavery clergymen and laymen envisioned.[19]

When writing for northern audiences, proslavery thinkers grandly pronounced that moral slaveholding was as modern as any organic system, true to nature and to God. Yet in preaching at home, they found there was room for more cautionary evaluations. Calvin Wiley, for instance, directed his fury at those hypocrites who treated slaves "as chattel for profit and comfort" and who, to avoid a master's responsibilities, called the institution "an evil, a curse," in the manner of Thomas Jefferson. "This is not merely unchristian philosophy," he said. "It is supreme selfishness."[20]

Moving in religious and respectable circles, the clerical ideologues,

19. Thomas S. Clay, *Detail of a Plan for the Moral Improvement of Negroes on Plantations* (N.p., 1833); Wiley, "The Christian Duty of Masters"; Donald G. Mathews, "Reform in the Old South: Charles Colcock Jones and the Southern Evangelical Crusade to Form a Biracial Community," *Journal of Southern History*, XLI (1975), 299–320; Kenneth M. Stampp, *The Peculiar Institution: Slavery in the Antebellum South* (New York, 1956), 156–62.

20. Thornton Stringfellow, "The Bible Argument," in Elliott (ed.), *Cotton is King*, 522; George F. Holmes, in *Southern Literary Messenger*, XIX (June, 1853), 324; Wiley, "The Christian Duty of Masters."

however, romanticized what they saw and ignored the unpleasant. Newcomers to slaveholding ranks were pushing their way up the social ladder with little regard for the niceties of Christian slaveholding, a chiefly upper-class posture. The advice literature aimed at the new additions as well as at those whose experience with ownership entitled them to set community standards. But the proslavery advocate seldom acknowledged that his idealizations soothed more than they uplifted the savage white heart. Compared with Yankee evangelical zeal, the fires of southern missionary fervor flickered rather unevenly.

A major reason for that failure was the inability of the southern polemicists to set a model of proper benevolence that could satisfy outside criticism. They could not make others see that slaveholding, however mild, and the dictates of conscience were compatible. The evangelical scheme required that all men, regardless of color or condition, seek salvation on their own terms, a stress upon individuality, inner constraints of conscience, and freedom to act for good (or ill). Southern slaveholding, however, was ethically based upon the ancient heritage of honor, even though its defense had moved to more enlightened ground. That moral ordering identified good conduct and social hierarchy, with each soul situated along a moral continuum, roughly parallel with the power attributed to that rank. Slaves were naturally below the circles in which honor was distributed. Maintenance of that order was the duty of individuals and communities of whites; without close supervision the ethical as well as the social structure of society would supposedly end in chaos and bloodshed.

Whereas the evangelical nineteenth-century ethic stressed conscience and guilt, the southern ethic referred to honor and shame. The former system encouraged self-examination and reform, both personal and social; the latter taught conformity to tradition and subservience to community will. Conscience stimulated individualism—the freedom to dissent from accepted ways in the search for salvation in heaven. Honor demanded that men channel their ambitions toward personal fame, earned by fulfilling community needs, not by challenging community values. As these differences became clearer in northern eyes, the proslavery effort became increasingly difficult. At best the apologists could fall back on the "peculiarities" of their situation and the exigencies of preserving the Union and racial peace.

For all its manifold weaknesses, Christian familism, both as polemical rationale and as plantation practice wherever it took hold, was a moral advance. Within the restricted boundaries of southern solicitude over slavery, it was the most humane and popularly acceptable way to assist the slave and restore southern reputation. Certainly, it had the support of the enlightened part of the southern elite from whence most social, economic, and political progress—in education especially—originated.

By the 1850s, the evangelical premises for Christian slaveholding were beginning to unravel, not on a popular level, but rather as the inspiration for the southern intellectual defense of the institution. Proslavery propaganda thrived on sectional controversies in politics and the widening economic and demographic differences between the sections. Even evangelical stalwarts like the Reverend James Thornwell were humiliated by the change among Yankee conservatives, former allies: "They pity us—they lament our lot—admit our case is bad—but then we are not so much to be blamed. They curse us in their sympathies." Nothing could pain the southerner more than the thought that he had lost esteem and with it power over his destiny. This deep sense of shame, more than any other single factor, explains how southern Americans came to contemplate the prospect of secession, the only recourse left, some thought, to regain self-regard and autonomy for their region. As will be explained more fully later, honor was intimately connected with public reputation, and only by refashioning the boundaries of the nation itself could that reputation be once more sustained. Only the insinuations of the Devil himself could possibly account for northern malignancy. Mary Jones, wife of the Reverend Charles C. Jones, architect of the Christian Mission to the Slaves, remarked after Lincoln's election, "'Forebearance has ceased to be a virtue'; and I believe we could meet with no evils out of the Union that would compare to those we will suffer if we continue in it." Not long afterward when the Confederacy was born, she added, "*We* have no alternative."[21]

Despairing of the usefulness of the Christian defense, contemptuous of northern "mobocracy" and "cant," outraged at Whig party treachery, mistrustful of the northern Democrats and frustrated by the South's own cultural inferiority and sluggishness, the late antebellum southern thinker sought better weapons with which to strike back. Among the gloomiest and most acidulous of these men was Edmund Ruffin. His solution was the establishment of a new nation, a response which most of those in the southern evangelical tradition were much slower to accept. Deeply troubled by "hypochondria" (the term for depression), Ruffin all but left behind his interests in agrarian reforms to promote his special vision, one which soon had a powerful following. He had never been particularly comfortable about Christian masterhood as an adequate defense. Suffering from a frail body, scarred by an unhappy childhood, and burdened with a disagreeable temperament, Ruffin made up for his inner sense of inadequacy as a man with belligerence toward enemies, real and imagined. Every critical remark, every sign of slight neglect, he seemed to feel, exposed him to public ridicule. He reacted throughout his life with stern criticism of even his friends, who naturally drew back in anger and diffidence. Long before he pulled the trigger that ended his life when the experiment failed in 1865, Ruffin knew the terrors of existential meaninglessness. He was aware of the cyclical character of his relationship with an unheeding southern public. It led him to hope for early death. "I could not (& never can) bridle my tongue," he wrote shortly after firing the first shot at Fort Sumter. Momentarily in public favor, he realized that when "my free censures & opinions [of others reached] their ears, I would be again building up for myself the load of disfavor & odium which I had before borne, & which my recent celebrity, & general applause, had served but partially to hide. . . . I feel, in sincerity & earnestness, that I have now lived long enough—& for my own future place in the opinion & regard of my

21. Thornwell, *The Rights and Duties of Masters*, 12; Mary Jones to Charles C. Jones, Jr., November 15, 1860, January 3, 1861, both in Myers (ed.), *Children of Pride*, 628, 641.

countrymen, it will be best for me to die very soon." Time, by which fame could be measured, was his enemy. Self-pity that masked self-loathing drove him to thoughts of death, but only when the shame of southern defeat suggested his own ineffectuality did he actually kill himself.[22]

Although temperamentally less bitter and pessimistic than Ruffin, George Fitzhugh also reflected the secularizing evolution of proslavery thought. "Twenty years ago," declared Fitzhugh in 1857, "the South had no thought—no opinion of her own." At that time, the region "stood behind all christendom, admitted her social structure, her habits, her economy, and her industrial pursuits to be wrong, deplored them as a necessity, and begged pardon for their existence." But, he boasted, a new order of things prevailed as other nations found "wage slavery" a system with grave defects and looked enviously upon the southern mode. "This, of itself, would put the South at the lead of modern civilization," he insisted.[23]

George Frederick Holmes, among others, was more than displeased with Fitzhugh's showy eccentricities. The southern philosopher accused "the Sage of Port Royal" of "that very intellectual anarchy" which Holmes believed was the curse of the era. Far from being original, Fitzhugh simply was repeating the same utopian musings that appeared in somewhat different form from the pens of the godless socialists of France and Germany. Certainly for the general reading public in the South, Fitzhugh was far too esoteric to gain a full hearing. Like Holmes, planters with some intellectual pretensions preferred the classic issues of religious concern: the fight over free will and Calvinist predetermination, science and theology, the future direction of Protestantism, the Christian applications to slavery. Nevertheless, Fitzhugh was a part of the movement away from

22. Betty L. Mitchell, *Edmund Ruffin: A Biography* (Bloomington, 1981), 104–120, 254–56; Ruffin, May 4, 1861, in *The Years of Hope, April, 1861–June, 1863* (Baton Rouge, 1977), 20. Vol. II of *The Diary of Edmund Ruffin*, ed. William K. Scarborough, 3 vols. projected.
23. George Fitzhugh, "Southern Thoughts," *De Bow's Review*, XXIII (October, 1857), 357; George Fitzhugh *Cannibals All! or Slaves Without Masters*, ed. C. Vann Woodward (Cambridge, Mass., 1960), esp. xxxiv–xxxviii; see also Eugene D. Genovese, *The World the Slaveholders Made: Two Essays in Interpretation* (New York, 1969), 195–201.

strictly theological argumentation and toward a visionary quest for the perfect slave society.[24]

More intriguing was the romantic impulse of Henry Hughes, about whom little has appeared in historical literature. Although unique, and therefore not representative, Hughes is worth examining. His self-infatuation illustrated a general problem for southern intellectuals. Although hoping to gain world respect as well as local standing, the southern thinker was driven back into himself by the provinciality of his own perspective and his sense of uselessness in a society and nation that failed to see his talents. At one time, as Drew Faust has observed, men of the caliber of Thomas Jefferson and other gentlemen-thinkers had served their country, region, and intellectual callings, for which sacrifices they were honored. American intellectuals, especially ones in southern backlands, could no longer hope for such rewards. Even the South had become too democratic for such dreams to be easily fulfilled.[25]

A product of the Southwest, Hughes's father was a planter in Mississippi. His mother came from Franklin, Louisiana, in the rich sugar-planting district of Atakapas. Like so many other southern men of letters, Hughes was a brilliant student of the classics, literature, and philosophy. Yet, his teachers at struggling Oakland College near Natchez presented to him no intellectual challenges, a problem that beset nearly all proslavery authors who were of southern origins. His senior class had only seven members. In 1848, when he was nineteen, Hughes started a diary, dedicating it to "my soul and to Fame" and pledging himself to be "unfailingly devoted on the sacred night of every week, to the purposes of recording my meditations, emotions, aims and circumstances." It would be of service, he thought, to "the future biographer."[26]

Certainly young men at Yale, Princeton, and other more learned spots than Oakland shared similar hopes in bright naïveté. But his ruminations had a special southern cast. Whereas northern roman-

24. Neal C. Gillespie, *The Collapse of Orthodoxy: The Intellectual Ordeal of George Frederick Holmes* (Charlottesville, 1972), 177.
25. See Faust, *A Sacred Circle.*
26. Henry Hughes Diary, January 1, 1848 (MS in Hughes Papers).

tics of similar gifts often worried about their godly faith, Hughes had other concerns. Like Edmund Ruffin, William J. Grayson, James Henry Hammond, and George F. Holmes—all proslavery recluses who felt alone even in the company of others—Hughes suffered from anguish and melancholia. The problem for all these men was partly the sense of personal inadequacy, as if intellectuality had unmanned them. They were seldom happy in the ordinary ambitions of life. They despised the everyday routines of planting or county-court pleading and the "groveling" to the masses required of office-seekers. As Drew Faust has remarked, men like Holmes, Hammond, Grayson, and Ruffin reassured each other that their beloved "South treated the man of mind—be he poet or scientific agriculturist—as a prophet without honor." Hammond, she continues, wrote to Ruffin, "I have no assistant, no sympathizer, no consoler." Likewise, Hughes simply despised his life as a country lawyer in Mississippi. Yet, he had left the opportunities of a New Orleans practice for the serenity of Port Gibson, perhaps because he feared hard competition. His thoughts on the subject were unusual: "Let me shuffle of[f] this mortal coil, and burst forth into unpenetrated regions of space where God dwells in solitude and rush around the Circuit infinety [sic]," the last phrase a reference to his occupation of following the judge from one county seat to the next. Boredom, limited choice of intellectual company, long drizzling days of winter, the heat of summer, and yet intelligence enough to yearn for intellectual excitement led to deep frustration. "My weariness," he wrote in 1849, "changes to impatience, impatience to ambition, till my frame quivers with passions which find no vent." Fantasies of other times and places furnished him small relief: "Oh for the Attic Sea-shore and cave."[27]

In his diary, Hughes recorded his preoccupation with the death of his father, the fleeting of time, and a mordant dread of dying ingloriously and forgotten. It almost seemed that his literary efforts and hopes for the future were a propitiation to his father Benjamin, who had died, Hughes wrote, "while my life was in its Spring." His

27. Drew Gilpin Faust, *James Henry Hammond and the Old South: A Design for Mastery* (Baton Rouge, 1982), 238; Hughes Diary, January 1, 1848, January 20, 1849, December 20, 1851, March 14, May 16, 1852.

musings on God the Father, and father the god, were sexual and violent: "My Father, you made me—let me talk so—I was your darling & hero; but if in what is thus done by me and through you, I am beguiled; if Oh my Soul, there is for me no Father, no caressing God; let then all Earth yawn its chops and gorge with men & blood its gut of fire; let all stars, suns and comets shoot into solid coal and flicker into ashy nothing. For a soul is lost, lost; a soul is, is lost! I fear then my soul is lost." His poetic inclinations bordered on the incoherent at times, a mixture of Blakean mysticism, visceral fury, and total egoism:

> Wherefore? Why? Open your lips:—What?—Fool!
> child, babe, dreamer. Oh! Eye of God! Oh, Jesus—
> bosom, Oh Holy Dove, coo in my ear. These fingers;—
> I clutch my hands; beat my bosom; tear my scalp;—
> swell veins & pop. There's blood; that: real. It
> is pain. That is in my mind; my mind is myself.
> Myself,—I, am—am—Planets, the blue deserts,
> wanderers of the camels foot, & night-bird's eye:
> that man of god of War & Glory. I am Glory's boy
> & Destiny's. Farewell. We will meet in—

In this passage he revealed a mental state that rather resembled Walt Whitman's, a poet whom he could not yet have read. Although his free verse was unsustained, Hughes at least had experimented with a new form, whereas Grayson had adopted the eighteenth-century heroic couplet for his *Hireling and the Slave*, an interminable proslavery pastoral. Hughes liked, as did Whitman, "working men. . . . I have been talking to engineers about improvements of steam-engines. Engineers are my favorites."[28]

Like Ruffin, Hughes was driven by his feelings of emptiness to dream longingly of death. "Thought on suicide, often have the wish, but something seems to detain me. But little binds to earth, me," he wrote in 1850. It is somewhat surprising to find in an antebellum intellectual the same fear of time, connected with suppressed anger and distress with a father, that Faulkner portrayed in Quentin Compson. Elated at times by yearnings for honor, Hughes, as a young college graduate, worried about the flow of time. "The yellow Tiber of Time," he lamented, "grows for me, too strong: Help, help me Cassius

28. Hughes Diary, June 27, 1851, October 19, 26, 1851.

or I sink." Hughes was referring to Shakespeare's *Julius Caesar*. Early in the play, to tempt Brutus, Cassius reports that he and Caesar had raced in the Tiber, but he had had to rescue Caesar, proof of Caesar's vulnerability as a mortal. Hughes linked the image of drowning and thoughts of his mother, who, he noted, was sitting nearby at the time of his writing the entry. Usually, however, Hughes identified time's passing with the death of his father. "My father, what is life; Time is gone." In a curious metaphor, Hughes added, "I wish that Time had a serpent's coil weighing down his wing."[29]

Hughes's narcissistic adumbrations upon themes of valor and slaveholding power led him to conjure up in his mind "A Universal Republic, Ultimum Organum, Longitude, Slavery Perfect Society; Myself, the God-beloved, the human supreme of Earth's Politics, Society, Philosophy, Economics, Religion & Aesthetics; Of these I am the devotee." Such thoughts were not merely the romantic effusions of a young man with immature ideas. They were evidence of a tragic psychological and cultural flaw in southern culture long before Faulkner depicted them in *The Sound and the Fury*. The soul-destroying character of egoistic honor was one of the novelist's most thoroughly articulated themes. Fixation upon that ideal had already caused southerners to turn inward and distorted their sense of reality before the Civil War began. Henry Hughes was among its victims in real life even as he was its votary, no less than Edmund Ruffin was. Where other statesmen—Lamartine, Richelieu, Caesar, Socrates—had failed, he said, "May I perfect."[30]

Consumed with a yearning to be the South's leading philosopher of slavery, Hughes also sought to be the epical hero or statesman as well. (Later, he won a state senatorship, though nothing grander.) He joined a secret club, "'the Order of the Lone Star which he thought might be the means to renown and nobility.' If this Order is honorable . . . I wish to use it in my life-aim of a Universal Republic." Humdrum politics, however, was not enough. "Calhoun, Clay, Webster, all are dead," he wrote in 1852. "I had rather not be than to be no

29. Hughes Diary, September 15, October 20, 1850, June 27, August 22, October 24, 1852.
30. Hughes Diary, October 21, 1851, October 24, 1852, April 3, 1853.

more than they were." Higher attainments, he ruminated at his office in sleepy Port Gibson, were possible: "'Perseverance keeps honor bright.'"[31]

The culture of the antebellum South was too antipodal, secondary, and dependent upon the good opinion of the metropolitan centers of the North and England to stand alone. The ethic by which white southerners lived was already dying. No late fantasies like Hughes's could breathe fresh life into it. Victorian morality, for all the impositions of the Christian mission to slaves and planters, was crowding the old traditions of unself-conscious masterhood from one side; the modern world of capitalism and mass society was pressing in on the other. Southern planters themselves were becoming piously Yankee-fied, an ironic result of the Christian effort to improve southern manners and ethics. At the same time, changes in the market world were compelling planters to become ever more commercial themselves. As his funeral orator said in admiration, Hughes was personally immune to thoughts of "money and money-getting, in a climate which enervates and in a community which falls down in prostrate adoration before cotton bales." Others were not.[32]

Like Fitzhugh, Hughes sought to change the character of slavery, less by moral instruction, than by endowing it with secular objectives. Aware that the name itself was cause for world disapprobation, he called it "warranteeism" in his *Treatise on Sociology* published in 1854. The concept may have been new to the South, but one suspects that he, in a manner akin to Fitzhugh, borrowed the approach from Thomas Carlyle. In *Past and Present*, Carlyle had romanticized Abbot Samson and his monks at Bury Saint Edmunds as a way to challenge the mechanistic society of middle-class England. As if the slaves were peasants under a beaming supervisor at a twelfth-century priory, Hughes pictured "the happy warrantees [who] shall banquet in plantation refectories, worship in plantation chapels; sit in plantation saloons, at the cool of evening, or in the green and bloomy gloom of cold catalpas and magnolias, chant songs, tell tales; or, to the

31. Hughes Diary, October 31, 1852.
32. Hughes Diary, October 24, 1852; W. D. Moore, *The Life and Works of Col. Henry Hughes: A Funeral Sermon* . . . (Mobile, 1863), 24.

metered rattle of chanting castanets, or flutes, or rumbling tambourines, dance down the moon and evening star." The Reverend Hightower in his rhapsodies about glories that never were could not have improved upon Hughes's ecstasy. But unlike Carlyle, Hughes did not believe that a return to the serene faith of medieval times could redeem the South in its own view or restore national regard.[33]

Hughes had studied in Paris under the positivist philosopher Auguste Comte, who shared his religious doubts. Borrowing from Charles Fourier and other European socialists, Hughes strove for an indigenous modernity. Conscious that the South had emerged from barbarous beginnings, he proclaimed a new era of slaveholding, based not upon faith, family, or benevolence but upon current trends in the Western world. "We know that our peculiar establishment is with a rapidity unparalled [sic] and marvelous perfecting itself; and hastening to set before civilized nations . . . a labor system . . . they must copy . . . to prevent pestilence, starvation and countless crimes." A believer in earthly perfection that any good Calvinist like Thornwell would consider blasphemous, Hughes announced the total withering away of the savage aspect of bondage. That form of slavery, "a system of inhumanity and injustice," he confessed, had existed at the time of the Revolution. Its horrors had moved the northern Founding Fathers to emancipate northern slaves, even as southern heroes, like Washington and Jefferson, despaired that the system could ever be reformed. Knowing only the polarities of free and slave arrangements, they failed to see, Hughes claimed, the potentiality for another mode of labor discipline. But, he continued, this third form had evolved in the nineteenth-century South, a system that Hughes called "liberty labor." By the term, Hughes meant a labor-capital association, ruled by "moral duty, civilly enforced."[34]

The young American romanticist made no direct attack on Chris-

33. Henry Hughes, *Treatise on Sociology: Theoretical and Practical* (1854; rpr. New York, 1968), 292; Thomas Carlyle, *Past and Present*, ed. Richard D. Altick (1843; Boston, 1965), 72–136.
34. *Southern Commercial Convention, Vicksburg, Miss. A Report on the African Apprenticeship System, Read at the Southern Commercial Convention by Henry Hughes. Held at Vicksburg, May 10th, 1859* (Vicksburg, 1859), 2–3, 12; Hughes, *Treatise on Sociology*, 91.

tian patriarchalism, but, like so many other Victorian intellectuals, he had lost faith in revealed religion. Out of a sense of duty, however, he held religious classes for blacks in Port Gibson and later for Confederate soldiers under his command in Virginia. For himself, though, he reserved a conviction in the absolutes of morality, enjoined not by divinity but by the state. Thus, "moral duty, civilly enforced" became the instrument of his slave millennium. Strangely enough, his disposition, his search for a utopia divorced from church institutions, resembled some features of Garrison's theology of moral absolutism. Hughes, an ardent secessionist, raised the figurative banner "No Union with *Non*-Slaveholders."[35]

Unlike most southerners, Hughes admired the power and uses of the state, which he defined as "the economic sovereign. It is the supreme orderer. The capitalist [or slave master] is its deputy orderer." Thus, he maintained, slavery was an agency of the state, though management was delegated to owners. In this reading, the planter was a state functionary, a lay magistrate, exercising powers for the benefit of the commonwealth. To be sure, Hughes granted the familial concept a place in the scheme, describing the laborer and the capitalist as members of "the same family," with the head of the household warranting "subsistence to all." The planter's motive was neither personal profit nor paternal solicitude; instead, he undertook slaveholding responsibilities because of a sense of "civic duty." Honor, not submission to Christ, was Hughes's imperative, as it was for Ruffin. The difference was Hughes's fascination with state power, albeit of a purely abstract kind. Ruffin, one imagines, would not have approved.[36]

However eccentric and blind to realities Hughes was, his dreams illustrated the trends and problems of the day. Like his fellow southern thinkers, Hughes feared "mobocracy" in the North or the South, but he wanted slaves in every home, a program requiring the reopening of trade with Africa. The advantages, he thought, were compelling: a lessening of white class antagonisms; the reorientation of the Upper South toward slaveholding neighbors; increased regional

35. Moore, *The Life and Works of Hughes*, 28–31; Ronald T. Takaki, *A Pro-Slavery Crusade: The Agitation to Reopen the African Slave Trade* (New York, 1971), 86–102.
36. Hughes, *Treatise on Sociology*, 110, 113, 256; see Genovese, *The World the Slaveholders Made*, 167, 181, 188, 236–37.

prosperity; greater congressional representation. Other zealots were making similar expansionary pleas in the 1850s, but Hughes had something more in mind than simply alleviating problems of labor shortage.[37]

In speeches and newspaper columns, Hughes championed what he called "African Contract Labor," whereby imported blacks would serve fifteen-year apprenticeships. Their numbers, he believed, should be so massive that their presence would alter existing slave arrangements. Gradually the contract form would apply universally, perhaps within twenty years. Careful not to appear subversive of perpetual bondage, Hughes left unclear whether the African coolies would subsequently become permanent slaves or whether resident slaves would merge into semi-autonomous peonage. So long as whites retained control of black destiny, it probably mattered little to him.[38]

Intrigued with the possibilities of civil bureaucracy as a source for progress and internal security, Hughes envisioned new regulations under state auspices. Through the taxing power, for instance, the state could ensure a safe proportion of whites to blacks, native or otherwise, in any region. Furthermore, even prior to the reintroduction of African workers, there had to be new laws restricting the subservient race to noncompetitive, unskilled employments, thereby enabling poor whites to fill the positions that an expanding, diversified economy created. At the same time, Hughes told a commercial convention at Vicksburg in 1859, the state must regulate "the negroes' hours of service, holidays, and food, raiment, habitation and peculium, and the other elements of their wages."[39]

Satisfied though he was that slave criminals had already gained sufficient protections, he offered a few "minor betterments" of his

37. Henry Hughes, "Warranteeism and Free Labor," *Eagle of the South* (Jackson, Miss.), March 28, 1859, and "Re-Opening of the Slave Trade," *Southern Reveille*, July 30, 1859, both clippings in Hughes Scrapbook.
38. Henry Hughes, "A Quartette of Objectives to African Labor Immigration," March 9, 1858, clipping, in Hughes Scrapbook; see also Stella Herron, "The African Apprentice Bill," *Proceedings of the Mississsippi Valley Historical Association, for the Year 1914–15* (Cedar Rapids, 1916), 135–45.
39. Henry Hughes, "Negro Mechanics," *Eagle of the South*, October 16, 1858, and "Large Slaveholders and the African Immigration Scheme," New Orleans *Delta*, February 14, 1858, both clippings in Hughes Scrapbook; Hughes, *Treatise on Sociology*, 112, 199–200, 233–34; *Southern Commercial Convention*, 12.

own. The state, he suggested, ought to pay full, not partial, compensation to owners of convicted slaves in order to encourage masters to surrender suspects instead of rushing them off to another state for sale. Also, he urged Mississippi legislators to provide penitentiary sentences for slave convicts to replace some capital and corporal mandates. All these plans required an expanded public service to rationalize race controls. Like T. R. Dew and other proslavery thinkers, Hughes believed that the expansion of southern population, newspaper networks, education, and transportation systems had made it easier, not harder, to control the underclass.[40]

In October, 1862, Henry Hughes, a colonel at the head of the 12th Mississippi Regiment, died from a war-related illness at his home in Port Gibson. He lived to see neither the defeat of the nation of which he had dreamed as the "Ultimum Organum," nor the enactment of the black codes of 1865. These fiercely suppressive laws to subvert Yankee-imposed emancipation came closer to what Hughes had in mind than did any arrangement in the slave regime for which his schemes were designed. An earnest advocate of Christian masterhood preached the funeral oration at the Methodist church in Port Gibson. The Reverend W. D. Moore could scarcely conceal his distress that Hughes had lived a life of religious doubt. Although disturbed at Hughes's admiration for "the socialistic writers" of Paris, Moore took solace in his friend's search for truth. As a Christian, Moore was proud of his opposition to Hughes's plan for African contract labor, given the dismal record of the old trade and the continued imperfections of men.[41]

For those who believed in the more familiar, domestic vision of servitude, Henry Hughes had pushed too far ahead, toward the bureaucratic impersonality of an industrial apartheid.[42] By the time that system of exploitation was adopted, the proslavery argument was thoroughly repudiated and Hughes long since consigned to obliv-

40. Henry Hughes, "Compensation for Executed Slaves," Port Gibson (Miss.) *Herald*, June 18, 1856, and "Re-Opening of the Slave Trade," *Southern Reveille*, July 30, 1859, both clippings in Hughes Scrapbook.

41. Moore, *The Life and Works of Hughes*, 9, 10, 17, 30–31.

42. Ronald T. Takaki, *Iron Cages: Race and Culture in 19th Century America* (New York, 1979), 205.

ion. Fortunately, Yankees had intervened before so grim a transformation of slavery had really begun in earnest. At least, in a manner of speaking, Jim Crow at the start of the twentieth century was not literally a ward of the state, as Hughes had planned, or a possession of a condescending, Bible-toting patrician, as the clergy and pious laymen had sought to fashion. Hughes was at once the most introspective and most forward-looking of the proslavery zealots. Foolish and romantic, he dreamed of a corporate servitude that would have met outside criticism by conferring some nominal rights to the slaves. But the oppression of the black race would have continued as inexorably as ever. In the latter part of the Victorian age, as evangelical enthusiasms further declined and tenets of racial Darwinism, industrial boosterism, and imperialistic destiny arose, what room would there have been for the flowering of sentimental Christian mastery in the southern states? The speculation that the country, spared both the Civil War and emancipation, might well have become a richer, more powerful version of South Africa may be fanciful. C. Vann Woodward and George M. Fredrickson have already called attention to the parallels between the two biracial societies during the post-Reconstruction years, but as Fredrickson said, their paths "diverged" after the First World War, a change that surely would have been severely limited in a South free to pursue its own fate. In this tragic context, the Union dead, it seems, had not bled in vain.[43]

In his funeral speech in 1863, Moore promised the dead hero of Port Gibson immortality in the memory of grateful descendants, always the primary reward for men of valor. The thought was homeric, but the reality was scarcely epical. Hughes's failure was the bankruptcy of the late proslavery movement itself. Modernity and tradition could not be so easily harmonized as he and others thought. Still worse, the attempt helped to set a pattern that would not be broken for many years. The cause of white supremacy lived on in new guises. It was no more static in the postwar years than it had been prior to Lincoln's election. There was a constant struggle to match changing

43. C. Vann Woodward, *The Strange Career of Jim Crow* (3rd rev. ed.; New York, 1974), 111–12, 121–22; George M. Fredrickson, *White Supremacy: A Comparative Study in American and South African History* (New York, 1981), 329–82.

conditions with fresh, plausible reasons for holding the blacks in bondage for the sake of southern honor, however tawdry it had become and perhaps always had been ever since Sir Walter Raleigh had first dreamed of ruling El Dorado.

The tribute exacted was the intellectual's compulsion to dream, not to think boldly, to cajole ordinary southerners into continuing to believe that he was Christian and honorable and his assumptions right and true. Although self-convinced of guiltlessness by any moral gauge, the southern apologist was alienated not only from the greater world of letters but from himself as well. Not until a second catastrophic war once again confronted the South with fresh moral assumptions was the southern intellectual freed, at least in part, from the shackles of the past.

As a spokesman for a social order fast slipping away, Hughes was no less innocent in 1863 than he had been as a young romanticist a decade earlier. In contrast, such leaders of the post–World War I Southern Renaissance, such as William Faulkner, were at last enabled to feel the guilt for ancient and present wrong that abolitionists had tried so hard to impress upon Hughes's generation. The breaking of the old southern ethic had made that transformation in sensibility possible. But for Hughes and his colleagues in the pro-slavery effort, the persistence of a traditional culture protected them from a sense of tragedy and wrong that could have been the beginning of self-knowledge. Visionary to the end, Hughes whispered to his Methodist friend three deathbed words: "Nos sumus purificate." Perhaps, as the Reverend W. D. Moore intoned from the pulpit, "a few moments after he was indeed purified forever from earthly sins and sorrows."[44] The same could not be said for the South he died to save.

44. Moore, *The Life and Works of Hughes*, 35.

VII

HONOR AND SECESSION

Send Danger from the east unto the west,
So Honour cross it from the north to south,
And let them grapple. O, the blood more stirs
To rouse a lion than to start a hare!
                    Hotspur, in *I Henry IV*, I, iii, 195–98

THE AIM of this final chapter is more modest than its title and location in the book suggest. Who nowadays would dare to substitute another theory for the long-standing view that slavery was the sole cause for the great catastrophe? According to Civil War historian Philip S. Paludan, "We know with some precision why the South seceded." Lincoln's election, he explains, was a threat to the "survival of slavery, the foundation for the Southern way of life." Linking the issue of southern devotion to liberty with the maintenance of slavery, William J. Cooper, Jr., has driven home the same idea in two major studies. At a time when scholars agree about very little, it would be perverse to cast doubt on so acceptable a proposition.[1]

Evidence for the centrality of slavery in southern political thought and action is ubiquitous. Politicians endorsed the arguments of the proslavery intellectuals: R. K. Call, governor of Florida, argued in 1860 that "slavery, like all other institutions, is on the line of progress and improvement. . . . It is no longer a remnant of barbarism, but an agent of civilization." In 1861, Alexander H. Stephens, Con-

Paper delivered at the Southern Historical Association meeting, November 4, 1982, Memphis, Tennessee.
    1. Philip S. Paludan, "The American Civil War as a Crisis in Law and Order," *American Historical Review*, LXXVII (1972), 1013; William J. Cooper, Jr., *The South and the Politics of Slavery, 1828–1856* (Baton Rouge, 1978), and *Liberty and Slavery: Southern Politics to 1860* (New York, 1983). For an excellent historiographical overview, see Daniel W. Crofts, "New Perspectives on Southern Politics: The 1850s and the Secession Crisis" (MS in possession of Crofts).

federate vice-president, carried the point still further when he proclaimed that the new government's "corner-stone rests upon the
great truth that the negro is not equal to the white man; that slavery—subordination to the superior race—is his natural and normal
condition." Such differentiations, he continued, were "in conformity
with the ordinance of the Creator."[2]

Nevertheless, it is also true that direct jeopardy to the institution
was distant, despite the results of the 1860 contest. Judge I. B.
McFarland, a Texas Unionist, asked, "Why all this hot haste [to se-
cede]?" The incoming president will be "left powerless for either good
or evil—he cannot even form his Cabinet without the consent and
concurrence of a Democratic Senate." As the judge and other thoughtful contemporaries recognized, most Yankees would much prefer
peace and constitutional regularity to a confrontation over the election. Under those circumstances, the Republican administration
would have been totally irresponsible to tamper with southern property rights. In addition, the Democrats were still ready to serve as
watchdogs. Although momentarily divided into quarreling Douglasite, Buchananite, and Southern Rights factions, the Jacksonian
party continued to uphold ideals southerners embraced: limited government; agrarian policies (in particular, low tariffs); and above all,
white supremacy. Northern Democrats had little trouble including
the slaveholding states in their sense of nationalistic unity.[3]

Moreover, recent studies have cast doubt on the once popular view
that disunionism was exclusively the work of the wealthiest Lower
South slaveholders defending their gains and livelihood. Instead, the
planter class was sharply divided on the right response to Lincoln's
installation. Shortly after the election results were known, Alexander Stephens, for instance, begged his fellow Georgians not to "yield
to passion [and] take that step" which would only make everyone

2. R. K. Call, *Address to the People of Florida* (Lake Jackson, Fla., 1860), 15; Alexander Stephens, "Speech Delivered on the 21st March, 1861, in Savannah, Known as
'The Corner Stone Speech,'" in Henry Cleveland, *Alexander H. Stephens in Public and
Private with Letters and Speeches, Before, During and Since the War* (Philadelphia,
1866), 721.

3. McFarland quoted in Frank H. Smyrl, "Unionism in Texas, 1856–1861," *South-
western Historical Quarterly*, LXVIII (1964), 187; Jean H. Baker, *Affairs of Party: The
Political Culture of Northern Democrats in the Mid-Nineteenth Century* (Ithaca, 1983),
317–54.

"demons" ready to cut each other's throat. Nor was the Georgia senator's a lone voice. The wealthy James Henry Hammond was another who believed that the best course would be a revival of the old cross-sectional conservative alliance that had held the Union together in the past.[4]

The reluctance of those with the most to lose was only one of several indications that more than just slavery was at work in the secessionist dynamic. Slavery was itself inseparable from other aspects of regional life, most especially from the southerners' sense of themselves as a people. That self-perception can be called the principle of honor. In modern times the term has so little meaning that it occupies, says sociologist Peter Berger, "about the same place in contemporary usage as chastity." Nevertheless, though sometimes seen as simply a "romance" to prettify the harsh reality of race control, it was a powerful force in the nineteenth-century South.[5]

Honor may be described in a number of ways, both characterologic and social. It can be considered as general demeanor or gentlemanliness; virtue, that is, trustworthiness and honesty; entitlement; or class rank. Certainly southerners believed that dependability for truth-telling was a prime aspect of honorable character, but it was more than that and also more than a fascination with titles like Colonel and Judge, forms of address that southerners were notoriously prone to crave. Honor will be used here in two separate sociological and ethical senses: the southern mode, which might be called traditional honor, and the mid-nineteenth-century northern one. The latter represented, to use Berger's term, an *"embourgeoisement"* of the concept—diminishing its feudal and communal overtones and adding an institutional, impersonal, and middle-class element.[6]

In regard to traditional honor, the concept involves process more

4. Alexander Stephens, "Speech Against Secession" [November 14, 1860], in Cleveland, *Alexander Stephens in Public and Private*, 704–708; Lawrence T. McDonnell, "Struggle Against Suicide: James Henry Hammond and the Secession of South Carolina," *Southern Studies*, XXII (1983), 115; Drew Gilpin Faust, *James Henry Hammond and the Old South: A Design for Mastery* (Baton Rouge, 1982), 331–59; Ralph A. Wooster, "The Secession of the Lower South: An Examination of Changing Interpretations," *Civil War History*, VII (1961), 117–27.
5. Peter Berger, "Excursus: On the Obsolescence of the Concept of Honor," in P. Berger and H. Kellner, *The Homeless Mind* (New York, 1974), 83.
6. *Ibid.*, 87.

than merely an idealization of conduct. First, honor is a sense of personal worth and it is invested in the whole person. Yet that whole covers more than the individual—it includes the identificaton of the individual with his blood relations, his community, his state, and whatever other associations the man of honor feels are important for establishing his claim for recognition. The close bonding of honor with an extended self, as it were, contrasts with the kind of honor that would place country before family, professional duty before other matters of importance. Second, honor as a dynamic connecting self and society requires that the individual make a claim for worthiness before the community, and third, it involves the acceptance of that self-evaluation in the public forum, a ratification that enables the claimant to know his place in society and his moral standing. "I am who I say I am" (or, more accurately, "I am who I seem to be"), says the man of traditional honor. We more likely might say, "I am who I am because of what I do." The timocratic community replies, "You are who you say you are." The exchange is completed with the registry of that reply upon the tablet of the individual's personality. He incorporates what is said and thought of him as part of his identity. Although honor can be directly internalized—to act *as if* a public were watching—it has few inner referents. Unlike the man of conscience, the individual dependent on honor must have respect from others as the prime means for respecting himself. Shifting fortunes, personal rivalries, worrisome doubts that one has been properly assessed make the ethical scheme an elusive, tense, and ultimately insecure method of self-acceptance. Western man has always known that traditional honor, being dependent upon public sanction, is a fickle mistress. Outward shows or honors—"place, riches, and favour,/ Prizes of accident"—sometimes matter as much as or more than merit, to borrow from Shakespeare, the southerners' most admired playwright.[7]

Ambiguities abound. On the one hand, moderation, prudence, coolness under duress, and self-restraint are admired and even idealized. The southern "Nestors" who urged calm deliberateness before

7. *Troilus and Cressida*, III, iii, 82–83.

entering on secession hoped to have these qualities approved in the public arena. On the other hand, the man of honor feels that defense of reputation and virility must come before all else. Otherwise, he is open to charges of effeminacy and fear. As Ulysses complains of his warrior colleagues:

> They tax our policy and call it cowardice,
> Count wisdom as no member of the war,
> Forestall prescience, and esteem no act
> But that of hand.[8]

In political terms, honor was not at all confined to those at the top of the social order. It is the nature of the ethic that it must be recognized by those with less status; otherwise, there would be none to render honor to claimants. In the American South, common folk, though not given to gentlemanly manners, duels, and other signs of a superior élan, also believed in honor because they had access to the means for its assertion themselves—the possessing of slaves— and because all whites, nonslaveholders as well, held sway over all blacks. Southerners regardless of social position were united in the brotherhood of white-skinned honor—what George M. Fredrickson has called herrenvolk democracy, though we might refer to it as people's timocracy.

It was upon this basis that John C. Calhoun and others came to admire the Periclean Greeks, devoted as the ancients were to *timē* (honor), democracy, republicanism, and small-community autonomy. In the Greek city-states "the passionate drive to show one's self in measuring up against others," said Hannah Arendt, was the actual basis for politics. To some extent, the same held true in the South. Politics was an arena in which peers—not necessarily the greatest magnates—were rivals for public acclaim and power. As a forum for self-presentation and public service, politics was a simple system to which elaborate bureaucracies, heavy taxes, statutory refinements, and other complexities were alien. Even the notion of party organization, as opposed to community consensus and unanimity on key principles, was suspect, at least among the firebrands for disunionism. In

8. *Ibid.*, I, iii, 197–200; see the essays in J. G. Peristiany (ed.), *Honour and Shame: The Values of Mediterranean Society* (London, 1965).

all societies where honor of this kind functions, the great distinction is drawn between the autonomy, freedom, and self-sufficiency of those in the body politic and the dependency, forced submissiveness, and powerlessness of all who are barred from political and social participation—that is, slaves or serfs. For the southern free white, dependency posed the threat of meaninglessness. Slaveholding ennobled, that is, enhanced one's status and independence because ownership provided the instruments for exercising power, not over the slave alone, but over those without that resource. By the same social perception, thralldom degraded and humbled. "The essence of honor," says one writer, "is personal autonomy" or freedom to do what one wishes, and its absence indicates powerlessness.[9]

Under these circumstances, the reasons why the southerner felt so threatened by northern criticism should be clear. The dread of public humiliation, especially in the highly charged political setting, was a burden not to be casually dismissed. In general terms, whenever the public response to claims for respect is indifferent, disbelieving, hostile, or derisive, the claimant for honor feels as blasted, as degraded as if struck in the face or unceremoniously thrown to the ground. He is driven to a sense of shame—the very opposite of honor. The response is twofold: first, a denial that he, a persecuted innocent, seeks more than his due; and second, his outraged "honor" requires immediate vindication, by force of arms if need be. This was especially true for the antebellum southerner because he could hardly escape doubts that his section was perceived by the world as inferior, morally and materially. "Reputation is everything," said James Henry Hammond. "Everything with me depends upon the estimation in which I am held," confessed secessionist thinker Beverley Tucker. Personal repu-

9. Paul A. Rahe, "The Primacy of Politics in Classical Greece," *American Historical Review*, LXXXIX (1984), 265–93; Arendt quoted in Michael Walzer, Review of M. I. Finley's *Politics in the Ancient World*, in *New Republic*, December 12, 1983, p. 36. On fears of modern party manipulations, see J. Mills Thornton III, *Politics and Power in a Slave Society: Alabama, 1800–1860* (Baton Rouge, 1978), 365–71, and Pauline Maier, "The Road Not Taken: Nullification, John C. Calhoun, and the Revolutionary Tradition in South Carolina," *South Carolina Historical Magazine*, LXXXII (1981), 1–19. Orlando Patterson, *Slavery and Social Death: A Comparative Study* (Cambridge, Mass., 1982), 79–101; Julian A. Pitt-Rivers, "Honor," in David L. Sills (ed.), *International Encyclopedia of the Social Sciences* (18 vols.; New York, 1968), VI, 505.

tation for character, valor, and integrity did not end there. Individual self-regard encompassed wider spheres. As a result, the southerner took as personal insult the criticisms leveled at slave society as a whole.[10]

Before dealing with southern honor more extensively, we must briefly differentiate it from the northern concept. By the mid-nineteenth century, according to historian Edward L. Ayers, it had come to mean individualistic dignity. The possessor of this quality settled disputes by peaceful means for the sake of state-regulated order and relied upon the dictates of conscience in all his dealings. "In a culture of dignity," Ayers says, individuals were supposed to avoid those conflicts over insult that southerners could not let pass. "Call a man a liar in Mississippi, an old saying went, and he will knock you down; in Kentucky, he will shoot you; in Indiana, he will say You are another." In the North, one could be brusque, even dismissive, without risk. On the other hand, in the South, especially the Southwest, it was wise to follow the rituals of a disarming politeness which was most effective when natural and effortless.[11]

To be sure, such characterizations can ignore diverse styles of behavior as well as ones common to both sections. Obviously, Yankees still believed in the same ascriptive hierarchies, male over female, white over black, native born over foreign born, that southerners valued. In addition, northern cities were often as afflicted by personal violence and mob actions as were southern ones, and largely for the same reasons: honor and group prejudice against the unfamiliar and threatening. The difference lay, though, in the way such disorders were viewed. Southerners were willing to tolerate more individual and group violence out of fear of encroachments upon individual liberty and self-respect. In the North, displays of institutional weaknesses in the police force and the judicial system were no occasion for

10. George M. Fredrickson, *The Black Image in the White Mind: The Debate on Afro-American Character and Destiny, 1817–1914* (New York, 1971); see Pitt-Rivers, "Honor," 503–511; Hammond and Tucker quoted in Steven Mac Stowe, "The 'Touchiness' of the Gentleman Planter: The Sense of Esteem and Continuity in the Ante-Bellum South," *Psychohistory Review*, VIII (1979), 6–15.

11. Edward L. Ayers, *Vengeance and Justice: Crime and Punishment in the 19th-Century South* (New York, 1984), 20.

quiet satisfaction. Personal dignity was enhanced, not thwarted, by the protections of law; in the South, where lynchings and vigilance activity were notorious, honor sometimes took precedence over civic order of the most elemental sort.

In regard to the specifics of the slavery conflict, these sharp distinctions must be somewhat modified because, of course, the northern concept of "dignity" did involve inherent manliness, republican loyalty, and individual liberty, matters which the man of honor would scarcely have repudiated. But by no means were the antislavery forces so free of imperfection that principle alone guided their actions. Some Republican party leaders were as materialistic as southerners thought all Yankees were. Such individuals objected to the South less on moral than economic grounds—slaveholders' antipathy toward giving "Protection to domestic industry, Rivers and Harbors" and toward developing the nation's economy, as Hamilton Fish of New York put it. Another New York politician, E. Pershine Smith, wrote to a friend: "The first thing is to destroy the Southern domination" in the upcoming 1860 election. Once done, then "we shall begin to think of our bread and butter—and not before." But in final analysis, a principle not of capitalism but of power dominated Republican thinking, a conviction related to honor itself. To let the South depart without a fight would be an eternal disgrace, a supineness unworthy of a free people, at least as Republican propagandists insisted in the late 1850s. With other parties subservient to the Great Slave Power, they said, "upon no organization, except the Republican party, can the country rely for successful resistance [to the] insolent and aggressive" demands of the South.[12]

Some of the most antisouthern Unionists were Democrats who became associated, as members or allies, with the Republican cause. Unionist Democrats like Frank Blair and Montgomery Blair, border state politicians, and Gideon Welles of Connecticut (still a Democrat when he joined Lincoln's cabinet) worshipped at Jackson's shrine. They were the ones most concerned about national honor and sec-

12. Fish and Smith quoted in Eric Foner, *Free Soil, Free Labor, Free Men: The Ideology of the Republican Party Before the Civil War* (New York, 1970), 192–93; Michael F. Holt, *The Political Crisis of the 1850s* (New York, 1978), 209.

tional treason. Like secession Tennessee's Unionist senator Andrew Johnson, such politicians were scarcely racial egalitarians, but they were convinced that the slaveholders had insulted the Union flag and should be taught respect and submission. As one former Democrat from Illinois thundered, "There is not a man [in the state] who will not raise his hand and swear to eternal God" that the Union would be maintained, "if our arms can save it." Even the most conservative and Whiggish members of the new sectional party referred at times to the choice between glorious self-defense and base subservience to slave-power demonism. For instance, an old-line Whig like Kentucky-born Orville H. Browning, a Quincy, Illinois, lawyer, could ring the changes on honor. At a Lincoln campaign rally in 1860, he pledged himself to stay in the Union and fight "for my right—if necessary with the sword. . . . Here I am within it, and here I mean to stand and die . . . defy[ing] all power on earth to expel me."[13]

Although the words and stylized presentation were the same as what a prosecession politician might use in speaking of his own self-sacrifice, Browning's honor did not carry all the weight of personal investment that the southern version did. Few Yankees would feel compelled to settle ideological differences on a dueling field. In a parallel to the description of northern ideals of dignity, the free-state citizen saw defense of honor as a last resort rather than a first consideration. As a result, in northern political discourse one finds less frequent use of such terms of honor as fame, glory, shame, infamy, and insult than in the South.

Behind these differences lay the bourgeois and highly institutionalized nature of Yankee culture. In the rapidly modernizing North, the strength of other institutions lessened personal dependency upon family and community opinion, especially in the cities, which absorbed a large share of the northern population. Even the few southern cities that existed were themselves more rural in culture and milieu than were their Yankee counterparts. As a result, a

13. Bissell of Illinois quoted in Foner, *Free Soil*, 179; Browning quoted in Halbert E. Gulley, "Springfield Lincoln Rally, 1860," in J. Jeffrey Auer (ed.), *Antislavery and Disunion, 1858–1861: Studies in the Rhetoric of Compromise and Conflict* (New York, 1963), 220.

more parochial view of Unionism prevailed, one that reflected the primacy of race and rurality in southern values. In contrast to Orville Browning's view of national allegiance, Alexander Stephens in 1845, for instance, offered a rather typical ranking of southern fealties: "I have a patriotism that embraces, I trust, all parts of the Union." Yet, he continued, "the South is my home—my fatherland. . . . These are my hopes and prospects . . . her fate is my fate, and her destiny my destiny."[14]

The primacy northerners gave national honor over community and even family honor distinguished North from South. True before the Civil War, it was even more evident in the course of the conflict, so much so that even the abolitionists, least honor-bound of all Yankee groups, felt its force. Ordinarily, the reformers made no distinction between godliness or conscience and honor, but the trying times and raging battles led to more convenient interpretations. The most telling example was the wartime incident in which Moncure Conway, a Virginia-born Unitarian minister, promised, in the name of "the leading antislavery men of America," to have the Union acknowledge southern independence if the Confederacy would at once emancipate the slaves under a "liberal European commission." The proposition was presented to James M. Mason, commissioner from the Richmond government, in London in June, 1863. Mason published it at once, in hopes of driving a wedge between the abolitionists and the Republican administration. Abolitionists repudiated Conway with a fury arising from deep embarrassment. Conway made them look like cowards eager to back away from the grim necessities of war. For years Garrison and friends had opposed military glories, offering instead Quaker-inspired pacifism. Also they denounced the "dishonor" to God and Right which the Constitution had placed upon all citizens in its sanction of slavery. According to Peter Walker's account in *Moral Choices*, Conway had "asked them to be true to their word" and Christian principles, but those who denounced him demanded, in effect,

14. David R. Goldfield, *Cotton Fields and Skyscrapers: Southern City and Region, 1607–1980* (Baton Rouge, 1982); Stephens quoted in Gladys F. Williams, "The Divided Mind of an Antebellum Statesman: Alexander Stephens, the South and the Nation" (M.A. thesis, University of Alabama in Huntsville, 1982), 52–53.

that patriotism had to come first, conscience second. By that means one could say, "My country right or wrong."[15]

Of all the groups in the heterogeneous North, the Democrats were by far the most comfortable with the southern view of honor as a rationale for white supremacy, sectional parity, and anticentralism. It is worth pointing out, however, that the Douglas wing of the party placed limits on its commitment to the southern persuasion when Stephen Douglas broke with Buchanan over Kansas. Because of administration bungling and prosouthern bias, and even the expedient of ballot fraud, the territory obtained a proslavery constitution. Douglas Democrats discovered that their honor no longer could permit further concessions to slavery expansion. In December, 1857, the Illinois Democrat said, "If this constitution is to be forced down our throats, in violation of the fundamental principle of free government, under a mode of submission that is a mockery and insult, I will resist it to the last." At the disastrous Democratic convention in Charleston, in late April and early May, 1860, the issue of honor figured in the controversy between the Douglas partisans and William L. Yancey and his followers. The fire-eaters demanded that northern Democrats repudiate "popular sovereignty," agree to Kansas statehood under the proslavery constitution, and submit to slavery's territorial expansion, policies that, Yancey assured them, would cost nothing—morally or politically. Outraged, George Pugh of Ohio replied, "You endeavor to bow us down into the dust. Gentlemen, you mistake us—you mistake us. We will not submit to dishonor." Pugh was not the only northern delegate to appeal to the manly code: a Michigan Douglasite declared that if asked to "yield up a principle of honor," his retort would be "never, never, never." After the firing on Fort Sumter, Democrats of this persuasion preferred war to passivity. As Jean Baker has noted, they fought to "restore the object of their allegiance—the Union," an identification of honor with an all-embracing nationalism as they had always understood it but which so many of their southern brethren had begun to repudiate in the 1850s.[16]

15. Peter Walker, *Moral Choices: Memory, Desire, and Imagination in Nineteenth-Century American Abolition* (Baton Rouge, 1978), 16–18.

16. Douglas quoted in Richard H. Sewell, *Ballots for Freedom: Antislavery Politics in the United States, 1837–1860* (New York, 1976), 344; Pugh quoted in Charleston

We can understand neither southern honor nor the intensity of re-action to Yankee criticism without recognizing the psychological force that the actual language of political and moral discourse exercised upon the southern mind. The words used were not empty gestures. Instead, as Murray Edelman has observed, "language forms [serve] a crucial function [in politics] by creating shared meanings, perceptions, and reassurances among mass publics." To be sure, the dramatic events leading toward war—the Kansas troubles, John Brown's raid, Lincoln's victory—served to excite passion and strike fear. But the very rhetoric in defense of the South and the words hurled against the region were equally significant.[17]

The importance of language as a means to express solidarity was closely related to the character of the southern local political setting. Family heritage and local loyalties were exceedingly important components. According to Robert Kenzer, it was not "ideological differences between the two parties," Whig and Democrat, in Orange County, North Carolina, a representative mixed farming district, which accounted for the bitter partisanship. "Rather, the parties were shaped by the county's neighborhood structure and ties of kinship." In antebellum Georgia upcountry politics, Steven Hahn has discovered, the same situation existed—a close-knit pattern of grocery-store and family relationships. As a result, with a few families and their relations dominating a local district's voting habits, pride of family and loyalty to friends helped to hold most voters to the same party, election after election. In addition, a process of secret balloting did not exist. In rural areas most especially, everyone *knew* each other's preferences. The powerful men influenced the votes of the

Courier, April 30, 1860 [quotation differs slightly from Murat Halstead, *Caucuses of 1860* (Columbus, Ohio, 1860), 48]; Stuart of Michigan in Charleston *Courier*, May 2, 1860; Baker, *Affairs of Party*, 319. Southerners rejected the Douglas Democrats' version of nationalism, but secessionism did not represent a fully developed southern nationalism. Traditional honor encouraged too parochial a view, so that slavery, states' rights, and kinship ties, not abstract nationalism, held the South together—imperfectly and only for a while. Compare John M. McCardell, *The Idea of the Southern Nation: Southern Nationalists and Southern Nationalism, 1830–1860* (New York, 1979).

17. Murray Edelman, *Politics as Symbolic Action: Mass Arousal and Quiescence* (New York, 1971), 65. On politics, patronage, and duels, see Bertram Wyatt-Brown, "Honor and the Code Duello in the Old South" (Paper delivered at Tennessee State Museum Symposium, September 28, 1984, Nashville).

common whites. The latter respected their leaders for their wealth, skills of command, and democratic manners. Certainly the yeomen did not intend their loyalty to be mistaken for meek obedience, but they did vote for men of wealth and education. Obligations of blood, past favors, present indebtedness, and other commitments cemented political allegiances. In a neighboring, rival township, the competing party might have held the preference, again with few to stray from the fold. As a result, elections were hotly contested. The language used was highly volatile because personal and group honor, rather than simply a partisan policy, was often at stake. Fierce family and individual rivalries sometimes led to challenges and even duels. By the standards of this system, the Yankees had changed the rules, introducing ideological and moral questions, uncertainties, and fears into a family-based, honor-bound exercise.[18]

Many examples might be used to illustrate the way in which honor and high-toned language pervaded local politics in the South. But only one will be offered here: a public letter sent to the early fire-eater John A. Quitman of Mississippi in 1851. The occasion was his release from trial over his violation of a federal neutrality act by aiding the ill-fated Cuba filibusterer, Narciso López. General Quitman, a hero of the Mexican War, had resigned the governor's chair after indictment, but now had the opportunity to regain the office sacrificed to save the state from association with his embarrassment. The committee used the formal language of deference in expressing gratitude for General Quitman's "chivalrous and patriotic defense not only of the rights of our common country but the rights of the

18. Robert Charles Kenzer, "Portrait of a Southern Community, 1849–1881: Family, Kinship, and Neighborhood in Orange County, North Carolina" (Ph.D. dissertation, Harvard University, 1982), 74–83; Steven H. Hahn, *The Roots of Southern Populism: Yeoman Farmers and the Transformation of the Georgia Upcountry, 1850–1890* (New York, 1983), and "The Yeomanry of the Nonplantation South: Upper Piedmont Georgia, 1850–1860," in Orville V. Burton and Robert C. McMath (eds.), *Class, Conflict, and Consensus: Antebellum Southern Community Studies* (Westport, Conn., 1982), 38–39; Paul F. Bourke and Donald A. DeBats, "Identifiable Voting in Nineteenth-Century America: Toward a Comparison of Britain and the United States Before the Secret Ballot," *Perspectives in American History*, XI (1977–78), 285; Harry L. Watson, *Jacksonian Politics and Community Conflict: The Emergence of the Second American Party System in Cumberland County, North Carolina* (Baton Rouge, 1981), 311; Whitman Ridgway, *Community Leadership in Maryland, 1790–1840* (Chapel Hill, 1979), 130–35.

South against the assaults of its enemies." Words such as *defamed* and *persecuted* referred to his injured innocence. The prosecutor's nolle prosequi was small vindication; only his return to the governorship could accomplish that. Preparatory to the upcoming campaign, the admiring supplicants offered to hold a barbecue in Quitman's honor, a distinctly informal affair compared to the style of the invitation. In reply, Quitman acknowledged that their celebration was "peculiarly gratifying." It demonstrated that they approved his conduct, and therefore he was "honored with their confidence and esteem." (He won nomination but later withdrew.) Although scarcely a major incident, the correspondence over the barbecue pointed toward a sectional distinction the significance of which might easily be dismissed. The late-nineteenth-century southern scholar William Garrott Brown once noted, "It is a superficial historical philosophy which dilates on the economic and institutional differences between the two sections, and ignores smaller divergences as appeared in the manners and speech of individuals."[19]

The formality of language made all interchanges less threatening. Ritual words of praise and acceptance ensured a feeling of trust. Words, thoughts, and gestures that ordinary southerners and their leaders knew so well provided that sense of reliability. It was so necessary in the absence of those institutional safeguards which Stanley Elkins described as mediational devices for social and psychological security. Ritual speech softened the harsh world of personal rivalry, vengeance, threat, and hierarchy. It made the common white feel secure and it strengthened the confidence and persuasiveness of the leader. The discrepancy between language and deed, between barbecues and ragtag parades on the one hand and lofty and punctilious deferences on the other helped to ritualize honor. Often such use of language in the Old South is perceived as meaningless, but it was genuinely functional. By these means the planters and militia officers who organized the occasion, the ordinary citizens who attended it,

19. C. S. Tarpley *et al.* to General John A. Quitman, March 10, 1851, and Quitman to Tarpley *et al.*, March 31, 1851, both in J. F. H. Claiborne, *Life and Correspondence of John A. Quitman* (2 vols.; New York, 1860), II, 127–38; James Brewer Stewart, "'A Great Talking and Eating Machine': Patriarchy, Mobilization, and the Dynamics of Nullification in South Carolina," *Civil War History*, XXVII (1981), 197–220; William Garrott Brown, *The Lower South in American History* (New York, 1902), 47.

and the former Mexican War general, John Quitman, running for the governor's seat reconfirmed shared attitudes. The exchange and celebration dedicated them all to the defense of the South against its enemies.

In still larger perspective, the employment of honor in its linguistic and political character helped immeasurably to reinforce the social order. The grandiloquent phrase, the references to manliness, bravery, nobility, and resolute action, for example, were scarcely reserved for politics alone, but political correspondence, public letters, editorials, and speeches all employed a tone that sounded bombastic and overblown to the unaccustomed ear. By and large, it was the rhetoric of gentlemen. Lesser folk often admired it. It sanctified the existing social system to lace speeches with Shakespearean and classical phrases, so long as they were familiar to the listeners. However exaggerated its character, the political vocabulary spoke to the most visceral feelings that southerners possessed.

Given the character of southern politics and its ethical framework, the road to secession does not seem so puzzling. In responding to northern criticism and self-assertiveness, the South's defenders had to emphasize vindication and vengeance. As a result, the purpose of so much southern rhetoric in the prewar period was to impugn the motives and policies of the abolitionists in and out of Congress. Any number of examples might be cited to show how southern anguish at criticism reflected the psychological processes of injured pride. Abolitionists like Garrison thought that their sermons against slavery would force the slaveholder to listen to his conscience, but the effort was futile. Instead, antislavery polemics evoked feelings, not of guilt, but of anger and indignation. As John S. Preston, a South Carolina proslavery advocate, declared, "There is not a Christian man, a slaveholder [in the South], who does not feel in his inmost heart as a Christian" that his fellow churchmen of the North have spilled "the last blood of sympathy [on the point of the] sword of the church. . . . They set the lamb of God between our seed and their seed." [20]

20. See Bertram Wyatt-Brown, *Southern Honor: Ethics and Behavior in the Old South* (New York, 1982); Preston quoted in George H. Reese (ed.), *Proceedings of the Virginia State Convention of 1861, February 13–May 1* (4 vols.; Richmond, 1965), I, 90.

Preston Brooks's assault on Charles Sumner in May, 1856, helps to illustrate the means for southern vindication. What outraged Brooks and his accomplice Lawrence Keitt, the South Carolina congressman, was the Massachusetts senator's tasteless vilification of Senator Andrew Pickens Butler, Brooks's kinsman, during the "Bleeding Kansas" speech. In addition, Sumner had dwelt upon the alleged ineffectuality, even cowardice, of South Carolina troops during the American Revolution. By the rules of honor, Brooks was under no obligation to call for a duel with Sumner because one fought on the field of honor only with one's social and moral peers. By southern standards, Sumner fell considerably below that status. In handling inferiors, a one-on-one horsewhipping was much more appropriate. The fire-eater Keitt explained the matter to the House after the event. By the ancient code, he said, "a churl was never touched with the knightly sword; his person was mulcted with the quarter-staff." This incident points to the sense of degradation that Yankees could feel when faced with southern aggression. "We all or *nearly* all felt," a Bostonian wrote the wounded Sumner, "that we had been personally maltreated & insulted." According to William Gienapp, the attack on Sumner, perhaps more than the troubles in Kansas, aroused northern opinion against the South. Even in conservative circles formerly hostile to the Massachusetts senator's course, concerns for northern self-respect and for free speech were evident.[21]

For both sides, Brooks's violence heightened an awareness of honor's demands. But before such means of vengeance, there had been an escalation of verbal confrontations. The abolitionist rhetoric need not be described; our concentration is upon southern epithet and abuse. Southern spokesmen inflated antislavery denunciations to the level of treachery, betrayal, insurrection, and devilish anarchy. Antislavery attacks stained the reputation by which southern whites judged their place and power in the world. Such, for instance, was the reason why slaveholders insisted on the right to carry their property

21. Keitt quoted in John H. Marchant, "Lawrence M. Keitt, South Carolina Fire-Eater" (Ph.D. dissertation, University of Virginia, 1976), 120; David H. Donald, *Charles Sumner and the Coming of the Civil War* (New York, 1960), 290–95; William E. Gienapp, "The Crime Against Sumner: The Caning of Charles Sumner and the Rise of the Republican Party," *Civil War History*, XXV (1979), 218–45, 224 (quotation).

into the free territories at will. It was not solely a matter of expanding slavery's boundaries, though that was of course important. No less significant, however, was southern whites' resentment against any congressional measure which implied the moral inferiority of their region, labor system, or style of life. Such reflections on southern reputation were thought vile and humiliating. For example, in late 1846, Robert Toombs, senator from Georgia, took exception to the Wilmot Proviso, by which slaveholders would be barred from bringing slaves into lands seized from Mexico. Southern whites, he argued, "would be degraded, and unworthy of the name of American freemen, could they consent to remain, for a day or an hour, in a Union where they must stand on ground of inferiority, and be denied the rights and privileges which were extended to all others." Fear for personal losses from antislavery territorial laws did not matter half as much as the symbolism of such antisouthern measures: its signification of still more dire consequences to come. As Toombs remarked in Congress during the sectional crisis of 1850, the right to enter any territory with slaves involved "political equality, [a status] worth a thousand such Unions as we have, even if they each were a thousand times more valuable than this." The issue was no small matter, in his opinion. He elevated the question of slaveholders' territorial prerogatives to the level of a casus belli, at least to his own satisfaction. "Deprive us of this right," he warned the Senate, and it becomes "your government, not mine. Then I am its enemy, and I will then, if I can, bring my children and my constituents to the altar of liberty, and like Hamilcar, I would swear them eternal hostility to your foul domination."[22]

The world of honor is Manichean—divided between Good and Evil; Right and Wrong; Justice and Injustice; Freedom and Slavery; Purity and Corruption. It was also apocalyptic—with the terms of reference being perfect peace or total war: stability or deference and affection toward the worthy, or servile rebellion, rapine, and slaughter of innocents. This style was scarcely incompatible with Protestant theology. But the primal character of the vision must be recog-

22. Toombs quoted in William Y. Thompson, *Robert Toombs of Georgia* (Baton Rouge, 1966), 42, 65.

nized, too. Dread of bloody revolt belonged to the world of honor, where few outsiders could be trusted. A telling example came from a speech of William L. Yancey at the Democratic convention in Charleston in which he vindicated the southern cause in these terms: "Ours is the property invaded; ours are the institutions which are at stake; ours is the peace that is to be destroyed; ours is the honor at stake— the honor of children, the honor of families, of the lives, perhaps, of all—all of which rests upon what your course may ultimately make a great heaving volcano of passion and crime." Harboring sentiments like these, southern leaders had no reason to question the use of violence as the best retort to obloquy. Thus, in 1858, Jefferson Davis roused a Democratic rally in New York City against Republican "higher law" politicians such as William H. Seward. The *"traitors* [to the Constitution], *these . . . preachers should be tarred and feathered, and whipped by those they have thus instigated."*[23]

In societies where honor thrives, death in defense of community and principle is a path to glory and remembrance, whereas servile submission entails disgrace. So it had been in Revolutionary America, at least as South Carolina nullifier Isaac Hayne portrayed the struggle for independence. The British imposition of "a three pence a pound tax upon Tea" had been just such a cause for revolution. With obvious reference to the current "tyranny" of unpopular tariff exactions, Hayne argued that the sums involved were not the issue at all. The Parliamentary tea tax would have driven no American into penury. But this and other British measures required patriots to accept meekly the statutory symbols of British imperialism, a surrender of liberty that was dishonorable and therefore unbearable. Nullifiers like Hayne, as well as secessionists later, often posed the splendors of honor against the degeneracy and cowardly temptation of peaceful capitulation. Robert Barnwell Rhett in 1828 assaulted the Unionist faction of South Carolina, stressing the dangers of lost self-confidence: "If you are doubtful of your selves . . . if you love life better than

23. Yancey quoted in Dickson D. Bruce, Jr., *Violence and Culture in the Antebellum South* (Austin, 1979), 192; Davis quoted in Dunbar Rowland (ed.), *Jefferson Davis, Constitutionalist: His Letters, Papers and Speeches* (10 vols.; Jackson, Miss., 1923), III, 337–38.

honor,—prefer ease to perilous liberty and glory, awake not! stir not!—Impotent resistance will add vengeance to ruin. Live in smiling peace with your insatiable oppressors, and die with the noble consolation, that your submissive patience will survive triumphant your beggary and despair." Dread of shameful subservience became a more pronounced southern theme after Lincoln's election. For instance, Alcibiade De Blanc of Saint Martin Parish introduced to the Louisiana secession convention a resolution that spoke to the southern fear of lost racial honor. The new president's party would force, he said, the southern people to accept an "equality [of blacks] with a superior race . . . to the irreparable ruin of this mighty Republic, the degradation of the American name, and the corruption of the American blood."[24]

As J. Mills Thornton puts the matter, the threat that Lincoln's election represented was "neither primarily material nor was its substance emancipation, except in the long run. The abomination with which the Republicans menaced the South was not freedom, but slavery," that is, the denial of southern equality in the realm of honor. As Thornton's careful statistics show, Southern Rights Democracy (Breckinridge's candidacy) and secessionism fared best not in the wealthier planter centers but in the small farm communities of Alabama. In fact, as political and economic historians of the South have argued, the most dynamic source for change lay precisely in the slaveholders' profits. Their reinvestment in other parts of the economy required speedy diversification and governmental activity for internal improvements, bank charters, and other "modernizing" instruments. Although politicians and constituents did not divide neatly according to class or even district on issues of economic expansion and change on the one hand and preservation of old ways on the other, all white southerners were aware that one world was dying and another fast rising—for better or worse. It was that tension,

24. Isaac Hayne, *An Oration Delivered in the Presbyterian Church in Columbia, on the Fourth of July, 1831* (Columbia, S.C., 1831), 4–5; Rhett quoted in Laura A. White, *Robert Barnwell Rhett: Father of Secession* (New York, 1931), 15; De Blanc quoted in *Official Journal of the Proceedings of the Convention of the State of Louisiana* (New Orleans, 1861), 9.

worry, and also the promise of a bright future that made so intense the issue of honor. It was a talisman, a symbol, and a code of high morality that shaped the debate over secession, a familiar set of beliefs with wide appeal for both the innovating and the traditionalistic forces in the social order.[25]

Nevertheless, the word *honor* had a more resonant meaning for those who disputed not only "submission" to Republican madness but also the South's own drift from familiar patterns of subsistence farming and antiquated commercial ways. Honor was the ethic of the small-scale community where loyalties remained personal and intense. Except in South Carolina, early advocates of secessionism did not stir southern minds. Antislavery dangers seemed too distant. Used to thinking in terms of immediate locale, subregion, and state, ordinary folk were only intermittently roused to feverish indignation against the South's critics in the North. Once Lincoln was elected, however, there was almost a tidal surge for secession in those parts of the South unused to rapid economic and social change. In such places men were terrified that the new political order would ruin the world they knew—insidiously and irrevocably. Farmers and planters in rural Georgia, for instance, were facing the consequences of wasteful agricultural practices—soil erosion, fewer food crops because of increased cotton planting, and shallow plowing. Such folk as these were the most vulnerable to political scapegoating. They were highly suspicious that factories, railroads, and banks which were penetrating a few parts of the rural South provided job alternatives and new ways of doing things that the old customs could not match. Bigger planters had more alternatives and the means for exercising power in a variety of options.

In offering this interpretation, I do not reject the significance of slavery. The South's vested interest in perpetuating slavery was the basis of the North-South conflict. Nor do I endorse the view of Mi-

25. Thornton, *Politics and Power*, 413, 414; George Crawford, "Preface to Revolution: Wealth, Opportunity and Crisis in Rural Georgia, 1840–1860" (Ph.D. dissertation in progress, Claremont Graduate School), Chap. 2; see also essays by William L. Barney, John T. Schlotterbeck, and Steven Hahn in Burton and McMath (eds.), *Class, Conflict, and Consensus*; and Harry L. Watson, *Jacksonian Politics and Community Conflict*.

chael Holt and J. Mills Thornton that "white freedom," rather than black slavery, was the source of the calamity. We must understand that the freedom in question was not the modern notion of individualism but instead the racially elitist concept that all white men were equal in their hegemony over blacks and in their right to seek esteem and power in the public arena according to the gifts of ascription and blood with which they were endowed. Thus, their *honor* depended upon the maintenance of traditional values of racial hierarchy, even though the seventeenth- and eighteenth-century plutocracy had given place to a less exclusive white political participation. In other words, honor was not an exclusive commodity to which bluebloods had sole access or claim. In the South, appeals to average citizens on the basis of community loyalty and honor could be made because "the sovereign people," as southerners often liked to say, decided for themselves what was honorable and what was not. Racism, white freedom and equality, and honor were not discrete concerns in the southern mind. They were all an inseparable part of personal and regional self-definition. To be sure, white supremacy, as Ulrich B. Phillips maintained long ago, was the "central theme" of southern culture. Yet the language for expressing it was largely framed in terms of honor and shame. To put it another way, white liberty was sustainable, it was thought, only on the basis of black slavery. Black freedom, on the other hand, necessarily meant white disgrace because it placed the southerner upon a level with blacks and Republicans.[26]

Nearly every major sectional issue from Tallmadge's amendment to the Missouri enabling act to the Free-Soil Wilmot Proviso had brought out expressions from proslavery advocates that connected slaveholding with southern honor and fear of shame. According to William L. Yancey's "Alabama Platform," the Wilmot Proviso was a "discrimination as degrading as it is injurious to the slaveholding states."[27] Words like degraded, shamed, demoralized, and humiliated all referred to the horrors of lost self-esteem. As northern contempo-

26. Ulrich B. Phillips, "The Central Theme of Southern History," *American Historical Review*, XXXIV (1928), 30–43.
27. Yancey quoted in Clarence P. Denman, *The Secession Movement in Alabama* (Montgomery, 1933), 10–11, 20.

raries believed, southern polemics far exceeded the actual causes. Just how would the Wilmot Proviso affect the ordinary planter in South Carolina or Alabama? Surely his control over his work force was scarcely less secure than before the measure was introduced in Congress. Loss of honor was the great issue, though by no means disconnected from slavery's protection.

So far, this exposition may have helped to explain the ethical language of the two sections, but it does not illuminate how honor played a role in the process of disunionism itself. At once, a vexing problem appears: the failure of all southerners to reach the same conclusion about the crisis. If honor were as pervasive as claimed, one might argue, then why such curious divisions throughout the South? The answer is complex and can only be touched upon here. Honor, like any ethical scheme from Christianity to Confucianism, provides only *general* rules of behavior, from which variety one may readily choose according to personal temperament, experience, or reading of circumstance. (One might as well expect uniformity about the dispensing of worldly goods in Christian doctrine.) Although traditional honor seemed the exclusive preserve of secessionists, the ethic could also be used to defend the status quo rather than revolutionary disunionism.

In ethical and strategic terms, the options were clearly drawn between the need for immediate vindication with a call to arms and the equally "honorable," Ciceronian course of moderation and coolness under provocation. Over the years, southern Unionists had roundly denounced and successfully turned aside the secessionist plea for hot-blooded action. Even at the close of the era, they did not believe that John Brown's raid or Lincoln's election required rebellious measures. Was there not a higher law of honor that demanded of the true-hearted southerner prudence after the results of the 1860 election were known? At the Alabama secession convention, delegate John Potter of Cherokee County, for instance, spoke to the issue. The secessionists tell us that "our honor must be vindicated," he observed. If that be the case, he said, then at least it was one powerful argument for disunion. But there is, Potter continued, "a morbid sense of honor" which often leads to extremes, and it "involves [men] in disgrace while they vainly seek to maintain their false view of true honor."[28]

Potter and many others urged a policy of calculation and patience. The slave states should confer about their grievances and weigh the costs of resistance before plunging into the unknown, they begged. From the time of Cicero to the outbreak of the Civil War, gentlemen had often responded to the passions of the moment by appealing to the Stoic-Christian tradition of honor that repudiated recklessness and intemperate behavior. But the Unionists of the South—by and large, the more securely placed large-scale planters—well knew that their calls for calm deliberation could be impugned as cowardice. For this reason among others, the Constitutional Unionists and those southerners who had voted for Douglas generally proclaimed themselves "conditional" Unionists. That position meant not only a readiness to negotiate or await the verdict of other slave-state allies but also a willingness to accept secession if that policy won overwhelming popular support. It was a part of the honor code itself that community consensus forced dissenters to surrender to popular decision even if the dissenters thought the policy foolish. Otherwise, one ran the risk of communal disloyalty.

Because of the fears for slavery's future that Lincoln's election engendered, the advantages lay with those in the Lower South who insisted that the inaction of continued Unionism would mean disaster and disgrace. The secessionists largely relied upon two tactics, one negative and the other more moderate. The first involved outright intimidation, sometimes violence. Nowhere was community will to repress dissent more evident than in South Carolina upon news of the "Black Republican" victory. Venerable, wealthy, and Unionist, the state supreme court chief justice John Belton O'Neall found that his neighbors no longer shared his sentiments or accepted his leadership. At the Newberry County Courthouse, he urged repudiation of

28. John V. Mering, "The Slave-State Constitutional Unionists and the Politics of Consensus," *Journal of Southern History*, XLIII (1977), 395–410; Potter quoted in William R. Smith (ed.), *The History and Debates of the Convention of the People of Alabama, Begun and Held in the City of Montgomery, on the Seventh Day of January, 1861* . . . (Montgomery, 1861), 107.

the autumn madness: "Freemen—descendants of the Patriots of '76—it is your duty to prevent such a disastrous [policy as secession]." In reply, the townsfolk pelted him with eggs.[29]

In other states the pressure toward consensus for disunion grew as well. In Atlanta, the *Daily Intelligencer* labeled Unionists "Southern Abolitionists [who ought to be] strung up to the nearest live oak and permitted to dance on nothing." In Alabama, boasted the Hayneville *Chronicle*, "not a half dozen papers" had the temerity to challenge the inexorable will of the outraged populace. The Unionist John Hardy of the *Alabama State Sentinel* in Selma received an offer of $10,000 to shut down his press. When the bribe failed, Yancey and friends pursued him with a libel suit. After two so-called abolitionists were killed by lynch law in Fort Worth, Texas, the local Unionist editor had to sell his paper to secessionists or face a similar fate. An Arkansas mob seized from a steamboat a traveling newspaper distributor from Saint Louis and hanged him for the crime of carrying Horace Greeley's New York *Tribune*. Such activities as these did not at all belie southern claims as liberty-lovers. Southerners simply meant something different by the term. As historian Donald Robinson points out, secessionist editors justified such suppressions of a free press "on the ground that the South was fighting for its very life and could ill afford dissension among its people."[30]

The power of popular coercion also intimidated the Unionist delegates to state secession conventions. At the Alabama meeting, for instance, Yancey darkly impugned the integrity of the Unionist opposition. He called them Tories no less subject to the laws of treason than the Loyalists of the American Revolution had been. At once Robert Jemison of Tuscaloosa leapt to his feet. "Will the gentleman go into those sections of the State and hang all those who are opposed to Secession? Will he hang them by families, by neighborhoods, by counties, by Congressional Districts? Who, sir, will give the bloody order? Is this the spirit of Southern chivalry?" Convinced that the South's

29. Lillian A. Kibler, "Unionist Sentiment in South Carolina in 1860," *Journal of Southern History*, IV (1938), 350–51.

30. Donald E. Robinson, *Editors Make War: Southern Newspapers in the Secession Crisis* (Nashville, 1966), 132–34, 152–55, 213.

material interests and even the safety of slavery lay in preservation of the Union, Jemison appealed to the higher laws of honor by which interpretation popular clamors should not deter the statesman from following the dictates of sound judgment. He put these concerns for public well-being and peaceful prosperity in terms of honor in order to meet secessionist objections that "principle" should overrule all other considerations, regardless of costs in blood, treasure, and risks to slavery itself. In like manner, Mississippi Unionists tried to show that genuine honor required a course quite different from the one secessionists proposed. A "fictitious chivalry," they said, offered only brave words but perversely claimed to be frightened of mannish Boston bluestockings and pious abolitionists. Honor, the Mississippi Unionists explained, demanded that the Gulf states do nothing precipitous: if they seceded at once, they would, in effect, leave their Upper South brethren in the clutches of hostile free-state majorities.[31]

Nonetheless, the submissionists, as they were dubbed, generally received the worst of this line of reasoning. Albert Gallatin Brown of Mississippi gave them the lie in 1860: "If it should cost us the Union, our lives, let them go," he cried. Better that than meekly to "submit to a disgrace so deep and so damning" as abject submission to Black Republican rule. The message that he and others delivered was not casually thrust aside. James L. Alcorn, a Unionist politician and a Delta planter with vast holdings, confided to a friend that the belligerence of the secession majority at the state convention had become almost intolerable. "Should we fail to commit ourselves [to secession], it will be charged that we intend to desert the South. . . . The epithet of coward and submissionist will be everywhere applied to us. We shall be scouted by the masses!" He and his Unionist colleagues signed the secession ordinance under duress, but they naturally had to claim that their action was as honorable and manly as their previous opposition had been. Both positions, they insisted, served the interests of the community and the glory of their state. When a similar

31. Jemison quoted in Smith (ed.), *History and Debates, Alabama*, 68–70; Donald B. Dodd, "Unionism in Northwest Alabama Through 1865" (M.A. thesis, Auburn University, 1966); Hugh C. Bailey, "Disloyalty in Early Confederate Alabama," *Journal of Southern History*, XXIII (1957), 522–28; Percy Lee Rainwater, *Mississippi: Storm Center of Secession, 1856–1861* (Baton Rouge, 1938), 182–83.

tide of secession enthusiasm swept North Carolina after Lincoln's mobilization order, former Whig Jonathan Worth sighed in resignation, "I think the South is committing suicide, but my lot is cast with the South and being unable to manage the ship, I intend to face the breakers manfully and go down with my companions." [32]

Antisecessionism came in different forms. In some parts of the Lower South, chiefly the upland districts, Unionism represented mountain independence and resentment of lowcountry planter domination. In such places the state capital seemed to pose a greater threat of centralism than did distant Washington, until, that is, the crisis deepened. In Huntsville, the major city in north Alabama, secessionists were outnumbered four to one in January, 1861, but by March they had gained a margin of three to one. Only a few antisecessionists in north Alabama or anywhere else in the upcountry Lower South were so loyal to the Stars and Stripes that they would accept Lincoln's election without significant Yankee concessions to assure southern parity. [33]

Whether mountain loyalists or Whiggish dissenters, most of secession's opponents sought delay in the verdict on Lincoln and the gaining of a satisfactory southern consensus by open assembly and discussion. Nevertheless, the Unionists, conditional and otherwise, had no clear-cut policy to correspond to the simple secessionist proposition. The result was demoralization and vulnerability to the blandishments and threats of others. Under such circumstances, Unionists found it easy to hide from decision-making by not attending elections and rallies.

Reaching conclusions compatible with Thornton's for Alabama, Peyton McCrary and his colleagues have discovered, by use of sophisticated statistical methods, that the greatest falloff in balloting occurred in the Black Belt districts and other large slaveholding areas where Whiggery and Unionist sentiment were strongest. Voters who

32. Brown in Jackson *Mississippian*, November 9, 1860; Alcorn quoted in William L. Barney, *The Secessionist Impulse: Alabama and Mississippi in 1860* (Princeton, 1974), 309; Worth quoted in Daniel W. Crofts, "The Union Party of 1861 and the Secession Crisis," *Perspectives in American History*, XI (1977–78), 370n61.
33. Thornton, *Politics and Power*, 438.

had supported John Bell's Constitutional Union ticket or else Stephen Douglas' candidacy on the national Democratic ballot in November, 1860, failed to vote in the elections for state secession assemblies a few weeks later. Breckinridge or Southern Rights Democrats, on the other hand, tended to support secession and fewer stayed home. This group, as mentioned earlier, was largely made up of farmers and small slaveholders. They were the southerners most attuned to the precepts of honor in its less sophisticated form, unsheltered, as many were, by wealth, advanced education, and urban connections. The Constitutional Union coalition, however, represented those who temperamentally sought less drastic means to defend vital interests. If these findings are supported by evidence from states other than Mississippi, Louisiana, and Alabama, from which McCrary had drawn his data, we can conclude that men chose their strategy at least in part on the basis of their ethical preferences. If class alone had mattered, then all slaveholders, especially the wealthiest, would have chosen secession. Instead, they were divided between what might be called the genteel, Whiggish element and the more primal, Democratic type. Rather than fight it out, however, the antisecessionists simply held their silence.[34]

Forcing the Unionists into silence or acquiescence had been the chief means for handling the minority opposition in the Deep South. That tactic had little chance in the Upper South, since there the Unionists commanded local allegiance prior to Fort Sumter, and they could be as mobocratic as the secessionists in the Deep South. As a result, a direct appeal to honor itself rather than threat of shame for cowardice had to be used: the reminder of blood brotherhood that united white southerners in a common destiny. It was especially prominent in the struggle to bring Virginia into alignment with the other departing slave states. A call for fraternal support was in es-

34. Peyton McCrary, Clark Miller, and Dale Baum, "Class and Party in the Secession Crisis: Voting Behavior in the Deep South, 1856–1861," *Journal of Interdisciplinary History*, VIII (1978), 429–57; William J. Donnelly, "Conspiracy or Popular Movement: The Historiography of Southern Support for Secession," *North Carolina Historical Review*, XLII (1965), 70–84; compare Steven A. Channing, *Crisis of Fear: Secession in South Carolina* (New York, 1970).

sence an appeal to Virginia pride as progenitor of the South itself. As William Freehling has so persuasively explained, Virginians of 1860 felt keenly the Old Dominion's loss of leadership to the Lower South. In so many ways, as one would expect, secession was a movement most attractive to the young, since honor was a martial and manly code. But the code also recognized the claims of venerability and length of service. Virginia's pride of place would certainly have been in jeopardy if the state chose, with the seven other remaining slave states, to stay with the Union in inert and toothless submission. That, however, was unlikely because the general populace east of the Alleghenies favored Unionism *only* so long as guarantees for slavery seemed possible through negotiations with the Republicans without loss of self-esteem. During the long secession meetings in Richmond before the installation of the Republican president, commissioners from the seceded states lobbied and spoke for Virginia's departure. One and all, they complained of the constant stream of "insults" and "unconstitutional" aggressions emanating from Yankee quarters. The commissioners had to counter the Unionism of the "northern yeoman" contingent from the counties west of the Blue Ridge, a vociferously anti-Tidewater faction that had many reasons for distrusting the eastern majority on questions of representation, allocation of state funds, and taxes. Hoping to divert attention from Virginia's complicated internal affairs, the commissioners focused on the common bonds of blood which all true southerners were obliged to acknowledge. Reciting what had become a familiar litany, T. Fulton Anderson from Mississippi reminded the Virginia delegates on February 18, 1861, that the southern people all shared the heroic heritage of the Revolutionary forefathers. A former Unionist himself, Anderson declared that "the hour has arrived when if the South would maintain her honor, she must take her destiny into her own hands." The people of Mississippi are "like you . . . the descendants of a revolutionary race [that] raised the banner of resistance. . . . They have decided . . . to trust for the safety of their honor and rights only to their own strong arms."[35]

35. Crofts, "The Union Party of 1861 and the Secession Crisis," 327–76; Marc W. Kruman, *Parties and Politics in North Carolina, 1836–1865* (Baton Rouge, 1983),

Even more dedicated to the tenets of blood loyalty and honor was the speech of John S. Preston, a noted orator and South Carolina hothead. Perhaps more than any other southern politician, Preston epitomized the rhetorical manner of ritual speech with its rolling cadences, repetitions, and reliance on the sonority of the long vowel. His purpose was not so much to convince as to confirm agreement on basic principles. Southern political oratory reminded listeners of the social and moral values that the region cherished. Familiar, even venerable ideas were put in forms just novel enough to please, and disturbingly innovative thoughts were seldom presented. For these reasons, Preston concentrated on achieving a cadence that resulted in some loss of coherence:

> Ah, gentlemen of Virginia, where[ever] outside the borders of Virginia the voice of a son of Virginia has spoken in this fight, it too has been renowned, because he spoke in the ancient tongue of his mother. . . . I, one of the humblest of her sons, told my countrymen, that before the spring grass grows long enough to weave one chaplet of victory, they will hear the resounding echo of that voice which has thundered into the hearts of your God-like sires—"give me liberty or give me death!". . . We therefore believe, that although you centralize a coercing power at Washington, stronger than the Praetorian guard when the eagles of Rome made one coalition of the Gaul, the Briton, and the Ionian. No community of laws, no community of language, of religion, can amalgamate . . . people whose severance is proclaimed by the most rigid requisitions of universal necessity.

Inspired by such sentiments, delegate after delegate rose to announce that the honor of the Old Dominion, the honor of blood kinsmen and friends in the Lower South, and their own personal honor demanded union with the departed slave states. Thomas Branch of Petersburg said, "If we are to be dragged either to the North or to the South, then in name of our ancient fame, by whom would we prefer to be dragged? Would you be dragged by the Northern Confederacy, your known haters or would you prefer to be dragged by your brethren of kindred ties and similar interests? . . . I had rather be ruled by King Davis

---

200–202; William W. Freehling, "The Editorial Revolution, Virginia, and the Coming of the Civil War: A Review Essay," *Civil War History*, XVI (1970), 64–72, esp. 67; Anderson quoted in Reese (ed.), *Proceedings of the Virginia State Convention of 1861*, I, 56, 59.

than by Autocrat Lincoln." Others felt the same way. The Charlottesville *Review* declared that Virginians "are humiliated" by not leaving with South Carolina and the rest of the Cotton South. "We are conquered. We could not hold up our heads in that Union any more." Fear of being called womanish and fear-ridden exerted a powerful force.[36]

Despite these sentiments, it was the actual outbreak of armed hostilities and the new president's mobilization order which stirred Virginia, North Carolina, Tennessee, and Arkansas to their fate. Thus, when Robert E. Lee, for instance, along with other former Unionists swore allegiance to their kinfolk, their state, and their region, they were neither mouthing pieties nor cynically prettifying the rationale for slavery. Southern whites could not separate defense of slaveholding from defense of family and community. The common denominator for both the domestic and the labor institutions was the exigency of honor. Ordinary citizens, not just politicians, felt obliged to close ranks behind the Stars and Bars on the fundamental principle of honor, family, and race supremacy, one and indivisible.[37]

The contest over secession was not one that involved matters of conscience or the more legally serious problem of treason. Rather, nearly all politically active southerners assumed the right of secession; the question was the wisdom of the decision. The secessionists, though, had always insisted that advocacy of peace and patience was simply another name for cowardice. Historian John Barnwell points out that the secession extremists proudly accepted their critics' charge of being Hotspurs whose fate served the South as an inspiring example to be followed—possibly into the grave. "Harry Percy failed," the hotheads retorted, not because of his rashness and arrogance but because his kinsmen and allies proved faithless. If southerners were

36. Preston and Branch quoted in Reese (ed.), *Proceedings of the Virginia State Convention of 1861*, I, 87, 113; Charlottesville *Review* quoted in William J. Cooper, Jr., "The Politics of Slavery Affirmed: The South and the Secession Crisis," in Walter J. Fraser, Jr., and Winfred B. Moore, Jr. (eds.), *The Southern Enigma: Essays on Race, Class, and Folk Culture* (Westport, Conn., 1983), 212.

37. William M. E. Rachal (ed.), "'Secession is Nothing but Revolution': A Letter of R. E. Lee to his Son 'Rooney,'" *Virginia Magazine of History and Biography*, LXIX (1961), 3–6; Captain Robert E. Lee, *Recollections and Letters of General Robert E. Lee* (New York, 1905), 25.

equally untrustworthy, then by the rules of manly honor they deserved defeat and disgrace.[38]

Like the Northumberland rebel, most southern radicals throughout the antebellum years were likely to be men on the threshold of their careers, not well-established and aging property holders. Benjamin Perry, a South Carolina Unionist, noted that the upcountry secessionists in the 1850s were "a set of young enthusiasts inspired with notions of personal honor to be defended and individual glory, fame and military laurels to be acquired." Critics might object to their choler and recklessness, but these truculent southerners had an answer. Even if the South's break for freedom were crushed by northern might, they said, the chance for vindication had to be seized. James Jones, one of the South Carolina ultras, predicted, "If we fail, we have saved our honour *and lost nothing.*" The alternative was too demeaning to be considered: the slavery of "*Submission.*" The honor that Shakespeare's Henry Percy represented could only save injured pride and animate a spirit of defiance. Perhaps it was fitting that the young should stand in the vanguard of secessionism. They were soon to be the first to meet enemy fire in the field. Whether that circumstance was just or not, the words of the victorious Prince Hal were, for many a fallen Confederate, soon and sadly to apply. He addressed Hotspur, slain and lying at his feet: "Thy ignominy sleep with thee in the grave, / But not rememb'red in thy epitaph."[39]

38. John Barnwell, *Love of Order: South Carolina's First Secession Crisis* (Chapel Hill, 1982), 188.

39. Perry and Jones quoted in Barnwell, *Love of Order*, 150, 188; *I Henry IV*, V, iv, 99–100.

EPILOGUE

MY CHIEF PURPOSE in this book has been to show that slavery alone did not separate North and South. How strange it is that so many historians have narrowed their focus to that single differentiation. By no means should the existence of black bondage be overlooked or reduced to a matter of secondary importance. Yet we must understand that slaveholding and black subordination in the South and free labor and ideals of universal (as opposed to discriminatory) liberty in the nonslave states involved a grave moral division, one based on distinctions of culture as well as ethics. Although William R. Taylor sought to dispel the long-popular myth of plantation grandeur, he put the matter well in noting that the North had developed by the 1830s a "leveling, go-getting utilitarian society and the South had developed a society based on the values of the English gentry." The cavalier and the Yankee, the southern planter and the northern merchant, did not share the same assumptions.[1]

Two areas of disagreement are worth mentioning even as this study comes to a close: attitudes about the prospect of human perfectibility and about the value of life itself. With the North chiefly in mind, Tocqueville observed that in America egalitarianism, individual enterprise, and notions of perfection all went hand in hand. Despite the dangers to the Christian that "Mammonism" was supposed to involve, the concept of perfectionism aided rather than discouraged economic innovation and profit-seeking. Both the philosophy and the appeal of business activity were based upon future hopes not defensive reliance upon the familiar and old. When Ezra Stiles Gannett,

1. William R. Taylor, *Cavalier and Yankee: The Old South and American National Character* (New York, 1961), 15.

214

a northern Unitarian clergyman, denounced what he labeled the inherent selfishness of the Yankee business ethic, Nathan Appleton, a wealthy Boston financier and congressman, gave a spirited defense: "That every individual shall be entitled to the benefit of his own acquisitions[,] the fruit of his own labour[,] is the fundamental principle" of progress and civilization. Assiduous labor, honest profit-taking, and exemplary charity made possible the religious and humanitarian reforms of the day. With considerable pride in his profession, the Boston merchant concluded that there was "no purer morality [than that of] the counting room."[2]

Nor were Appleton's thoughts by any means idiosyncratic. For instance, New York merchants Lewis Tappan and Arthur Tappan and others in their circle of philanthropic businessmen subscribed to sentiments of this kind. According to their perspective, individual transactions served the community at large. The money, skills, and experiences gained in business were God's gifts to be returned to him in the form of good works to advance moral and religious objectives. The spiritual and material capital so invested would hasten the day of millennial perfection. Few worried that change and perfectibility might turn out to be contradictory, that unreachable goals could constrict the heart, promote complacency, and blind the eye to ugly realities.

Steeped in Old World traditions that slavery helped to perpetuate, the southern antebellum mind remained skeptical of progress if it pointed toward the kind of human perfection of which reformers dreamed. Accustomed to the hierarchies of race and acquired social position in a democratic setting, southern whites did not "absolutely deny man's faculty of self-improvement," to borrow from *Democracy in America*, but they did "not hold it to be indefinite"; they could "conceive amelioration, but not change"; they fancied "that the future condition of society" could become "better, but not essentially different."[3] Though scarcely blind to the requirements of the market-

---

2. William H. Pease and Jane H. Pease, *The Web of Progress: Private Values and Public Styles in Boston and Charleston, 1828–1843* (New York, 1985), 215.

3. Alexis de Tocqueville, *Democracy in America*, ed. Phillips Bradley (2 vols.; New York, 1945), II, 34.

place, antebellum southerners were not inclined to see economic advance as a prime means for sweeping public reformation. Instead, acquiring possessions enhanced self and lineage. The man of wealth might choose a course of public charity, but seldom did conscience so dictate. The southern rich chiefly had to remember the needs and expectations of relatives or face the prospect of personal remorse and family recrimination. Public benefactions were not high on the list of financial options.

Gaining wealth also allowed the successful a means to play a public role, as exemplars of devoted civic service. To the southern leadership class, politics was not a profession or source of income, at least not ideally. Instead, as Kenneth Greenberg has documented, the political arena was supposed to be a forum where men who proved worthy received the honors of office as just reward for disinterested, even nonpartisan statesmanship. How different from the venal spirit of the northern politicians, thought members of the slaveholding class, was this concept of civic duty. Edmund Ruffin, among others, deplored the free suffrage that enabled "demogogues" to plunder state and federal treasuries. In May, 1860, Ruffin despaired because of the "great deterioration & corruption" of the Buchanan administration, the latest example of how a "formerly free government" had become "a government of the *worst*, instead of the *best* of the people."[4]

Whereas northerners made business their priority, southerners, despite dissatisfactions with evils in the antebellum party system, tended to put politics ahead of economic considerations. As a result, the lawyer and the politician were powerful figures not only in governmental affairs but in ethical concerns of society as well. That breed of men was to the South what philanthropists and evangelical ministers were to the North: models of public morality and sectional ideology. As the latter group became increasingly optimistic about human good and public progress, the former watched the moral change with growing dread.

4. Kenneth S. Greenberg, *Masters and Statesmen: The Political Culture of American Slavery* (forthcoming); Ruffin's remarks, May 14, 1860, in *Toward Independence, October, 1856–April, 1861* (Baton Rouge, 1972), 420. Vol. I of *The Diary of Edmund Ruffin*, ed. William K. Scarborough, 3 vols. projected.

Southern questioning of mankind's potentiality for good was closely related to another moral issue: the worth of human life itself. The vast waste that the southern moral code involved is something tragic to contemplate, even though most societies throughout history have been equally profligate. So often, as Elkins observed, societies with weak and simple institutional safeguards are the ones least willing to recognize the contributions of all their members, despite boasts about liberty and justice. Certainly in the American South, the slave system, post-emancipation peonage, and Jim Crow segregation must be seen as a gross misuse and distortion of human potentiality. With impressive statistics, Robert Fogel has revealed the favorable situation of American slaves when compared with the health, mortality, and living space which peasants, workers, and slaves elsewhere had to endure. It seems that the abolitionists had misread the economic and material conditions of bondage. The proslavery advocates had more of a case than we have thought.[5]

Nonetheless, no matter how successful slavery was, southern rules of race squandered the lives of thousands of black men and women, a fact that Fogel finds ironic and tragic. To be sure, blacks fashioned a rich culture of their own, as historians Lawrence Levine, Herbert Gutman, Charles Joyner, and Eugene D. Genovese have shown.[6] But how much greater that national resource might have been, had southern whites accepted the abolitionist perspective. Likewise, the scheme of honor placed burdens of manly fulfillment upon the dominant race. Southern whites behaved in this fashion not because they were sinners but because they were faithful servants of archaic custom. Perhaps there was a certain glory that was conferred on all Rebels. But if the purpose of the slaughter was in part the preservation of southern self-respect, the price of honor was certainly far higher than the proslavery enthusiasts ever imagined it would be.

5. Robert W. Fogel, *Without Consent or Contract: The Rise and Fall of American Slavery* (forthcoming).

6. Lawrence W. Levine, *Black Culture and Black Consciousness: Afro-American Folk Thought from Slavery to Freedom* (New York, 1977); Herbert G. Gutman, *The Black Family in Slavery and Freedom, 1750–1925* (New York, 1976); Charles W. Joyner, *Down by the Riverside: A South Carolina Slave Community* (Urbana, 1984); Eugene D. Genovese, *Roll, Jordan, Roll: The World the Slaves Made* (New York, 1974).

Surely there was waste in terms of talent as well as life in the fighting and dying of so many.

At the risk of appearing too present-minded, one may ask a final question, a point that became a cliché not so long ago: is the record of American moral politics in the past "relevant" to our present situation? The answer must be an emphatic yes. For all the suffering that the Civil War battles caused, the result was the advancement of human freedom. That theme had much to do with the moral character of the struggle against Nazi Germany and militarist Japan, a conflict which in turn helped to prepare the nation for the civil rights effort of the 1950s and 1960s. In World War II, invocations of military honor—valor, courage, and self-sacrifice—were a necessary source of inspiration toward that larger aim of democracy and freedom. No people can dispense with the ethical imperatives of warfare. It was a point that even the pacifist Garrison had come to recognize, once Lincoln's war began.

Southerners refused to march in step with the rest of the country toward the enlargement of human liberties and suffered the consequences of that decision. What was morally right, though, for Civil War Americans does not necessarily legitimize American coercions in international affairs. If history teaches any lesson at all, we must be sensitive to the concepts of justice and honor that prevail outside our parochial borders and be alert to the risks of imposing our notions of these concepts upon other nations. Ignorance of the values that inspire our antagonists can sometimes prove disastrous. For example, though the circumstances were far more complicated than can be summed up here, President Carter had no idea during the Iranian crisis that he had violated the Islamic laws of honor when he permitted the deposed shah to enter the United States. Sticking by a fallen friend, though well intentioned and honorable in its own way, involved the nation in a tragic blunder that a greater appreciation of Iranian ethics could have helped us to avoid. By Middle Eastern standards, the country that befriends an enemy *becomes* an enemy. Hospitality involves the notion that its recipients are temporary family members and enjoy the protections inherent in that status. The implication was clear to Ayatollah Khomeini and his theocratic allies over whom the secular authorities had little control during that stage of the revolution. The Americans, the Ayatollah and his colleagues assumed, would seek to reimpose the fallen tyrant. Appropriately the retaliation was against the fifty or more American embassy officials, the resident "guests" of the host country. For centuries, vast crowd demonstrations in Iran had been a religious and political means to express xenophobic resentments as well as opposition to central government and secular tyranny. Thus the humiliation of the captives in mass rites of shaming was more significant to the Iranian mobs than even the Americans' deaths would have been. The mullahs had deeper purposes in mind than just embarrassing the United States: the consolidation of the revolution. But the hostage situation aroused popular Iranian passion because of the perceived insult to Islamic pride.

Ironically, the president at that time was a southerner who might have recognized the possibility of misunderstanding on a point of etiquette for which his region was so long renowned. Carter had acted in what he thought was a forbearing, prudent spirit, while refusing, first, to surrender the shah to Teheran for trial and, later, to make abject apologies, the truculent, demeaning conditions successively demanded for the prisoners' release. Nonetheless, Carter's own moral sense was his political undoing. He would not risk the hostages' lives simply to show American grit, a tactic that Gerald Ford had employed in the *Mayaguez* incident, May 14, 1975, just as American influence in Southeast Asia had reached its nadir. (Forty-one marines died in that rescue mission, even though the ship's crewmen had already been released by their Kampuchean captors.)[7] By denying himself a similar display of determination, Carter appeared passive and indecisive. The result was puzzlement abroad and unpopularity at home, especially when the helicopter rescue-effort of April 24, 1980, failed so emphatically. Like all ethical systems, honor cannot

7. Paul J. Magnarella, "Iranian Diplomacy in the Khomeini Era," in M. Zamora (ed.), *Culture and Diplomacy in the Third World,* in *Studies in Third World Societies,* XII (1980), 544–46; E. Abrahamian, "The Crowd in Iranian Politics, 1905–1953," *Past & Present,* No. 41 (1968), 184–210; James A. Nathan, "The *Mayaguez,* Presidential War, and Congressional Senescence," *Intellect,* CIV (1976), 360–62.

resolve the hard choices, ambiguities, and contradictions that we must face. Carter's sense of honor was deeply Christian, the kind that General Robert E. Lee would have appreciated. But that tradition of concern for the helpless as a mark of high-minded generosity was only one of the strands running through the course of southern—and indeed American—ethics. Honor and justice as vengeance and legitimate defense were also part of the code upon which Carter might have drawn, however contradictory the two forms of honor were.

If the president from Georgia had made the right moral choice but had to pay dearly for it, another southern-raised chief executive had previously chosen the lustier kind of honor and likewise suffered heavy consequences. As heir to its aggressive, manly traditions, with roots deep in the lore of Texas heroes at the Alamo, at San Jacinto, and in the battles of the Confederacy, Lyndon Johnson made full-scale his war in Southeast Asia almost exactly one hundred years after Appomattox. "We love peace. We hate war. But our course," he declared in 1965, "is charted always by the compass of honor." Like the secessionists of 1861, Johnson feared more the ridicule of his fellow Texans and cold-war colleagues if he backed away from that course than he did the judgment of history or even the opinion of countrymen less keenly committed to the demands of the ancient faith. During the 1965 crisis over political instability in the Dominican Republic, the president called a friend in Johnson City, Texas, to ask if his deployment of marines to that island aroused objections there. The report came back: not a single critic could be found. He was gratified. However, honor based on defensive fear may prove no virtue. Instead, it can be an arrogation of power awesome in its consequences. In a work on Johnson's early career, Ronnie Dugger reminds us that "the fates of nations and peoples in the nuclear era may depend on one leader's concern . . . not to be thought a coward." During Johnson's term in the White House, Dugger remarks, "people trying to think, 'What is wise?' were pummeled [by the president] with the question, 'What is brave?'"[8] Fire-eaters had given the same retort to opponents of their scheme in the crisis of 1861.

8. Ronnie Dugger, *The Politician, The Life and Times of Lyndon Johnson: The Drive for Power, from the Frontier to Master of the Senate* (New York, 1982), 147–51.

EPILOGUE

For better or worse, honor did survive that earlier conflict. Confederate heroes lived on in the hearts and memories of their descendants, an immortality through fame that has always been hailed as the reward for the brave. But today the same spirit that brought the South to its fate would leave none to remember, none to praise, none to record who the heroes and who the cowards were. We ignore the implications of honor to the peril of human history itself.

INDEX